EVERYCAT

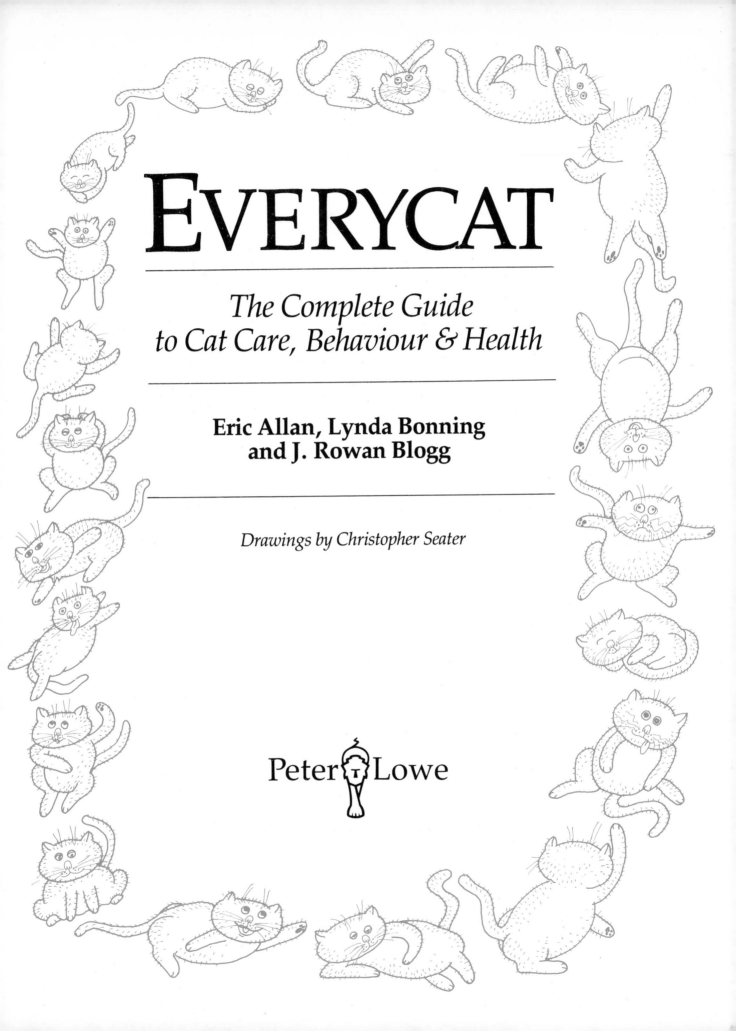

EVERYCAT

The Complete Guide
to Cat Care, Behaviour & Health

**Eric Allan, Lynda Bonning
and J. Rowan Blogg**

Drawings by Christopher Seater

Peter Lowe

ACKNOWLEDGEMENTS

We are extremely grateful for the generous help, freely given, by many people. Dr Peter Cullen gave invaluable assistance on the subject of reproduction, and we are especially indebted to him. Thanks also to Dr Jack Arundal, Dr James Greenwood, Uncle Bens of Australia, Mr and Mrs J. Chitty, Gayle McPhee, Dr Virginia Studdert, Dr Sonya Bettonay and in particular to Pam and Warren Bonning for their support. Lesley Abbott not only rapidly and accurately typed the manuscript, but was unfailingly co-operative and tolerant. Thanks also to Kingsley Abbott for cheerfully facing the drudgery of checking it all.

The chapter on 'The Eye' (pages 137–156) has been written by Dr J. Rowan Blogg: diplomate American College of Veterinary Ophthalmologists, Armadale Veterinary Eye Hospital, Australia.
The glossary (pages 243–266) has been prepared by Dr. N. Koch B.V.Sc.

| TAKE |
| GREAT |
| CARE! |

Caution: Do not attempt treatment marked with this symbol unless you are experienced with cats and/or it is a real emergency.

First published in 1985 by
Methuen Australia Pty Ltd
First British edition published 1986 by
Eurobook Limited

British Library Cataloguing in Publication Data
Allan, Eric
  Everycat: the complete guide to cat health,
  behaviour & care.
  1. Cats
  I. Title   II. Bonning, Lynda   III. Blogg,
  J. Rowan
  636.8'083   SF447
  ISBN 0 85654 653 4

Printed in Spain

Cover photograph: European silver tabby by Lacz Lemoine/NHPA

CONTENTS

INTRODUCTION

Everycat is written for all cat owners. It aims to give the sort of advice your vet would like to give you, if only there was enough time. We hope it will enable you to understand and enjoy your cat more.

Owners of cats are no longer content to rely on advice from friends or enthusiasts. They are increasingly seeking reliable, accurate information about their pets. This book encompasses the answers to the sort of questions vets are frequently asked in the consulting room and over the 'phone. Your own vet can provide many answers during routine consultations, but there are times when all you require is general advice or credible information. At other times, a crisis could arise. For example, you may suspect your cat has eaten a poison. The correct action on your part may ensure a favourable outcome.

We have covered all the common, and a lot of the uncommon, conditions of cats, plus their routine needs and the illnesses that can affect them. A lot of space is devoted to explaining the fascinating behaviour of cats and their unique senses.

Cat owners often ask how a vet can diagnose their cat's problem without being able to question the patient. The answer lies mainly in careful observation and recognition of abnormalities and signs of illness. This book should help you to do the same. Early recognition of disease can prevent unnecessary discomfort. The cat cannot take itself to the vet. Its welfare is in your hands.

Every effort has been made to use simple, non-technical language. The cartoons and illustrations help to avoid long, tedious explanations.

LIVING WITH A CAT

WHY HAVE A CAT?

The appeal of a cat is indefinable. Some owners admire their independent spirit, others their capacity for affection. Many are enchanted by the cat's personality or by its grace and beauty. Cats are clean, need little room and are relatively inexpensive to acquire and maintain. Almost anyone can own a cat — high rise apartment dwellers, people living in houseboats, large or small families or elderly people living on their own.

Think before you get a cat: there are certain responsibilities you must accept, there are different types to choose from and there are lots of little things that you might like to know about to make living with your cat more enjoyable. Read on.

Responsibilities — think before you buy
Kittens are extraordinarily appealing little bundles of fun. Unfortunately, a large number of people impulsively acquire a kitten without considering what they are taking on. Before you get a cat, you must be sure you are willing to house, feed and maintain it for the next ten to fifteen years. The cat will need regular meals. You may have to clean litter trays, groom the cat, and provide some exercise and entertainment. The costs of vaccination and neutering will have to be met, and the cat could have additional occasional problems, such as fleas, worms and sickness.

Too many cats are abandoned or destroyed because people haven't thought the problems through. In almost every major city in the world, thousands of cats are destroyed every week by welfare societies. This is an appalling situation, but you can do your part by being a responsible owner.

(A) Longhair

(B) Shorthair

There are a few points to ponder while you are mulling over your choice.

Type
Longhair or shorthair? The longhairs can look magnificent, but they do require *daily* grooming. They also tend to shed more hair on furniture and carpets, and are less suitable than shorthairs for hot climates.

Breed
There is a lot less variation between the characteristics of the cat breeds than there is between dog breeds. Nevertheless, there are some fairly well defined traits, although it should also be stressed that every cat is an individual. All these comments are generalisations.

Pedigree or non-pedigree?
Pedigree cats are more expensive, especially if sold for breeding and the show-ring. You could be offered a pedigree cat for a relatively low fee if it is unsuitable for showing due to some fault in coat, colour or conformation. This does not necessarily mean this particular cat will be unhealthy or unsuitable as a pet, but before you commit yourself to a sale, ask carefully what the faults are, and get your vet's comments and advice.

Sex
Unless you are a keen breeder, you should have your cat neutered. Once they have been neutered, there is little difference between the sexes, although females tend to be quieter, less inclined to roam, and usually less concerned with defence of their territory.

If you do not want to have your cat neutered, then a female is much easier to keep than a male. An 'entire' male (that is not neutered) is usually dominated by his sex drive. They can be very smelly and aggressive, especially towards other male cats. We strongly recommend that you have your cat neutered.

Male cats make much better pets if they are neutered

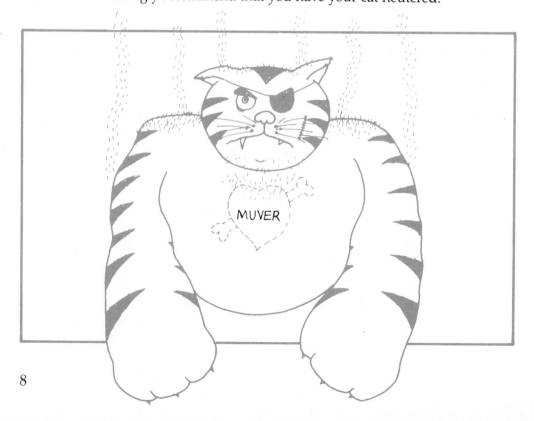

MUVER

BREED	TEMPERAMENT	VOICE	COMMENT
Shorthaired Siamese	A sociable cat, very outgoing personality. Can become strongly attached to owners. Very demanding of both attention and affection. Enjoys sitting on laps. Intelligent, but often highly strung and tendency to be neurotic. Good with children if brought up with them.	Very loud voice — a penetrating distinct meow, that they tend to use excessively. Can be hard to take (especially when queen is 'on heat').	Indiscriminate breeding has produced some faults in the breed e.g. crossed eyes, skeletal disease, kinked tails and abnormal temperaments. Observe parents before buying a kitten.
Burmese	Intelligent, easygoing and adaptable. Affectionate and attention-seeking. Good with children, but can be withdrawn with strangers.	Much less vocally demanding than the Siamese.	Increasingly popular breed.
Abyssinian	Gentle and affectionate, often shy and reserved. Apprehensive with strangers and can be nervous with children.	Quiet voice.	Becoming more popular.
Rex	Intelligent, inquisitive, extrovert. Often highly strung. Tendency toward sulky moods.	Not very noisy.	Relatively high incidence of slipping kneecaps in the breed. Don't shed hair like other cats, may be suitable in a household where someone is allergic to cat hair.
Longhaired Persian	Mainly placid, gentle temperament. Often reserved and shy. Not particularly demanding of affection or attention. Some have fiery tempers.	A melodious voice compared to Siamese. Don't vocalise often.	Usually adjust well to strange environments. Coats need to be groomed daily.
Himalayan	Gentle temperament with an outgoing personality. Not as demanding as Siamese and generally more affectionate than Persian.	Not very noisy.	A breed that is becoming more popular. Coat needs to be groomed daily.
Birman	Placid, friendly nature. Affectionate, but can be demanding.	Not very vocal until they want something.	Relatively uncommon breed, but growing in popularity. Coat needs daily grooming.
Angora	Gentle cat that can be highly strung and nervous.	Not a very vocal breed.	Loves water and swimming. Needs daily grooming.

Note: These comments are only meant as guide — there will be exceptions to these guidelines. There are many other breeds available that have not been mentioned.

The age to buy
The kitten is weaned from its mother at about four or five weeks of age. Shortly after this time, the kitten will adapt fairly easily to a change in environment, and could form a fairly strong bond of attachment to you. Eight weeks of age seems to be the optimum time to acquire a kitten. However, there may be situations where an older cat is more suitable. For example, elderly people may find a kitten too much of a handful, or a working couple may be unable to adequately feed and tend to a youngster.

Rearing a young kitten can be very rewarding. You can help to shape its personality. If you have children, it is best to get a young kitten which will grow up in the rough and tumble and learn to cope, whereas an adult cat may become distressed or frightened with boisterous behaviour.

WHERE TO BUY A CAT

Private homes
Private homes are usually the best source. The kittens will probably have been handled from early in life and this makes them much more socially adaptable. There is less risk of the kitten contracting infectious diseases (such as cat 'flu) and parasites than there is in breeding establishments or welfare homes. You can ask about the parents' personalities, and it will give you some guide as to what to expect from their progeny.

Pet shops
Pet shops can be good, but be careful. Be sure the kittens are kept under clean, hygienic conditions, otherwise you could be buying trouble. Many pet shops are excellent, but others are a source of feline enteritis, cat 'flu, ringworm, mange, fleas, ear mites and other conditions.

Humane or cat welfare organisations
These groups do a great service to cats. They are usually staffed by genuinely concerned cat lovers. But beware! Kittens from *some* of these homes can be sick, or incubating diseases. Sometimes you could be offered kittens of wild or feral cats and these can be very difficult to tame. They could be unsatisfactory as pets. If you choose a cat from one of these organisations, be very careful in your choice. Don't let your heart rule your head.

Advertisements in local newspapers

Your vet
Your vet may have clients who are looking for good homes for cats or kittens.

10

Pedigreed animals
Pedigreed animals can be obtained through the various cat fanciers' organisations. Telephone the secretary of the appropriate breed society for information and a list of breeders who currently have kittens for sale.

THE PICK OF THE LITTER

Given a bunch of playful kittens to choose from, how do you pick the one most likely to suit you?

First, be sure the kittens are healthy. Here is a list of points to check:
- Should be lively, active and well nourished.
- Feel the kitten — don't just look. The ribs should not protrude, nor should the kitten have a pot-belly.
- Coat: soft, with a light sheen, not dry or harsh.
- Eyes: clear and no discharge.
- Ears: clean and no discharge or offensive smell.
- Mouth: should have all the milk teeth.
- Legs: straight, not bowed.
- Should be properly weaned, and not still sucking.
- Look for evidence of diarrhoea. This matts the hair around the anus and may stain the hocks.
- Ask what worming has been done, what vaccinations (if any) the kitten has had. A vaccination certificate should be available.
- Should be used to being handled, otherwise it may be difficult to handle when older, and is especially likely to be wary of strangers.

THE KITTEN FOR YOU

If possible, see the whole litter together, look for a kitten that is alert and playful, and which responds to your approach with interest, not fear. This sort of kitten is likely to make a good pet.

The kitten that approaches you first is liable to have a dominant personality. Select it only if you want a strong-willed cat that is likely to be independent. The kitten that sits back or shies away is likely to be sensitive, and will need patience and gentleness. Do not choose this kitten unless you are prepared to spend time gaining the cat's confidence. It will not be suitable for young children or for a person who is intending to move around a lot.

It is tempting to feel sorry for the runt of the litter. Don't rush in without considering what you could be taking on. This kitten will almost certainly have some problems and may be liable to sickness. You will probably have the cat for many years — are you prepared to look after it? Some people gain great satisfaction and pleasure from rearing such a kitten, but it takes a special type of owner.

Avoid aggressive kittens. They almost invariably grow to be aggressive adults.

It is usually possible to make your purchase conditional on a satisfactory report from your vet. We recommend a veterinary examination, especially if purchasing a pedigreed cat.

If the kitten has a pedigree, take it with you to your vet. Look carefully for evidence of inbreeding (your vet will help you here). The pedigree should be complete and the kitten registered with the appropriate breed society.

Avoid aggressive or apprehensive kittens

11

Should you get two kittens?
You may consider getting two kittens to keep each other company, especially if you are away from home a lot. This is usually not necessary, as most cats are very independent and perfectly happy to be the sole resident of your home. If you want to have two cats, it is best to start them off together rather than introduce another kitten later as this second kitten could be rejected or resented. The best combination seems to be a male and a female. Two females usually get on well together, but two males are less predictable. Behavioural pressures of dominance and territorial rights may come between them, even if both are neutered (see 'Behaviour', page 47)

What will you need for the new arrival?
- Food and water bowl.
- Sleeping box or basket.
- Litter tray and litter.
- Cat food (see 'Nutrition', page 60).
- Perhaps a scratching post (see page 50).
- A cat collar.

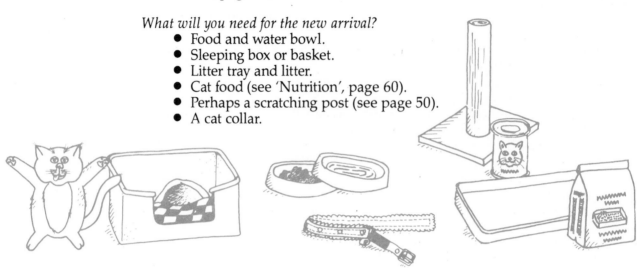

Not everyone agrees that a cat should wear a collar. We feel they should. If the cat is lost or injured you have a good chance of recovering it if you have an identification tag on the collar. Without a collar, the chances are very poor.

A cat collar is special. It has a soft, felt lining and a piece of elastic sewn in so that if the cat is caught by the collar it will expand to slip over the head.

Cats should be introduced to collars when young. It may be difficult to get an adult to start wearing one.

When a cat is used to wearing an ordinary cat collar, you can then get it to wear an insecticidal flea collar, if desired.

THE FIRST DAY

If possible, collect the kitten on a weekend or a holiday so that you have time to help the new arrival settle in.

Shut all the doors and windows.

Select where you want the kitten to eat and also a different spot for the litter tray. Keep these positions constant so that the kitten can develop a routine.

Put the kitten down on its bed. Then step back and allow it to move quietly about and explore. Don't overfuss or overexcite the kitten. Give it time.

You will be able to tell when the kitten has relaxed as it will sit down and begin to groom itself. At this stage offer some food. (And have a cup of coffee yourself. You probably need it!)

For the first few days, feed the kitten the same diet that the breeders had been feeding. Only gradually change to your own selection. (see 'Nutrition', page 60). Beware especially of giving too much milk as this will result in diarrhoea.

The first night can be a trauma. Give the kitten a source of warmth, such as a hot water bottle wrapped in an old jumper. A soft toy that the kitten can snuggle against may help. Some kittens are soothed by a loud ticking alarm clock. One theory is that the ticking substitutes for the mother's heartbeat. Perhaps it does, or perhaps it just provides something regular and reliable to break the solitude.

After meals, or when the kitten first awakes, put it on to its toilet area. Praise it if it obligingly urinates or defaecates.

Do not let the kitten outside until it has become used to its feeding place. Once that pattern is established it will return for food. It is dangerous to let the kitten out without supervision. You should *not* let the kitten out at night as it is likely to be harmed by prowling adult cats and there is also a high risk of it being run over on the road.

Cats like to sleep above floor level. As your kitten grows, you could put its basket up onto a suitable shelf in an attempt to avoid it making its own choice of chairs or other furniture. It is not easy to bend a cat's will, and most will make their own decision as to where they are going to sleep. Some cats will change their preferred sleeping area every so often, but most are consistent, although they have several resting or napping areas.

Meeting other pets

You have probably seen pictures of cats living happily with mice or birds or other little animals. Be warned. These are exceptions to the rule. The cat is a hunter, with strong instincts bred in over thousands of years. They do not usually get along with small mammals such as guinea pigs, hamsters, rabbits or mice. Nor with birds or fish. If you have other such pets, you must provide them with a secure hutch or cage and don't allow the cat to interfere with them. The tops of fish bowls should be covered.

If you have a dog, keep the two apart on the first day. Introduce them under supervision, preferably with a leash on the dog. Be ready to pull the dog away. Most dogs will accept a young kitten. They may even grow to be close companions. Initially, expect a few hisses and the occasional slap with a paw. If you have a puppy, be careful he is not scratched in the eye.

Always feed the dog and the cat in their own bowls, preferably in separate areas. The cat can be fed at a height on a bench or tabletop, so that the dog does not get at its food.

Vaccinations

Cats can be vaccinated against feline infectious enteritis (panleukopaenia), the feline respiratory diseases (cat 'flu), various other diseases, and in some countries rabies. Temporary vaccinations can be given from six weeks of age and 'permanent' vaccinations from twelve weeks. Read the chapter on 'Infectious Diseases' (page 104) and see your own vet for recommended dose regimes.

VACCINATION

Worming

You should worm your kitten when you get it, and then every two or four weeks. For details, see pages 192-7.

Flea control

If your kitten has fleas, you should try to remove them at once before too many eggs are laid, (see page 167).

Choose a name for your kitten as early as possible, then repeat it whenever you are stroking the kitten. Call the name when the kitten is walking towards you, when you are putting the food down and on greeting it first thing in the morning. The kitten will soon associate the name with itself.

Use simple, single words. A firm tone for commands is essential. Do not try for too much at once. Try these few for a start:

NO! When the kitten is removed from some undesirable activity, such as urinating on the carpet or demolishing a pot plant.

DOWN! As you put the kitten down off your lap or from a table or chair.

OUT! As you put the kitten out of the door, especially if this is to go to the toilet area.

It is useless to use phrases such as 'you are a naughty boy.' A simple NO is much more effective.

A cunningly hidden balloon full of water can dampen the cat's enthusiasm for the clothes basket

Reward, not punishment, is the best teacher. If you must punish, be aware that it is easy to establish distrust in the cat. However, if the cat behaves aggressively or dominantly you should establish *your* dominance immediately, firmly and consistently. Use a similar sort of body language to the methods the kitten's mother would use. Grasp the offender by the scruff, firmly saying NO! Or use a rolled up newspaper to slap the kitten on the snout. The noise and the domination of the act are enough. You should not give the kitten more than a light tap. Never physically hurt the kitten.

Reward the kitten for good behaviour with praise and affection, and perhaps with a treat or titbit. Never feed a cat after it has misbehaved. Wait for at least twenty minutes. Otherwise, the cat may interpret the food as a reward associated with the offensive activity.

Habits that are cute in a kitten can be a real problem when the cat grows up. Do not let the kitten sleep on your bed, or get away with scratching the furniture, crawling up your trouser leg or biting your hand.

For constant misbehaviour other than aggression, do not use physical punishment. Instead, use 'aversion therapy.' The idea of aversion therapy is to get the cat to associate the unwelcome activity with something unpleasant. If possible, the cat should not associate you with the unpleasantness, as this can lead to a lack of trust. An ideal tool is a water pistol, or you could throw a rolled up ball

Aversion therapy: the object is to get the cat to associate the undesirable activity with an unpleasant result

of paper at the cat or throw a bunch of keys near the cat to startle it. Every time you see the cat attempting the undesired activity such as scratching the furniture, give a quick squirt, but try not to let the cat see you doing the squirting.

In some cases, you can 'set up' the cat. For example if the cat has developed the unwelcome habit of sleeping in the clothes basket, you could put in a balloon filled with water almost to bursting point, then cover it with some old clothes. After a couple of wet surprises the cat is very unlikely to return. If the cat is pulling clothes from a drying rack, then put a water balloon inside a tempting sock.

Toilet training

Most kittens have already been toilet trained by their mother, or will automatically seek out somewhere to bury their excreta.

If the kitten is not already trained, it is usually easy to do so. Put the kitten into the litter box or toilet area immediately after feeding or on waking. Hold the front paws and make digging actions, showing it how to scratch amongst the litter. (The kitten will use its *back* paws, but they usually resent you pulling at them.) The kitten will generally catch on quickly.

The litter should be cleaned daily. Many cats will not use soiled litter, and may therefore soil elsewhere. If you find your cat will not use litter, try sand or soil. If possible, establish an outside toilet area as well.

Praise and stroke the cat to reward it for correct toilet habits. If you actually catch it in the act of soiling the floor, use harsh voice tones or the aversion technique. Do not use physical punishment. Definitely do not rub the kitten's nose in the mess. This is likely to cause mistrust and make the problem worse since it stresses the cat.

The chapter on 'Behaviour' (page 47) discusses how to deal with inappropriate urinating as well as other subjects such as furniture scratching and killing birds.

EXERCISE

Cats need exercise. They are athletic creatures. Constant confinement without an outlet for exercise and play can lead to a dull, apathetic cat or to the development of destructive behaviour. Bored cats may damage plants or soft furnishings or may become neurotic.

Two kittens will exercise each other, rolling and romping happily without the need of any props. Single cats should be provided with some playthings — for example a ball with a bell inside, or a stick with a ribbon or rope attached with a tassel on the end. Give the kitten a box to play in. Cut a few holes so it can crawl in and out or run through the box.

If you can, let the kitten play outside. An enclosed run is ideal, especially if fitted with a few shelves or a tree to climb on.

A small cat door or cat-flap can be fitted to allow the cat free access inside or out without requiring your help or interfering with the security of your house. At first, leave the cat door open. When the cat is used to using it, close the door. Most cats soon discover how to open it themselves.

The cat door can be locked at night if you do not want the cat to wander.

Some owners are able to train their cat to walk on a harness and lead, and exercise them that way.

TRAVELLING

If the cat is not used to travelling in a car or other vehicle, you must confine it in a strong, secure container. Specially designed cat carry baskets or bags are available. You can make do with a box, but it must be strong and capable of being securely fastened. Cardboard boxes are usually unsuitable as the cat is likely to urinate and a wet box loses its strength.

A nervous cat can be a dangerous passenger

A zip-fastening bag will do for things like a trip to the vet. The cat will not smother. If the journey is a long one, it will be necessary to provide more room and better airflow than a zip-up bag allows. Don't make the mistake of leaving the zip partly undone. Cats can squeeze out through remarkably small gaps.

Withhold all food and water for several hours before the journey. Unless you are travelling for more than twelve hours it is not necessary to provide food. If it is hot, be certain the box is well ventilated and the cat has access to water.

Some cats travel well. Some don't. If your cat is a nervous traveller it may be advisable to give a tranquilliser first. (Do not experiment with drugs or dose rates. Seek the correct advice from your vet.)

Do not be tempted to travel with your cat roaming free in the car or sitting on your lap. A frightened or hysterical cat is extremely dangerous, especially when trapped inside a moving vehicle.

You can help the cat to become used to travelling without trauma by introducing it to the experience gradually. Sit with the cat in a stationary car, with and without the motor running. Feed a few treats. Indulge in a little play session, then try a few short drives — up and down the driveway first, then around the block.

Travel by air, rail and sea
Organise your cat's transport well in advance if possible. All transport companies have specific requirements, and they will usually send you a list of these, plus some guidelines to follow.

If you are travelling abroad there may be vaccination and other regulations to comply with. Some countries have strict quarantine requirements. Check with the Ministry of Agriculture, Fisheries and Food. Your vet will probably know who to contact.

Boarding your cat
The vast majority of cats will settle perfectly happily into a boarding cattery, contrary to the expectations of the vast majority of cat owners. It usually takes one or two days for the cat to become familiar with the new surroundings and to realise it is safe and secure and that food is available. After that, they generally seem content.

It is worth taking the time to select a good cattery.

Ask friends for their recommendations. Here are a few guidelines you might bear in mind when making your choice:

● Look for clean, hygienic conditions. The smell inside the cattery will give you some guide.

● There should be no opportunity for direct 'nose to nose' contact between cats. There should be solid partitioning or a space between the cages.

● Cats should not be admitted without a current vaccination certificate.

● Cats do not need a huge area, but they should have enough room for separate eating, sleeping and toilet areas.

● Ask what the cat will be fed. Does the cattery cater to individuals which are choosy, or require a special diet?

● Ask what the proprietor would do if your cat fell ill.

Advance bookings are usually necessary, especially on public holidays or in summer. Plan ahead, or you may have to settle for a second rate establishment.

FIRST AID

GIVING MEDICINE

Getting a cat to take the medicine it needs but probably doesn't want can be a problem unless you use the correct techniques. Get yourself organised first, with the tablet ready and a blanket handy.

It is easier to put the cat on a table than to try and struggle on the floor. If the cat is likely to struggle and scratch, envelope it tightly in a blanket first, leaving only the head exposed.

To give a tablet, try the following method:

● Hold the cat's head in your left hand, with your thumb on one corner of the jaw and forefinger on the other, so that your hand spans the cat's head just behind the eyeline. The ears should be under the palm of your hand. By holding the head in this manner you can get a firm grip without hurting the cat.

● Do *not* grip the cat around the neck. The cat is liable to panic and you could be severely scratched or bitten.

● Tip the cat's head back.

● With your right hand, open the cat's mouth by putting the nail (only) of your forefinger on the teeth of the cat's lower jaw and pull down. The mouth will usually open easily.

● The pill must be placed right at the back of the cat's mouth, over the hump of the tongue. Throw the pill to the back of the mouth and quickly push it out of sight. You could use your finger, but a pencil or similar may be safer. Keep your finger in the *centre* of the mouth — do not come in over the side teeth, or you could easily be bitten.

● If the cat struggles or claws, envelope it in a large towel or blanket, leaving only the head exposed.

The tablet must be pushed right to the back of the throat, over the hump of the tongue

17

If you have trouble actually physically giving a tablet, here are a few ideas on how to give the medicine in other ways.

It is not sufficient simply to hide the tablet from view. Cats detect these unwelcome additions to their food mainly by smell. For example, if you had fifty pieces of meat and you picked up one piece, then put it down again, the chances are the cat would leave that particular piece. It will at least examine it closely before consuming it, even though it contained no drugs. It is your odour that the cat detects. Any unusual smell will immediately alert the cat. So if you handle a single piece of meat to insert a tablet, the cat will usually detect it.

If the tablet can be crushed (some must not be crushed: they may have a protective coating to diguise a bitter taste or to protect them from stomach acids) then you may succeed in disguising it if you mix it with a strong-smelling food. First, powder the tablet. It is not enough just to break it into a few pieces. Then mix it thoroughly with a food you know your cat likes, and which has a strong odour, for example fish or cheese. Let it sit for about twenty minutes before feeding it to the cat.

If the tablet is not suitable for crushing, cut a deep hole in a piece of meat or cheese, and push the tablet in. Do not simply wrap the food around the tablet. If you have had to handle the doctored piece of food, handle all the others as well before offering the food to the cat. A gravy poured over the lot may help.

If these methods fail, crush the tablet and mix it with a little yeast extract or honey, and smear the mixture onto the cat's forepaw. The cat's fastidious nature will usually drive him to lick the paw clean.

If you have no success with tablets, ask your vet if the required medicine is available in liquid form. These are generally easier to give than tablets (assuming only a small volume is required).

To administer a syrup, paste or liquid, simply hold the cat's head as described above, tip it back slightly, and introduce the nozzle of the loaded dropper or syringe into the mouth just behind the canine tooth. There is a gap in the teeth here, so there is no need to prise the cat's jaw apart.

HANDLING AN INJURED CAT

Be cautious when handling any injured animal. A cat that is frightened or in pain can be dangerous. Be gentle and patient. Do not take risks if the cat is unco-operative.

The co-operative cat
If the cat is quiet and tranquil your main aims are to minimise further damage and to use handling techniques that minimise pain and discomfort.
    First: Before attempting to lift the cat, reassure it by speaking in a calm, level voice. Stroke the cat softly, with a slow soothing action.
    Then: Pick the cat up using one of these techniques:
(a) hand under chest and rump; or
(b) scruff of neck and rump.

The unco-operative cat
Beware of the frightened cat. Teeth and claws can inflict severe damage. Even your own normally placid cat can be unpredictable when frightened.
    Warning Signs: If the cat watches you with wide open (dilated) pupils, has the ears flattened and hisses at your approach, then DO NOT attempt to pick it up.

18

If possible, leave the cat alone until it has calmed. Take your time. Stay at a safe distance. Reassure the cat by talking quietly. Do not stare into the cat's eyes as this has an unsettling effect. In many cases, the cat will gradually calm and will then be able to be picked up.

If urgent attention is necessary or if the cat is in a dangerous position, such as lying on a roadway, or if the cat's attitude is unlikely to improve, the following technique may be used:

- Get a large blanket, towel or coat.
- Drop it over the cat, enveloping it.
- Scoop the entire bundle up, tucking the edges firmly into the bundle. All four limbs and head must be included. Don't worry, the cat will not smother.
- Put the entire bundle — blanket, cat and all — into a secure box, or you could carry the cat directly to the vet.

If first aid treatment of a limb or the head is essential, expose ONLY that part, keeping the blanket firmly wrapped around the rest of the cat.

ABSCESS

An abscess is a localised collection of pus. A 'wall' of thick, fibrous tissue encompasses this pus. Most abscesses form as a result of puncture wounds inflicted during cat fights. Other possible causes include a reaction to a foreign body, such as a grass seed or wood splinter. Infection can develop within a deep cut or abrasion or even a surgical wound. Abscesses sometimes flare due to some chronic irritation such as an ingrowing toenail, or a tumour. The abscess may rupture spontaneously, discharging the thick, yellow or brown foul smelling liquid pus. Or the abscess may have to be opened (or 'lanced') by you or your vet.

Abscesses usually take three to five days to form after the initiating wound. By this time they can be seen or felt as soft or fluctuating, painful swellings under the skin.

The most common sites of abscesses in cats are on the side of the face (this is especially so in tom cats), or around the base of the tail.

Because of the cat's thick coat, the full size of the infected area may not be readily apparent, especially for the first two or three days after the initiating wound. Usually, all you see is a swollen, tense and discoloured area of skin.

If the abscess is large (that is, over a centimetre in diameter) or if the cat is in pain or is lethargic or off its food, then veterinary attention is advisable.

Should the abscess be opened (lanced)?
If the abscess has not spontaneously burst, you may be able to bring it to a 'head' by gently bathing with a mild solution of salt or bicarbonate of soda. If it has not ruptured within twenty-four hours, it may have to be lanced. This is best done

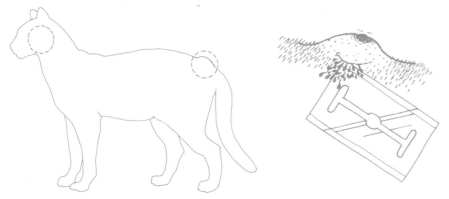

*These are the two most common sites for bites, and therefore for abscesses. If you **must** lance the abscess yourself, cut into the lowermost part so that all the discharge can escape*

by your vet but if necessary you may be able to do it yourself using a very sharp, sterilised knife blade, or a razor blade.

The cut is made in the lowest part of the abscess. Cut into the tense skin covering the swollen mass. The aim is to allow all the pus to drain away.

After lancing, the abscess cavity is flushed with a mild antiseptic solution (such as 2% hydrogen peroxide). Antibiotics may be required to eliminate bacterial infection completely and so prevent the abscess re-forming.

Keep the drainage hole open for at least twenty-four hours and preferably forty-eight hours. Gently bathe away any scab that forms. The more discharge that escapes, the better.

If the abscess has already burst, what is the next step?
Try to keep the abscess draining. Aim to clean out as much of the discharge as possible. Most will drain out, but there are usually residues that could prevent resolution of the infection or even lead to the abscess re-forming.

Usually the cat will lick away the pus. This may seem nauseating to us, but it does not seem to do the cat any harm. If the cat cannot reach the abscess to clean it, then clean it as follows.

If the abscess has burst, try to gently massage out all the pus – if the cat will let you

TAKE GREAT CARE!

When to call the vet
- Cat is lethargic, off food or in pain.
- The abscess is extensive.
- Abscess ruptures but is not clearing up, or has re-formed.

If you *know* your cat has been bitten it is best to go to your vet straight away. Penetrating bite wounds are almost always infected. It is better to get immediate treatment than to wait for an abscess to develop.

Beware: What may appear to be a small abscess could be only a part of a more extensive problem. Don't delay your visit to the vet if your cat is clearly ill.

BLEEDING (HAEMORRHAGE)

The primary first aid aim is to minimise blood loss. Fortunately, cats usually don't bleed much, even from quite severe wounds. However, if a major blood vessel is damaged, the cat could lose a lot of blood in a short time.

Beware: The cat may resent your attention. Be cautious when dealing with an injured cat.

The simplest way to slow or stop bleeding is to apply pressure directly over the site, if this is possible:
- Get bandages. Gauze is ideal. In an emergency a handkerchief, tie or strips of cloth will suffice.
- If possible, first coat a gauze pad with a little white petroleum jelly. This prevents it sticking to the wound and pulling the clot off later.
- Apply this pad to the wound.
- Press down on the pad, applying pressure with your fingers. Don't press too hard or the cat will resent it.
- Wrap a bandage or cloth strip over the pad. The bandage should be firm, not tight.

To stop bleeding: apply pressure on a pad placed over the bleeding area

20

- If blood seeps through, apply another bandage *over the first*. Do NOT remove the lowest pad or you will disturb any clot that is forming.

Tourniquets

Tourniquets may be used if there is severe bleeding of a leg or tail. Tourniquets should only be used as a *last resort* as they can cause further damage. Many cats will not tolerate them.

Tourniquets must be loosened for half to one minute in every ten, or serious tissue damage can occur due to lack of oxygen.

To apply a tourniquet: Use a broad belt, tie or piece of cloth. Apply this well above the bleeding area. Insert a piece of wood or a pen into the circle of cloth and twist it tight.

When to call the vet?

After any episode of severe bleeding, veterinary advice should be sought.

Tourniquets can be life saving, but are dangerous. Read the text

BITES

Cat bites

Cat fights are common, especially in spring or when a cat moves into a new territory. The two most frequently bitten areas are around the face and neck, and around the base of the tail.

A common complication of a cat bite is infection. The cat's canine teeth make deep puncture wounds. Bacteria from the cat's mouth and from the victim's skin are virtually injected into the wound. It can be difficult to locate the wound as the small punctures are concealed by the coat. Bleeding from the wound site is usually minimal. Assuming you do find the wound, and the cat is co-operative, you should first gently clip away the surrounding hair. Then clean the area with a dilute antiseptic such as 2% hydrogen peroxide. Finally, paint it with an antiseptic. A 'tamed' (doesn't sting) iodine preparation is quite effective.

In many cases you will be either unware of the initial bite or will be unable to find the wound until three or four days after the event. By this stage, the bacteria will have established themselves and multiplied. The affected area becomes red, swollen and very tender. By the fourth or fifth day an abscess may develop (see page 19).

Antibiotics are usually indicated if such an infection has developed.

If your cat has been bitten but you cannot effectively clean the wound, a consultation with your vet is worthwhile. The vet may prescribe antibiotics to prevent infection developing. A short course given early can save a lot of problems later.

Dog bites

A dog bite can cause severe bruising and deep tissue injury as well as producing irregular, torn wounds in the skin. What you can see on the surface may be only a small part of the actual damage. Veterinary attention and treatment for shock, infection, bruising and possibly internal damage is strongly recommended following a dog bite.

First aid

Large, open wounds should be covered with a pad of clean, preferably sterile, absorbent material such as gauze. A handkerchief may do. Bandage this firmly in place, with a roll bandage or strips of cloth. In an emergency, a scarf, tie or handkerchief will suffice. Do not remove the lowermost pad or you may disturb partly formed blood clots.

In areas where rabies is present it must be determined whether the biting animal has been vaccinated. If a vicious attack by a wild animal has occurred, every effort should be made to destroy that animal and have it examined for rabies.

Beware: Do not touch an animal if you suspect it may have rabies, even when it is dead. Wear gloves, and wrap the body in a large plastic bag or a blanket before picking it up.

BROKEN BONES (FRACTURES)

There is a common misconception that a 'fracture' is somehow worse than a 'break' in the bone. This is not so. The terms are synonymous.

Signs
- *Loss of function:* The cat will not use a broken leg or tail. It will dangle and is usually held at an abnormal angle.
- *Pain:* Cats usually tolerate a fracture remarkably well, although they will object strongly if the broken bone is moved or handled roughly. Otherwise cats usually cope with pain without much apparent fuss.
- *Swelling:* The affected limb usually becomes very swollen. The swelling can be difficult to see if the femur (upper hind limb) is broken. If one of the lower bones is broken, swelling is generally obvious by an hour after the accident.

First aid
It is rarely either necessary or possible to apply a splint. Your main objective is to transport the cat to your vet in the most comfortable, practicable manner. Your aim is to cause the minimum extra trauma.

Preferably, put the cat into a cat basket or a secure cardboard box where it cannot move around too much. If a suitable box is not available and if the cat is calm, you should carry the cat (refer to the diagrams). Allow the injured limb to hang free.

Foreleg fracture
Hold cat by scruff and support the weight by placing a hand under the rump.

Hindleg fracture
Hold cat by the scruff and support the weight by placing a hand under the chest.

Fractured pelvis
As for hindleg.

VET TREATMENT
URGENT

Back (spinal) injury
If there is loss of function or sensation in both hind legs, or in all four legs *beware:* The cat may have suffered spinal damage. Handle the cat with extreme care to avoid further damage.

It is essential to transport the cat with the absolute minimum of movement of the suspected fracture site.

Do *not* bend the cat's back at any stage.

Put the cat on to a large, firm board, or place the cat carefully into a large box so that it can lie flat.

22

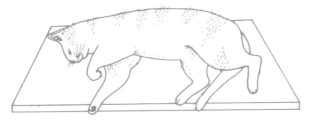

Transport a cat with suspected back injuries on a flat, firm board

A blanket can be used, but because it sags you should support the cat's weight by placing one or both hands under the blanket and cat as it is being carried along.

At all times keep the back as straight as possible.

CHOKING

Signs
Mouth agape, tongue protruding and saliva flowing. Cat makes convulsive coughing and choking noises and may paw at mouth. Legs splayed, head down and neck extended.

Note: Vets are frequently telephoned by owners who believe that their cat is choking to death. In the vast majority of these cases, the cat is merely gagging on some irritating matter such as phlegm or a wad of hair. The noise produced as they make these expulsive efforts mimics the sounds a human makes when he is indeed choking. In the cat, these retching and coughing sounds and efforts can be alarming. If the cat is not particularly distressed there is usually little to be concerned about. However, if the signs listed above *are* present, see your vet immediately.

First aid
Do *not* put your fingers into the cat's mouth or you will be bitten.

If you can see the object and it is *not* irregularly shaped or sharp or pointed, then you may be able to grasp it with needle – nosed pliers or tweezers and pull it out.
Or: Place one hand flat over each side of the cat's chest and give a quick squeeze. The sudden thrust of air that results may dislodge and eject the foreign body from the cat's throat.
Or: Hold the cat by the scruff of the neck and by the hind legs. Turn the cat upside down and shake him vigorously for a few seconds.
Or: Mouth to mouth (see picture). If the cat's gums are turning blue and his eyes are bulging, then this is an emergency. Then place a chock in the mouth so that the cat cannot bite you. A piece of wood, a knife handle or a ruler will do. After chocking the mouth open so that it cannot close around your finger, try to hook the object out with a finger.

This is one way to try to dislodge matter stuck in the throat

ARTIFICIAL RESPIRATION

Artificial respiration may be needed after:
- Drowning.
- Smoke inhalation.
- Choking.
- Electric shock.

Mouth to mouth
If the cat's gums turn blue and its eyes bulge it needs oxygen urgently. Before trying to remove anything from its throat, breathe air in through its nostrils for 2–3 seconds. Repeat if necessary.

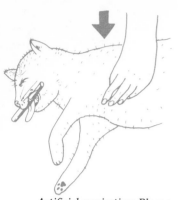

Artificial respiration: Place a chock in the mouth if necessary. Keep your fingers clear

Situation

Breathing has stopped but the heart is still beating.

- Remove any foreign matter from the mouth. (Use tweezers or pliers, NOT your finger.)
- In the case of drowning, hold the cat upside down, shaking it gently.
- Lie cat on side.
- Stretch neck forward, with head up.
- Pull tongue out as far as you can. This opens up the throat.
- Press down over the chest with the flat of your hand using a short, sharp push that forcibly ejects the air. Repeat this push every five seconds until the cat begins to breathe spontaneously.

FITS AND CONVULSIONS

The spectacle of a cat having a fit can be alarming. Don't rush in with an ill-considered attempt to help. In most cases there is little you can do until the convulsive episode is over. Most fits last only a minute or so and end spontaneously.

Signs

Some of the following may occur:

- Muscle twitching and spasm.
- Cat may collapse, usually onto one side.
- Neck arches back.
- Legs held rigid, or paddling with forepaws.
- May pass urine or faeces.

Most fits only last from two to five minutes. Some last only a few seconds, and owners frequently fail to realise the episode was a fit. In some cases the fit may last half an hour or longer, or there may be recurring fits with only short intervals between.

After the fit there is a variable period when the cat will seem a bit dazed. It may react in a quite abnormal, even bizarre fashion. Some become frightened and run to hide. These cats should be approached only with caution as they are unpredictable until they settle down, and may uncharacteristically bite or scratch. Others will seek out their owner for sympathy or comfort.

First aid

If possible, leave the cat alone until the fit has passed. It is dangerous to handle a convulsing cat. The cat will not recognise you, and you may be bitten or scratched.

The cat could give the impression of being in pain. In fact it is not in pain, and we believe it will remember nothing of the actual fit later.

If the cat is in a dangerous position such as in the middle of a road or on the balcony of a high-rise building, it may be essential to move it. First, throw a blanket, coat or large towel over the cat then, after wrapping it up, move the whole bundle to safety.

Keep the convulsing, or recently recovered, cat quiet and undisturbed, preferably in a dark room. Remove or extinguish any potentially dangerous objects such as electric heaters or fans. Draw the curtains. Switch off any source of noise such as the TV or radio.

If the fit is continuous or recurring, you need a vet's help urgently. Move the cat only if absolutely necessary, and then do so with caution, preferably with the cat enveloped in a large, thick blanket.

24

Possible causes of fits:
- Poisons (refer to pages 35, 38, metaldehyde, lead, anti-freeze).
- Infections. (e.g. toxoplasmosis).
- Eclampsia (milk fever).
- Chronic kidney and liver diseases.
- Epilepsy.
- Brain tumour.
- Post-accident blood clot or scarring.
- Worms (especially in kittens).

HAIRBALLS

Because cats are fastidious about their coats they normally groom themselves daily. Inevitably some dead hairs are raked out by the cat's barbed tongue and subsequently swallowed. The cat's digestive system is perfectly capable of handling even quite large amounts of hair without the cat suffering any discomfort. At certain times, for example in spring or when the cat is sick, quite large amounts of hair are consumed, and a 'hairball' may be formed in the cat's throat or stomach.

When a mass of hair balls up in the stomach it may prevent the normal passage of food. Eventually the hairball will either pass through into the small intestine or the cat will vomit it up as a cigar-shaped mass. This vomiting may appear disagreeable but it does not cause the cat any harm. It is natural and normal, and not a cause for alarm.

A cat with a hairball may feel hungry but eats only a little at a time, presumably because the hairball gives it a bloated feeling.

First aid
You can ease the passage of a hairball by giving a non-toxic lubricant, such as mineral oil, liquid paraffin or white petroleum jelly. We prefer liquid paraffin, half to one teaspoon daily until the hairball is cleared.

There are many commercial hairball 'cures' available. These are generally prepared so as to be quite attractive to cats and are therefore often easier to administer than liquid paraffin.

Prevention
Regular brushing or combing will reduce the formation of hairballs and perhaps even prevent them altogether. Extra grooming is especially valuable in spring when most cats moult.

Hairballs are just a part of life for many cats. Having to watch a cat vomit a hairball can be disturbing for many owners. Don't get too upset. Once the cat has expelled the offending mass of hair it will feel much better. If, however, the cat continually gags and retches but fails to produce the offending irritant, then you should contact your vet.

A non-toxic lubricant such as liquid paraffin (from the chemist, not the garage) helps to ease the passage of a hairball.

HEATSTROKE

Signs
Open mouth, rapid breathing, salivation. Gums very red at first, but later becoming bluish. Cat becomes very distressed. Eventually will collapse into a coma. Death could follow.

Treatment
You must cool the cat and provide good ventilation.
- Remove it from the hot area (for example, parked car with windows shut).
- Allow plenty of fresh air.
- Cool the cat, using a water spray or cloths soaked in cool water *or* immerse the cat up to its neck in a cool water bath.
- After recovery, allow free access to clean drinking water.

The cat's condition should improve within about ten minutes, although you may have to continue cooling for up to half an hour. *Beware:* Do not overdo the cooling as the cat could become chilled. The water should be cool but not icy.

Veterinary advice should be sought after the cat's temperature has been brought down. There is some danger of cerebral oedema (swelling of the brain) developing.

Causes of heatstroke
Heatstroke is usually associated with confinement in a hot, poorly ventilated area such as a parked car, in a cat box exposed to direct sunlight or in a tin shed. Deprivation from water exacerbates the situation.

Cats with flat faces, such as Persians, are more susceptible to heatstroke, as are very old or very young cats.

Prevention
Prevention is mainly common sense and forethought.
- Never leave your cat confined in a parked car or similar confined space when the weather is hot (over 25°C).
- On hot days, allow the cat plenty of air circulation and free access to water and shade.

COLD INJURY (HYPOTHERMIA)

Cause
Exposure to cold water or freezing temperatures, especially if cat is wet or in a debilitated state. Sometimes cats are accidentally locked in a fridge. Newborn kittens are highly susceptible to cold stress. If the cat's body temperature falls below 32°C (90°F), normal body functions are severely depressed.

Signs
At first, shivering. As the body temperature drops, the cat becomes lethargic and eventually unconscious. The body is very cold to the touch, especially at the extremities, such as ear tips. Breathing is slow and shallow.

Treatment
If the cat is wet, first dry it thoroughly. Avoid all draughts. Then apply heat.

26

Important: Do not try to heat the cat too quickly as the sudden application of heat can cause shock and collapse, and perhaps extensive tissue damage.

Put the cat into a warm room, but not too close to the heater or fire.

If the cat has collapsed, or in the case of a chilled newborn kitten, immersion in a warm water bath is an excellent way of heating the cat. After the cat has warmed, remove it from the bath and dry it thoroughly. Then keep it in a warm, draught-free area for several hours.

Warm milk and food may be offered. If the cat is not interested, do not attempt to force feed it.

FROSTBITE *(especially of ear tips and tail)*

Signs
Affected area feels very cold and lacks any sensation. It may be very pale or a bluish colour.

Treatment
Apply warm cotton wool pads. First soak the pads in warm water, then squeeze out excess fluid. Do not rub the injured area, or the skin may be damaged. Keep changing the pads or re-warming them.

Seek veterinary advice. If the damage is too severe the affected area may require amputation.

OBJECTS CAUGHT IN THE MOUTH

Fish hook in lip
Do not try to pull the hook out. If possible, have your vet remove the hook. Otherwise, cut the hook in half with wire cutters or pliers so that the barb falls off. Then the hook can quickly be slid out of the cat's lip.

Thread
Beware: There could be a needle on the other end. Cats enjoy playing with thread but the thread can easily become hooked around the barbs on the cat's tongue. It is then inexorably worked back into the throat, and swallowed. If you suspect a needle could be on the other end, you should *not* attempt to pull the thread out. Seek veterinary advice immediately.

Other foreign objects (e.g. bones, hair or grass seeds)
Do not put your fingers into the cat's mouth. Even very placid cats can unintentionally bite. The cat has a very sensitive throat and you may inadvertently trigger off a reflex reaction, causing the cat to bite down on your finger.

Use a pair of tweezers or needle nose pliers if you are trying to remove foreign matter from your cat's mouth. Thread, grass or other debris tangled around the teeth can usually be removed by lifting the lip back. Work from the outside of the teeth. This is easier than trying to open the jaws and probe around inside.

If you need to open the mouth and probe inside, for example to remove a bone lodged across the roof of the mouth, you should prepare well first. Get someone to help in restraining the cat. Preferably wrap the cat in a towel first. Put the cat on a table where the light is good. A pencil torch is helpful and can be held in your mouth, leaving both hands free. *Remember: Do not* put your fingers into the cat's mouth. Use tweezers, pliers or similar.

MOTOR CAR ACCIDENTS (or similar trauma)

After an accident the cat will be in a state of shock. It will be frightened and perhaps in pain. Approach carefully and slowly. The cat is liable to be very defensive, and could be aggressive even to people it knows well.

Talk to the cat quietly. Don't make sudden movements or grab for the cat. Even if the cat is lying dazed, be careful — it may partially recover and scratch or bite in fear.

Ideally, you should wear long leather gloves such as motorcycle gauntlets. These will only rarely be available, so use the best substitute you can. A coat, large towel, or rug may be thrown over the cat and it can then be picked up. If the cat is fairly calm, expose its head (but *only* its head).

Be prepared — the cat will probably wriggle and struggle. Don't let go unless you absolutely must. Any future attempts to catch the cat will be far more difficult than the first.

If you pick up the cat — hold it by the scruff and place it as soon as practicable into a cat box or other suitable container.

If the cat escapes — do not chase it helter skelter. Watch where it goes, then approach slowly. A calm approach has a much better chance of success.

Depending on the nature of the cat's injury, proceed as outlined for shock and/or bleeding, fractures, cuts and bruises.

STINGS AND INSECT BITES

Bees, wasps, hornets, ants and other insects
These stings can cause considerable distress. Kittens indulging in play-hunting are especially liable.

Signs
Intense pain at the site of the sting. Site becomes swollen, red and hot to the touch. With spider bites or multiple wasp or bee stings, there may also be:
- Vomiting.
- Muscle twitching.
- Shivering.

If the bite is around the mouth there could be localised swelling in the throat or tongue. This is an emergency. Urgent veterinary attention is required. There are no effective first aid measures if the cat's throat is obstructed by swelling. *Otherwise:*
- If the sting is visible, pull it out with tweezers.
- If the cat will co-operate, apply cotton wool soaked in vinegar to the bitten area. An antihistamine cream, if available, may help.

SNAKE BITES

A venomous snake bite leaves two puncture wounds. Non-venomous bites leave a U-shaped row of teeth marks. Both types are difficult to see unless the hair is shaved off

Cats are rarely bitten by snakes. The common adder (*Vipera berus*) is poisonous but most European snakes are not. In North America and Africa many snakes are poisonous, and in Australia almost all are.

The wound produced by the bite of a poisonous snake generally has only two deep puncture wounds. Non-venomous snakes leave a semi-circular or 'U' shaped row of teeth marks.

28

Treatment
For a *non-venomous* bite, treat the wound as for any bite wound. Assume contamination with bacteria. If possible, clip away the hair and wash the wound with mild soap and water, then rinse with water mixed with 2% hydrogen peroxide. Most cats will resent any handling of the wound, but will generally clean it themselves. If swelling persists or a discharge develops, consult your vet.

If you suspect a bite from a *venomous* snake:

● Slow the spread of the venom. If possible, apply a pressure bandage to the bitten area. Apply a cold compress. Keep the cat as quiet and inactive as you can. Ideally, put it into a small box or cage.

● Transport immediately to a vet. Telephone ahead to allow the vet to prepare.

BURNS AND SCALDS

Technically, a burn is caused by dry heat such as a flame or a hot surface, while a scald is caused by hot liquids, fat or steam. The result is the same and the treatment is the same.

The skin of the cat rarely blisters. This sometimes leads owners into underestimating the extent of the damage. The presence of a thick coat can also help to mask the severity and extent of a burn and (especially) of a scald.

Burns are usually extremely painful. The loss of skin cover leads to the development of shock and dehydration through pain and fluid loss. The barrier to invasion by bacteria is reduced and infections can quickly develop. Extensive burns lead to dehydration.

Treatment
Cool the damaged area immediately. Immerse the cat in a sinkful of water, or spray or gently hose the affected part. Cold soaking with wet cloths will do, but be sure to re-soak the cloths frequently and do not rub at the wound. Continue this treatment for 5 to 15 minutes.

Do *not* apply ointments or grease or butter to the affected area. This not only helps retain the heat but the cat is also likely to resent its application and presence and will sometimes lick it off despite the pain and additional damage that this causes.

Do *not* pull any matter stuck to the cat's coat, and do not remove any crusts or scabs. This could expose more raw tissue, making the onset of shock more rapid. Leave the cleaning of an extensive burn or scald to a vet.

Cats with more than a very minor burn or scald should be examined by a vet. This is especially true for burns over 2cm in diameter and/or where the eyes or mouth are affected. Cats can tolerate much greater heat than humans (see p.46). While we find temperatures over 45°C (113°F) uncomfortable to the touch, cats show no great discomfort until above 52°C (126°F).

TOAD POISONING

Toads produce a venom in the glands of their skin. The venom of European toads is relatively weak in comparison with some species in Africa, the Americas and Australia. If a cat picks up a toad, this venom can cause the lining of the mouth to become extremely swollen and inflamed.

If the cat is bitten by a poisonous snake, try to slow the spread of venom. Keep the cat as quiet and still as possible and apply a pressure bandage, starting at the foot. This will not completely constrict the blood flow but will help to prevent the venom from spreading too quickly. Take the cat to the vet.

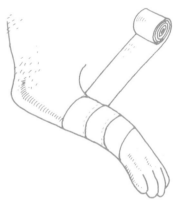

Signs
- Profuse salivation.
- Retching, drooling.
- Vomiting.
- Loss of consciousness could occur but is uncommon.

These signs persist for 8 to 12 hours.

Treatment
- Provide plenty of fresh, clean water.
- If the cat will allow it, flush out the mouth with copious quantities of water.
- If the cat is very distressed, your vet can give injections to reduce the swelling and salivation and to control the pain. In most cases this is unnecessary.

STRAINING

VET TREATMENT URGENT

Beware! If you notice your cat hunched in its litter tray or in the garden it may not be constipated. It could have an infection or even a blockage of the bladder.

A blocked bladder is an emergency. It occurs almost exclusively in neutered male cats. Many of these cats have been inappropriately treated for constipation for several days by their owners before being taken to the vet.

If the blockage is not relieved, the cat will die within four days, usually less. See page 205 for more details.

GLUE ON THE COAT

Allow the glue to dry, then clip off the glue and affected fur. Beware! Do not apply solvents to the glue or severe skin and internal damage could result.

POISONING

See pages 33–41 for a list of symptoms, causes and treatments.

SHOCK

A state of 'shock' is serious. *Shock* does not mean just a 'fright.' Shock is a series of physiological changes that occur in the body after injury.

SHOCK CAN KILL

Many cats injured in road accidents or severely burned, etc., die from shock.

Some causes of shock
- Severe diarrhoea and vomiting.
- Blood loss.
- Fluid loss, for example from burns.
- Severe bruising.
- Blood poisoning, for example from extensive bite infection.
- Snake bite.
- Car accidents.

Signs
- Rapid, shallow breathing or panting (cats rarely pant — if they do so they are generally in considerable distress).
- Pale, cold or bluish coloured gums. (Lift the side of a lip back to examine these.)
- Paws and ears feel cold.
- Pulse or heartbeat is weak and rapid.
- Cat may be immobile and unwilling to stand, flopping down again if picked up. May be very flaccid and unresponsive.
- Fails to respond normally to being called, stroked or picked up.
- Pupils dilated (wide open). May have a 'glazed' look about the eyes.

Treatment
Time is important. Start treatment as soon as possible. Don't let shock develop.
- Keep the cat warm, dry and draught free. If necessary, wrap the cat in a blanket and put into a warm room or apply heat indirectly, for example, using a water bottle. Beware of overheating the cat. Do not place it too close to a fire or place the hot water bottle directly onto the coat. Overheating can make shock worse.
- Reassure the cat — calm, quiet talking and slow, gentle stroking can be an extremely effective method.
- Don't disturb the cat too much if it resents attention.
- If the cat wants to drink, give warm milk or glucose and water. DO NOT try to force liquids.

Where shock is severe, veterinary attention is necessary. If you have to transport the cat, keep it warm and move it gently. It is better to drive slowly than to race anxiously and further alarm the cat.

VOMITING

A cat vomits to clear its stomach of any irritating or noxious substances, for example, hairballs, spoiled food or toxic chemicals. In many instances, once the offending matter has been eliminated, the problem is over and there is no need for treatment other than to 'rest' the stomach.

Sometimes vomiting can be a sign of a serious disorder. Vomiting may occur as one clinical sign in the following conditions. This list is not exhaustive:
- Obstructions of the bowel.
- Liver, pancreas or kidney disease.
- Swelling within any abdominal organ, for example a tumour of the spleen or a blocked bladder.
- Food poisoning.
- Viral infection, for example feline infectious enteritis.

If your cat has vomited but otherwise is alert and not in pain, proceed as follows:
- Remove all food and water.
- After eight to twelve hours offer a small amount of food. A spoonful is enough. Give a food that you know the cat likes, but avoid fatty, oily or rich foods. Cooked, minced chicken or fish is suitable.
- Offer water, but do not allow the cat to drink more than about a tablespoonful at a time.
- For the next twenty-four hours offer only small meals.
- Return the cat to the normal diet gradually.
- Don't rush. Take two to five days. This allows the stomach to settle down.

31

Consult your vet if
- The vomit contains blood.
- Vomiting is frequent or persistent.
- Vomiting is accompanied by profuse diarrhoea.
- The cat is lethargic, distressed or in pain.

DIARRHOEA

Many cats are private or secretive about their bowel motions. You may not actually be able to see a motion. Suspect diarrhoea if your cat is making frequent trips to the toilet area, or if the fur around the anus and hocks is matted or stained, or if the anus is raw and inflamed.

(*Note:* Frequent trips to the toilet area can also indicate cystitis.)

Most cats will have an occasional bout of diarrhoea. In many cases no treatment is necessary, but if the diarrhoea is severe or persistent then read the section on page 181 and consult your vet if necessary.

Treatment for mild diarrhoea
- Withhold food for twelve hours.
- Give water only. No milk.
- After twelve hours, offer small amounts of a readily–digestible food such as cooked, minced chicken. Add boiled rice if the cat will accept it.
- Only gradually return to the normal diet.

There are various anti-diarrhoea preparations commercially available. These could help to speed a cure. For example, use Kaomagma (aluminium hydroxide gel) or Kaopectate. Dose: half to one teaspoon twice daily.

Consult your vet if
- The cat is very lethargic.
- Vomiting accompanies the diarrhoea.
- There is blood in the motion.
- Diarrhoea persists or recurs after treatment is withdrawn.

FALL FROM A HEIGHT

Over–ambitious or frightened cats may jump from a height that is beyond their capabilities. Sometimes a cat may jump at a bird that lands on a windowsill, or perhaps a branch may give way as it climbs a tree.

Usually a cat will survive if it falls from below a height of three storeys. Above that the outcome depends on the nature of the ground it falls upon.

Cats almost always land on all four feet. In some cases the cat's chin will smack onto the ground, so a fracture of the lower jaw is a common result of a fall from a height. The cat may also lose teeth and split the roof of its mouth. One or more legs could be fractured.

Other injuries could possibly include shock and perhaps rupture of internal organs such as the liver, kidney and spleen.

POISONING

Cats are very careful about what they eat. As a result malicious poisonings are rare. But there are other ways in which a cat may be exposed to toxic doses of a variety of dangerous compounds. Sometimes an owner may inadvertently give drugs that the cat's system cannot cope with. There are many substances that are relatively non toxic to humans, but which are dangerous to cats. Cats cannot readily detoxify or degrade these substances into harmless by-products. Common examples are aspirin, paracetamol, benzoic acid (a preservative) and phenolic compounds. Another relatively common way in which cats are exposed to poisons is when their coat is contaminated by them. The cat's meticulous grooming instincts drive it to clear away any foreign matter. Unfortunately, there could be potentially toxic substances present such as insecticides, disinfectants, cleansers, lead paints or adhesives.

The correct first aid procedures, applied as soon after exposure as possible, can be critical to the outcome.

Do not induce vomiting until you check the list to see if this is the correct procedure

In some cases inducing vomiting can cause further serious damage. DO NOT induce vomiting in the case of ingestion of the following: petrol, turpentine, acids, caustic cleansers, dry cleaning fluid, paint thinners, kerosene, flyspray or furniture polish.

Inducing vomiting
There are various ways of stimulating the cat to vomit. DO NOT try to stick a finger down the cat's throat — you will inevitably be bitten, no matter how placid the cat, as its jaw will clamp shut in a reflex action.

Give *one* of the following:
- Syrup of IPECAC — Dose: 2 mls per kg body weight (usual dose for adult cat: 8 mls).
- Salt and water: make up a solution by dissolving two heaped teaspoons common table salt in half a cup of water. Try to give the cat 10 mls or more.
- Half teaspoon salt placed on the back of the tongue.
- One teaspoon raw mustard.
- Hydrogen peroxide (3% solution). Dose: 5 mls.

Do not induce vomiting if the cat is not fully conscious

Cats sometimes ingest poisonous substances when they groom themselves

33

NAME	COMMON SOURCES	SIGNS	IMMEDIATE HOME TREATMENT	COMMENTS
Acetamin-ophen	Paracetamol — type of pain killer.	Gums dirty brown colour. Difficulty breathing. Blood in urine. Jaundice and facial swelling.		*Don't* give paracetamol to cats. Even small amounts are toxic. Cats rarely accidentally eat these products. Signs may appear many days after ingestion.
Acids	Battery acids, some cleaning polishing and bleaching agents.	Severe chemical burns on skin. Abdominal pain, blood stained vomiting, mouth burns. Shock.	*Do not induce vomiting.* Give neat evaporated milk, milk or water, milk of magnesia or aluminium hydroxide mixture. See vet as soon as possible. Acid on skin: flush with lots of water.	Cats don't usually drink acids voluntarily, but will lick them off their skin if spilt on it.
Adhesives	Glues and pastes.	Drooling, lip smacking, abdominal pain.	Give milk.	Not usually attractive to cats but can be quite toxic.
Alcohol, methylated spirits	Alcoholic drinks, perfumes and after-shaves, industrial alcohol.	Depression, vomiting, collapse, dehydration, coma and death.	Induce vomiting *if* conscious then give activated charcoal in water.	Not usually attracted to strong–smelling products. Some cats may be induced to drink alcoholic drinks for 'fun.' Such 'fun' can be fatal.
Alkaline (strong bases)	Fluid cleaners, e.g. drain cleaners and solvents.	Severe chemical burns on skin. Abdominal pain, blood–stained vomiting. Possibly mouth burns or ulcers.	Alkali on skin — flush with lots of water. *Do not induce vomiting.* Give neat evaporated milk or water with 50% lemon juice or water with 25% vinegar to neutralise the alkali. See a vet.	Cats don't usually drink alkaline products but will try and lick it off if spilt on their coats.
Alpha-choralose	Rodenticide. Also used for stupefaction of pigeons.	Depression, lethargy, cold.	Wrap cat in blanket and put in warm room. No other treatment needed.	
Ammonia	Household cleaner.	Signs due to inhaling fumes: sneezing, salivating, drooling. May vomit.	Fresh air.	Rarely a problem because cats are repelled by the smell.

NAME	COMMON SOURCES	SIGNS	IMMEDIATE HOME TREATMENT	COMMENTS
Antibiotics	Dispensed tablets for human or animal infections.	*Penicillin:* Vomiting and diarrhoea if large number consumed. *Streptomycin:* Nerve damage, head tilt, circling. *Nalidixic acid:* (Used in humans for bacterial bladder infection.) Vomiting, hypersensitivity, back arching, loss of balance. Coma or fitting may follow.	Induce vomiting. Induce vomiting. See vet as soon as possible. Induce vomiting. See vet as soon as possible.	Nerve damage may be permanent.
Anti-depressants	Valium (diazapam).	Depression, loss of consciousness and coma.	If still conscious induce vomiting.	Take to vet immediately.
Anti-freeze (ethylene glycol)	Radiator preparation to prevent the water freezing.	Depression, ataxia. Sometimes vomiting. Convulsions followed by coma.	Immediate intensive veterinary attention is needed. Often kidney damage irreversible.	Cats like the sweet taste.
Ant-killers	See 'Arsenic' if it contains arsenic.	If it contains chlordecone there are usually no signs.		
ANTU (alpha-naphthyl thiourca)	Rat poison. Not commonly used.	Restlessness, anxiety, perhaps vomiting. Breathing difficulty and coma.	Immediate veterinary attention. No antidote available.	Usually fatal.
Arsenic	Ant, cockroach and rat poisons, herbicides and insecticides	Restlessness, abdominal pain, vomiting and bloody diarrhoea. Dehydration.	Induce vomiting. Give milk. See your vet immediately. An antidote is available.	Urine, bowel motions or vomit should be kept and submitted to your vet for analysis if malicious poisoning suspected.
Aspirin (acetyl salicylic acid), Disprin, Aspro	A common, widely used household pain-killing drug.	Inco-ordination, loss of balance and falling. Hypersensitivity and loss of appetite. Vomiting occurs, sometimes it may be bloodstained.	Induce vomiting. Give water or milk plus activated charcoal.	This drug is toxic if given in large doses or in smaller doses over a number of days.

NAME	COMMON SOURCES	SIGNS	IMMEDIATE HOME TREATMENT	COMMENTS
Baby oil	Baby oil.	Nil. Perhaps diarrhoea twelve hours later.	Nil.	
Barbiturates	Some sleeping tablets and tranquillisers.	Depression and sleepiness. Loss of consciousness followed by coma.	If conscious, induce vomiting. Keep the cat moving and take to vet as soon as possible.	
Baysol — (*see* Organophosphates)				
Benzoic acid	A preservative in some pet meat and tinned pet food.	Inco-ordination, muscle tremors. Apparent blindness. Supersensitive to touch, may convulse.	Take to vet immediately.	High concentrations can be fatal. Also accumulative effect of low doses over long period of time.
Bleach	Laundry products.	(*See* Alkalis.)		
Carbamate — (*see* Organophosphates)				
Carbon monoxide	Car exhaust fumes. Cat may be locked in garage or boot with fumes building up.	Poisoning occurs rapidly. Gums cherry red. Breathing distress.	Encourage activity to increase blood flow to vital organs. Place in fresh air. If unconscious, artificially respirate — place your fingers and thumbs either side of the chest with your palm straddling the breast bone. Firmly depress the chest then release. Repeat 15 times per minute.	After recovery, the cat may be staggering for several hours.
Carbon tetra-chloride (fumes)	Some worming preparations. Rarely used now. Some dry-cleaning fluids.	Breathing difficulty and respiratory failure.	Artificial respiration. Fresh air.	

NAME	COMMON SOURCES	SIGNS	IMMEDIATE HOME TREATMENT	COMMENTS
Chlorinated hydro-carbons (in-secticides)	Flea rinses. Benzene hydrochloride, Dieldrin, BHC, DDT, Gammexane, Lindane, toxophene, chlordane, methoxychlor. They are absorbed through the skin.	Apprehension, muscle–twitching and very sensitive to touch. Progresses to epileptiform convulsions, often triggered by handling.	There is no specific antidote. The aim is to reduce the amount of poison absorbed. If convulsing, take straight to vet in a box or basket to reduce handling. Don't pet the cat in reassurance as it will trigger fitting. If not convulsing, wash poison off body with soap and water. Induce vomiting. *Don't* give milk.	Samples of vomit or bowel motions should be collected if malicious poisoning suspected. If cat submerged in Lindane, death usually follows. Dieldrin is sometimes used to dress grains before sowing. Rodents eating such seeds become inco-ordinated and stagger, making easy targets for cats or birds. A cat that eats one of these rodents will also be poisoned.
Chlorine	Water steriliser, swimming pool contains too low a concentration to cause acute poisoning.	Reddened eyes and sometimes mouth if strong solution contacted.	If in eye, wash out well. If much is swallowed, give milk.	
Cosmetics		Most are fairly non-toxic. Highly perfumed ones contain a lot of alcohol but cats rarely touch them.		
Detergents		If used to bath cats, may cause itchy, red skin. If licked off coat, frothing or foaming at the mouth. Vomiting.	Rinse off coat. Use mild baby shampoo to rewash. Rinse thoroughly.	Don't use detergents to bath cats. Low toxicity when ingested.

Dieldrin — (*see* Chlorinated hydrocarbons)

Disinfectants — (if contains Phenol — *see* Phenol)

Drain cleaners — (*see* Alkali)

Ethylene glycol — (*see* Anti-freeze)

NAME	COMMON SOURCES	SIGNS	IMMEDIATE HOME TREATMENT	COMMENTS
Flea collars	Organophosphates, dichlorvos, propoxur.	Allergic reaction, red, irritated skin around neck and eyes.	Remove the collar. Don't use a flea collar with the same active ingredient again. If severe reaction see your vet.	
Kerosene	Heating and lighting fuel. Cleaning fluids.	If spilt on cat — red skin, may burn. When ingested, causes abdominal pain. May have lip and tongue ulceration.	Wash in vegetable oil several times then mild soap. Rinse thoroughly. If swallowed give vegetable oil orally and then induce vomiting.	Take to vet.
Lead	Lead-based paint — not used in modern household paint but old painted objects are a source e.g. stripping paint off wood before renovation. Linoleum, batteries, putty, some lubricants, solder, plasterboard and roofing material.	First the cat has gut signs. Nervous signs follow. *Gut signs:* abdominal pain, vomiting, loss of appetite. *Nervous signs:* very variable. Anxiety, restlessness, perhaps hysteria. Dislike of light (photophobia), inco-ordination, staggering, periodic convulsions, eventual paralysis.	Lead poisoning can be fatal if untreated. Induce vomiting if lead has been eaten within the previous half hour. Take to vet. Your vet may perform blood tests to confirm lead poisoning. An effective antidote is available.	Unusual poisoning in the cat. More likely to occur due to curiosity. A slow build-up of lead can occur before signs become obvious. Skin absorption of lead from used motor oil is significant enough to produce lead poisoning.
Lindane — (*see* Chlorinated hydrocarbons)				
Mercury	Mercurial ointments e.g. mercurachrome.	Abdominal pain, vomiting, droppings blood-flecked, decreased urinary output.	Wash off any remaining ointment. If has been used over a long period of time — see your vet.	Don't use mercurial ointments on the skin of cats as they will lick it off.
Metalde-hyde	Slug and snail poison ('Defender').	Continuous salivation (foaming at mouth), muscle-twitching and convulsions.	Induce vomiting. If not convulsing go straight to vet. If treatment prompt, outlook reasonable.	Cats find the pellets attractive. When using them on gardens don't heap the pellets but scatter them over a wide area.
Methylated spirits — (*see* Alcohol)				Poisoning rare as cats don't like the smell or taste.

NAME	COMMON SOURCES	SIGNS	IMMEDIATE HOME TREATMENT	COMMENTS
Organo-phosphate carbamate (Baysol)	Snail and slug killers. Insecticides absorbed via skin, mouth or lungs. Some worming preparations e.g. dichlorvos, diazinon, malathion, ronnel, trichlorfon.	Continuous salivation, vomiting and diarrhoea. Muscle-twitching, inco-ordination and convulsions. Increased tear production, laboured respiration.	If on skin, wash off with soap and water. Go straight to vet. Antidote effective if treated early.	Common.
Paint	Housepaint. Usually spilt on coat.	Relatively non-toxic.	Leave on coat to dry then cut off painted hairs. *Don't* put paint solvents such as turpentine on or near the skin.	
Paracetamol — (*see* Acetaminophen)				
Paraquat	Weed killer.	Produces gut signs first then breathing problems 3-4 weeks later. *Gut signs:* vomiting, abdominal pain and depression. *Later:* difficulty breathing, rapid respiration at rest. Irreversible lung consolidation.	Early veterinary treatment essential. Mineral absorbants such as kaolin or Fuller's Earth can be used to absorb paraquat from the stomach.	Rare in cats. Requires cat to eat grass that has been sprayed with the herbicide.
Petroleum products	Oils, greases, benzenes, hydrocarbons etc. May be ingested or absorbed through skin.	*Ingestion:* weight loss, liver and kidney problems (slow to develop). *Skin:* red, irritated. Becomes thickened with time. May burn when exposed to strong sunlight (photosensitisation).	Wash the cat thoroughly with soap and water (any poison on the coat of the cat will be licked off). See your vet if chronic skin problem present.	White cats or cats with white patches are prone to photosensitisation.

NAME	COMMON SOURCES	SIGNS	IMMEDIATE HOME TREATMENT	COMMENTS
Phenols	Many disinfectants and household cleaners. Fungicides, wood preservatives, some photographic developers.	Skin burning. If ingested, twitching staggering and coma. Usually fatal.	If treated immediately on ingestion or if only a weak solution ingested: give neat evaporated milk or milk and olive oil. Then induce vomiting. Wash off coat immediately using methylated spirits then soap and water.	See your vet. Never use disinfectants on cats.
Phenyl-butazone	Tablets prescribed for human or animal arthritic problems.	Loss of appetite, weight loss and depression. May induce chronic kidney problems.	Induce vomiting. Go to your vet.	Not common.
Sodium chlorate	Weed killer.	Small dose — no signs. If large dose: vomiting, depression, coma and death.	See your vet.	Rare poisoning in cats. Cat must ingest recently sprayed grass.
Strychnine	Pesticides.	Apprehensive and irritable. Tense and stiff. This progresses to violent convulsions stimulated by loud noises or by touching the cat. Often fatal.	Induce vomiting if *not* convulsing. Go immediately to your vet. Transport in a box or basket. Avoid loud noise or sudden movement.	Most commonly used in malicious poisoning. Any suspected source or vomitus should be collected for analysis.
Thallium	Rat and other rodent poison. Often used by commercial exterminators.	Depression, abdominal pain and loss of appetite. Vomiting and diarrhoea, muscle spasm and paralysis may follow. If recovery from these signs occurs 5-7 days later, striking changes in the skin occur: red, crusty peeling areas of hairless skin all over body.	Induce vomiting. Go to your vet immediately. An effective antidote available if treatment begun early.	Poisoning more likely to occur in cats that scavenge around new buildings or construction sites.

NAME	COMMON SOURCES	SIGNS	IMMEDIATE HOME TREATMENT	COMMENTS
Toad poisoning	Skin glands over toad's body express poison when cat has the toad in its mouth. Poison is rapidly absorbed regardless of whether the toad is swallowed.	Local reaction: severe reddening and swelling inside mouth. Excessive drooling and retching for 5-12 hours. Body reaction: severe abdominal pain. Continuous exhausting vomiting. Difficulty breathing. Inco-ordination. Glazed expression in eyes.	Provide plenty of fresh, clean water. Flush out the mouth with water. In tropical countries, see your vet immediately.	The venom of European toads causes discomfort rather than serious poisoning but some tropical species are dangerous.
Tobacco	Cigarettes.	Vomiting due to stomach irritation.	Charcoal tablets.	
Toxaphene — (*see* Chlorinated hydrocarbons)				
Turpentine	Paint solvent.	Burning of skin, lips and tongue.	Wash cat thoroughly with soap and water. If skin very irritated see your vet.	
Warfarin ('Ratsac')	Rat and mice poison. Other similar products: Coumateryl (Racumin), Coumachlor and Chlorophacinous (Drat).	A blood anti-coagulent (stops blood clotting). Therefore signs are related to bleeding and vary according to the site of bleeding. These may be breathing difficulty, sometimes blood in the droppings or vomit. Heart rate is rapid and weak. Small haemorrages or blood spots on the gums. Weakness progresses to staggering, collapse and death.	Treat gently. Do *not* knock, bump or handle roughly as this may increase internal bleeding. Keep warm. Go to your vet as soon as possible as antidote is highly successful when given early.	Cats probably not poisoned by eating pellets directly, but by eating rats or mice that have been slowed down by their last meal of bait.
1080 (sodium fluoroi-acetate)	Vermin poisons for rats, rabbits, foxes, etc. Odourless and tasteless.	Signs start 4-10 hours after eating. Aimless wandering, confused, disorientated behaviour. Unusual vocalisation. Vomiting, urination and repeated bowel motions. Frothing at the mouth, laboured breathing and convulsions.	None. Go to vet immediately.	Cats are less susceptible to 1080 than dogs. Treatment may be successful if commenced early.

THE SENSES

How well does a cat see, hear or smell? The cat lives in a world of sensations very different to the ones we perceive. In trying to understand the cat's behaviour we try to find explanations in terms of our own senses, but we will never be able really to comprehend the feline mind.

HEARING

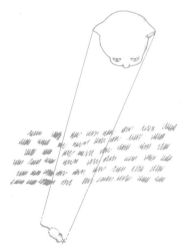

The cat can accurately detect the direction from which a sound has come. The cat knows where the mouse is even though a hedge screens it from view

The cat has developed a hunter's sense of hearing. Prowling cats hear sounds that are inaudible to the human ear. Their hearing ranges far into ultrasound, well beyond our capability. Cats do more than just detect sound — they can also locate its source. The cat has twelve muscles in each ear that can accurately direct the ear towards a sound source, allowing the cat to zero in on a potential meal or source of danger. A cat can discriminate between two sound sources only five degrees apart — that is, the width of only four fingers at a range of over a metre.

Cats are born deaf, but their hearing develops quickly. Try rustling a piece of crumpled cellophane near a ten-week-old kitten. The high frequency noises mimic the sounds made by small prey and usually trigger play-stalking and catching actions.

The cat's sense of hearing remains 'on guard' even when the cat is asleep, or 'cat napping'. The slightest unusual sound arouses the cat back to full alert. Cats are also sensitive to vibrations felt through the pads of their feet, and are said to 'hear' with their feet.

As acute as their sense of hearing is, the cat cannot hunt effectively in total darkness. Sight and touch are also essential for successful hunting.

With advancing age, the cat's hearing acuity diminishes. This is because the sensitive structures of the inner ear become less mobile and respond less efficiently to sound waves. The nerves that relay signals from the inner ear to the brain also degenerate slowly, resulting in various degrees of deafness.

Blue-eyed white cats are deaf. This is due to a genetic defect. The specific colour combination of white coat and blue eye is found only on a gene that also produces a defect in one of the structures of the inner ear, resulting in the prevention of the passage of sound waves. If a white cat has only one blue eye, it is deaf in the ear next to the blue eye, but may hear with the other ear.

SIGHT

The cat has large, deep set eyes that gaze forwards, allowing the field of vision from each eye to overlap and produce a three dimensional image. Compare this to the rabbit, horse or cow where the eyes are set on either side of the head to give a wide field of vision. The cat, as a result, has a narrower field of vision, but the three dimensional sight that is gained allows it to judge distances accurately when jumping and climbing, or pouncing on prey.

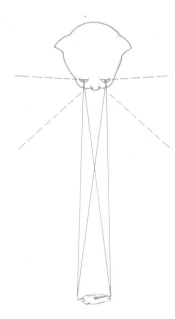

By focusing on its prey the cat can judge its distance and size. The cat's 'peripheral' vision is about 180° and is shown by the dotted lines

The back of the cat's eye is lined with a mirror-like structure (the Tapetum lucidum). This reflects any light not initially absorbed by the retina, (where the sight image is formed) and so creates a 'second image'. This greatly increases the cat's visual sensitivity in dim light. Cats can see in light that is six times dimmer than light in which humans are capable of seeing.

It is this reflecting shield that gave the cat its God-like status in Ancient Egypt. The Egyptians believed that the cat's eyes continued to reflect the sun during the night, so they shaped their sun God 'Ra' in the form of a cat so that Ra could work against the malevolent powers of darkness.

The cat's sight and hunting
The cat needs to see well at night because its main prey are small mammals or rodents which are most active at night. The cat's eye is acutely sensitive to movement. Once a tiny movement has alerted the cat, it can then concentrate accurately on that spot, sublimating all other movement, such as wind-blown grass.

How does a cat's sight compare with man's?
The cat's eye may be more sensitive in dim light than man's, but it lacks the ability to focus and produce a clear, sharp image. It is estimated that our ability to focus is ten times better than the cat's. Sight has evolved as man's primary sense. Our ancestors needed close, precise focus for activities such as tool-making. It also enabled them to choose ripe fruits correctly and to avoid poisonous herbs and plants. Acute sight was essential to successful hunting and defence. To the cat, the sense of sight is less important. Their sense of sight is integrated closely with other senses, especially those of hearing and smell. The cat places less reliance on a single sense than we do.

Can cats see colour?
Tests suggest that cats can differentiate between blue and green, but probably see mainly in shades, much like a colour TV out of tune. Their colour perception is better than that of the dog, but is far less developed than man's.

When does a kitten see properly?
Kittens are born blind. Their eyes remain closed for the first seven to ten days of life. All kittens' eyes are blue at first, and only gradually mature to reach full development at around three months of age. It is doubtful if kittens see well until they are about six weeks old.

BALANCE

The cat has a remarkable sense of balance, enabling it to perform almost uncanny feats of agility. The cat's sense of sight helps in orientation but it is the inner ear that plays the major role in the cat's balance. Nerves link the ear to a part of the brain called the cerebellum, where information from the inner ear is analysed.

Good balance is essential to cats as they are tree climbers. A well developed 'righting reflex' protects the cat from injury if it falls. During a fall, the cat extends all four legs, which act like shock absorbers when they hit the ground. The pads of the feet further cushion the force of a fall, reducing the chances of spinal or internal injury.

Cats sometimes make mistakes. A cat is especially liable to misjudge if it is carrying something in its mouth. Or it may misjudge the height it is at and make an over-ambitious leap. These errors can result in fractures of the jaw or limbs.

A cat reaches maximum speed of descent after twenty metres; so in theory if a cat can survive a fall of twenty metres it can survive a fall from any height, even from a skyscraper. Survival after falls from enormous heights have been recorded. A cat always has a reasonable chance of survival so long as the fall is onto soft ground.

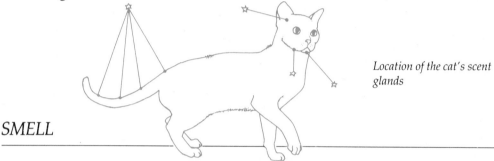

Location of the cat's scent glands

The cat has a remarkable ability to turn itself around to land safely on all four feet

SMELL

The cat's sense of smell is phenomenal in comparison with our mediocre ability. The cat is able to identify individuals solely by their unique smell, and can detect the presence of this smell long after the person or animal has departed.

Cats possess multiple scent glands that produce a specialised secretion with a persistent, personalised odour. We cannot detect this odour. These scent glands are located on each side of the cat's forehead, on the chin and lips and all along the tail. When a cat smooches up and gives you a friendly rub with his head and draws his tail over your legs he is covering you with his scent.

The use of the sense of smell starts from birth. The presence of scents termed 'pheromones' attract the newborn kitten to the mother's nipple. Smell continues to play an important role in eating. Food is always thoroughly sniffed before being accepted. This partly explains why cats are rarely poisoned. They do not rush up and gulp food the way some dogs do. Cats only rarely eat carrion. Most find the smell of tainted food offensive.

If the cat's sense of smell is affected, the result can be catastrophic. During a bout of the 'flu, congestion of nasal passages causes obstruction of the sense of smell. A severely affected cat usually refuses to eat; or will only be tempted with pungent foods such as cheese or smoked fish. Other habits, such as toilet habits and scent-marking, are also upset. Clearing the nasal passages to restore the sense of smell is a priority in sick cats to hasten recovery.

TASTE

Tastebuds are spaced along the front, edges and base of the tongue. We humans perceive four basic dimensions of taste: sweet, salt, bitter and acid. The cat differs from us in showing little response to 'sweet'. Cats do not rely on taste to the extent we do. Smell dominates. The cat's sense of taste is at its most acute when the cat is young. For example, a day-old kitten can detect the difference between salted

44

and unsalted liquid. As the cat matures, the sense of taste diminishes.

Jacobsens organ:
Another dimension to taste and smell. Cats possess a sensory organ termed the Vomeronasal organ, although it is more commonly called Jacobsens organ (after its discoverer). This provides a *third* chemical sense in addition to those of taste and smell. It is complementary to both. Jacobsens organ sits in the roof of the cat's mouth, just behind the incisor teeth. A duct opens from this organ into the mouth. By pressing the tongue up against the duct, odourous chemicals are forced up into the organ. When the organ is stimulated, the cat extends its neck, opens its mouth and lifts the upper lip. We may be tempted to interpret this as a gesture of disgust, but in the cat it is often closer to ecstasy. Such a reaction is most commonly seen in males responding to the sexually stimulating smells of a queen on heat, when 'turning on' to catnip or when smelling each other's anal regions.

The catnip experience
The catnip plant (nepeta cataria, also called catmint) emits an odour that is compelling to most cats. Typically, a cat will sniff, then lick or chew the catnip, then stare blankly into space. Perhaps it may shake its head or rub it against the plants, or roll on the ground, purring ecstatically. These episodes last for five to ten minutes and then cannot be repeated for an hour or more.

The catnip's leaves contain an oil that is an hallucinogen called nepetalactone that is related to marijuana. When the cat presses this oil up into Jacobsens organ it apparently sends the cat on a mild drug induced 'trip', hence the space-staring and rolling behaviour.

Some manufacturers of cat products utilise the attractiveness of catnip by producing playthings stuffed with catnip leaves or scented with its oil. Up to two thirds of the cat population are attracted to catnip. Age or sex makes no difference.

However, be warned. If catnip is used excessively it can result in an unpleasant change in the cat's personality.

TOUCH

The cat's foot pads and nose are particularly sensitive to touch. Throw a kitten an unfamiliar toy: first the kitten will reach out with one paw to touch the object lightly, then touch it more firmly. Finally the nose and whiskers are used to make a closer inspection. The cat's nose is quite sensitive to heat. While sniffing at food, cats are also testing the temperature, and they will quickly step back if it is too hot. Cats rarely burn their nose or mouth on hot foods due partly to this heat sensitivity, and partly to their natural caution.

The cat's foot pads are sensitive to touch and to vibrations. Cats will touch their prey to see if it is dead or pat each other or their owners with their pads as an affectionate gesture. They can detect vibrations such as footsteps long before we are aware that someone is approaching. Because of this sensitivity, many cats hate to have their feet touched or stroked.

The cat's whiskers are sensitive to stimulations as delicate as air currents. In dim light, the cat relies quite heavily on its whiskers, and can detect objects by their deflection of these air currents. The whiskers also act as a defense for the eyes. When the whiskers are touched the cat instinctively blinks.

Most cats love to be stroked and petted, and will brush against legs and nuzzle against other cats or people. The stimulation of stroking has been shown to slow the cat's heart rate, relax the body and increase the rate of digestion in the bowel.

The cat's skin is less sensitive to heat than ours is. A cat may sit on a stove too hot for a human to touch, and may even sit near enough to a heater to burn its fur without displaying any apparent discomfort.

THE SIXTH SENSE

Is it ESP?
Perhaps we don't give the cat enough credit. Certainly, they are intelligent and can solve problems, and can then adapt the solution to different problems. For example, opening doors or retrieving a seemingly inaccessible object. Cats will explore and investigate, apparently purely out of curiosity. This is something which less developed or intelligent animals will not.

Sometimes owners wonder how their cat seems to sense when they are depressed, or are going away or are about to get out the flea powder. Cats are acute observers and read our activities, behaviour and routine with surprisingly accurate perception. Some cats may choose to ignore a modification in the daily routine. Others are more demonstrative and follow the owners from room to room, refusing to leave them alone, or alternatively dash for cover and refuse to be induced out. This is not ESP. This is achieved by reading and reacting to our behaviour with a sensitivity of observation that is surprising.

Feline analysts have come up with four major categories of unusual behaviour. For the first three they offer a logical explanation. For the fourth they cannot.

1. Showing foreknowledge of impending danger or events
As cats are very sensitive to vibrations, felt mainly through the pads of their feet, they may detect minuscule tremors that humans cannot perceive, heralding events such as an earthquake, an eruption or imminent building collapse. They can smell rain or the faint odour of fire long before humans can.

All these sensations are threatening and unfamiliar to the cat, and may trigger quite bizarre behaviour. It is often this unusual behaviour that alerts the owner, and may warn him that something is amiss.

2. Foretelling an unexpected return home by the owner
The cat can detect and recognise the familiar vibrations created by such things as the owner's footsteps, or the family car. We are usually totally oblivious to these slight vibrations. Reports of cats jumping up to greet their owner up to five minutes before their actual arrival have been attributed to ESP but it is probably only due to the cat's far greater sensitivity to a whole range of stimuli.

3. Finding a way home after being lost
It is believed that the cat has an acute sense of time, plus a sensitivity to the earth's magnetic field. These sensory perceptions combine and result in the cat's 'biological clock'. The cat senses from the sun's position at a certain time of the day just where it is in relation to its 'home' base, and can therefore tell in which direction home lies.

4. 'Psi-trailing': Locating its owner in a place where the cat has never been before
There are many accurately recorded cases of cats that have been left behind when the owners move — sometimes up to hundreds of miles away to a new home — and have eventually tracked their owners down. Distances from twenty to two thousand miles have been recorded, and one cat took over two years to reunite itself with its owner.

The explanation for these cases is elusive. Perhaps the cat does have extrasensory powers.

BEHAVIOUR

CATS LIVING WITH CATS

Cats are commonly thought of as solitary animals, preferring to be alone. Certainly while hunting, the cat prefers solitude, but contrary to popular belief most cats can live happily as part of a group. When a number of cats live together, a social structure will be formed within the group with a definite hierarchy, rules and accepted patterns of behaviour.

A basic bond within a group of cats is the mother-kitten relationship. While some males prefer a solitary nomadic role, others become quite paternal and fit comfortably into a family unit. Within a group, cats will groom, nuzzle and rub against each other, play together and sometimes sleep huddled together. Females will look after one another's kittens and may even feed kittens from other litters.

Social hierarchies are formed. Amongst females the order is fairly loose, but rank is rigorously observed by the males. The dominant male commands the greatest territory, but unlike a dog pack leader he does not necessarily mate with all, or even a majority, of the females.

The order of the male hierarchy is determined by fighting. Whenever a new male arrives, fighting will occur. Several toms must be challenged before ranking is established. Fights are short and vicious but never to the death. Fighting will also occur when a queen comes on heat.

The winner does not necessarily enjoy the spoils of victory — the queen decides which tom she will mate with.

Female hierarchy is based mainly on breeding ability. While nursing, a queen enjoys a privileged status and with each litter moves up the social scale. If a female is spayed she will quickly lose her status.

TERRITORIES

Every cat needs its own territory, comprising a home base and a home range. Cats will vigorously defend their territory and comply with a complex code of

These four blocks of land have been broken up into territories of varying size and shape by three cats.

 This neutered male requires only a small territory

 An entire (unneutered) male commands a relatively large area

 A female with kittens will protect her territory aggressively

 Areas are set aside that cats can move along without encroaching on another's territory and where they can meet on neutral ground

territorial behaviour which includes marking out their claim, the establishment of common ground (or neutral areas) and even rules of the road between holdings.

A cat's 'home base' may be no bigger than a sleeping area. In a group, every cat has its own base which the others respect. The home 'range' comprises sleeping, watching and playing areas as well as hunting runs. The size of the range depends primarily on the availability of food. In domestic cats this factor is controlled, but in feral cats it is critical. Where food is scarce, a range may have to be twenty hectares or more. In contrast, many cats can successfully inhabit an area where rodents are plentiful, such as a granary or a rubbish dump. Other factors influencing the size of a cat's range include its sex, age and temperament. Older or neutered cats usually have to be content with small territories.

Pathways between territories
Elaborate systems of permissible pathways are developed to allow cats to pass between territories or move to neutral areas, or areas set aside for hunting, mating or as communal meeting grounds. These pathways, although invisible to us, are clear enough to cats. There are definite right-of-way rules on the pathways. Once a cat has entered a pathway he generally has right of way, and even a more dominant cat will wait its turn before entering. When two cats meet at an intersection the dominant cat has precedence. The inferior cat has to back off. Fighting can occur, especially if it has been a chance meeting. Surprisingly, females are less tolerant towards one another in these encounters than males.

Territories in households with several cats
Each cat establishes a favourite sleeping area as its home base. Some cats will have more than one of these. In other cases, one cat may hold priority over a

48

particular area during the day, but relinquish it to another cat at night.

The home range of a group is generally larger than that held by a single cat. Responsibility for defence of the range is shared by members of the group.

The group also sets aside areas for meetings on a common or neutral ground. The reason for these gatherings is not clear, but they only occur outside the mating season. Cats meeting in these areas can sit close to one another without fear of hostility or aggression. Indeed they will often groom one another.

Moving house

When you move, your cat must establish a new territory. You will already have established your rights by negotiating prior to moving — presumably without bloodshed. Unfortunately, your cat must fight a way in. The garden of your new house may already 'belong' to another cat. Unneutered males are especially liable to have many bloody battles before territorial boundaries are re-drawn and they become established in a new domain.

Marking territories

The claimant of any territory must mark out the boundaries. Scent markings are the primary signal, but clearly visible claw scratch marks may also be left on trees or posts.

The scent glands of the cat are located around the lips, temples, tail and anus. When claiming a possession the cat will leave a scent marking on every convenient object — for example on trees, the legs of furniture and walls. By rubbing the scent glands of the head against an object, or curling the tail around it or by wiping against it with the anal area, the cat deposits a persistent, individualised scent. Other cats will smell the area carefully and may then superimpose their own scent. The urine of male cats contains chemicals termed 'pheromones' which have a particularly pungent, pervasive odour. When marking an object, the male performs a little ritual. After examining the area he will back up to the object and then accurately spray it with a fine jet of this strongly scented urine. (The male cat's penis points backwards except during an erection.)

Females and castrated males usually do not spray urine, but may do so if they feel stressed or threatened — for example after moving to a new house or when a new cat moves in to threaten his or her territory.

The urine of a queen on heat also contains 'pheromones'. This is a signal to males that she is on heat and available for mating. This scent message is not territorial marking. The queen will usually urinate at ground level rather than spraying walls and trees.

As you move into your new home, your cat's territorial battles are about to begin

49

SCRATCHING

Cats scratch trees and posts for two reasons. One is to mark territory, the other is to keep their claws sharp by removing loose scales. The ritual of claw-sharpening is part of the cat's body language and can also be used to intimidate watching cats.

When a cat scratches an object, scents from glands in the foot pads are also deposited. Males will usually reinforce this smell by also spraying the scratched object with urine.

Claw-sharpening can be a big problem if it is misdirected onto valuable furniture or walls. If you intend a cat to live inside it is prudent to accustom it early in life to a scratching post. This is a standing post mounted on a solid, heavy base and covered with fabric, bark or carpet. To introduce a kitten to the post, sit it in front of the post, place its front feet on the material and gently mimic a scratching action with its paws.

Once a cat has developed the habit of scratching furniture, it is difficult to break the habit but one of the following procedures may work:

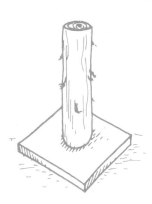

A scratching post can save furniture

- Place the scratching post near the damaged furniture or wall. Spray the objects to be protected with a cat repellant spray (available from vets or pet shops) or use a strongly scented polish or similar. Do *not* use any product containing ammonia as this could exacerbate the marking behaviour.
- Trimming the cats nails yourself may suffice. This is not hard to do if the cat co-operates. Ask your vet to show you how much nail to clip off if you are uncertain.
- De-clawing cats (that is, removing the entire nail surgically) is advocated by some. This should only be contemplated if the cat is exclusively indoors, otherwise it needs the claws for climbing and for defence. The attitude to de-clawing varies between vets and from country to country. If you wish to have your cat de-clawed talk it over with your vet first — it may not be necessary.

HUNTING

The cat is an excellent hunter adapted to catch small rodents, but capable of successfully hunting other prey such as birds, snakes, frogs or even fish, depending on their territory. It was the cat's hunting prowess that first led to its domestication as a ratter.

Cats are solitary hunters. Patient, observant and intelligent, they are capable of planning a hunt, locating their prey with senses tuned to detect the slightest

Cats are patient and persistent

movement or smell and then exercising enormous patience waiting for their prey to make the wrong move that provides them with an opening. Cats have been known to sit for days waiting for their quarry to emerge from cover.

Training for hunting starts at about four to six weeks of age. The cat has strong, inherited hunting instincts, but if it does not receive instruction in hunting by the time it is about four or five months old, then it may never learn to hunt or will do so only with great laboriousness.

The mother first introduces the kittens to hunting by bringing them dead prey. When the kittens become accustomed to this, and have commenced play-hunting games, she will bring live prey. Hunting instincts and efficiency are refined and polished by accompanying the mother on hunting expeditions.

The cats' habit of toying with their prey may be repulsive to us, but this seemingly cruel behaviour may be necessary to hone their hunting reflexes and techniques. Some believe it is an avenue of tension release.

Common questions regarding hunting cats

Can I stop my cat killing birds?
Many cat owners are extremely unhappy that their cat kills birds. Others refuse to have a cat because of this tendency. The cat's hunting instinct is deep rooted. Once a cat has learned to kill it is difficult to deflect this drive. The best way to tackle this problem is to prevent the kitten from learning to hunt. If the mother is not a hunter you will probably have little trouble. If she is, then you should try to eliminate any access to prey. This means keeping her locked in at night, or preventing her from getting back to the kittens with the fruits of her hunt. This could be quite simply achieved by locking her out and letting her back in with the kittens only after you have removed any trophy she is returning with. If the kittens are not exposed to hunting training, there is a good chance they will not realise their hunting potential.

Once the cat has learned to hunt, your aim is to try and break the habit or try to protect the birds. Attaching a bell, or better still, *two* bells, to the cat's collar may help to alert the birds, although usually the cat will learn to move without jangling the bells.

'Aversion' techniques may succeed. An old-fashioned idea that occasionally works is to tie a dead victim to the cat's collar, but this can be aesthetically unpleasant. Another is to 'set the cat up'. This takes some planning and effort. Your aim is to get the cat to associate hunting with an unpleasant sensation. As the cat is stalking a bird, the owner waits for the penultimate moment, then shoots a jet of water at the cat. Something equally startling or unpleasant such as letting off a cracker or firing pistol blanks could be used instead of the jet of water. It may be necessary to repeat this procedure many times before it takes effect. Do not let the cat see you doing the squirting or similar. It must associate the unpleasantness with the activity *not* with you.

To give the birds a better chance, make sure any bird feeding areas or nesting boxes are sited in open areas where the cat cannot use cover to approach or lie in wait.

Why do some cats bring home birds or mice? Are they showing off?
These cats are probably expressing a concern for their owner's wellbeing rather than showing off or looking for praise.

This behaviour is presumably a modification of the natural instinct of a mother to bring back food to the nest. It does not warrant punishment. This would only confuse the cat. If you don't want to encourage these small presents it is best

to make no response at all, either negative or positive. Ignore the cat if you can, and dispose of the body when the cat is not observing you.

Do cats make better mousers if they are starved?
Surprisingly, cats are more efficient mousers if they are fed properly. The explanation offered is that the well-fed cat lacks any element of anxiety about food and is more clinically efficient in the kill.

Contentment

BODY LANGUAGE

Body postures, positions and actions are fundamental methods of communication between cats. Together with facial expressions and vocalisation, a cat can accurately convey its feelings to other cats. We can learn a lot about our cat if we understand a little of this body language.

Body posture and facial expressions are very important in communicating different moods.

A contented cat will have relaxed muscles, erect perky ears and may groom itself with long slow licks.

Pleasure at seeing its owner is indicated by the cat standing with the head lowered, hindquarters raised and tail held straight up. The tip of the tail is usually bent slightly forward and wavers slowly from side to side. In this case the cat rises and approaches slightly stiff-legged. It then rubs its cheeks, chin and whiskers against the owner's legs often winding the tail around simultaneously. The cat may also purr and make rhythmic kneading motions with its feet (see vocalisation, page 54). When the cat is being petted the eyelids become half closed, the third eyelid may slip partially across the eye, the whiskers are relaxed and the ears erect.

If the cat is greeting another friendly cat then sniffing around the head, nose-touching and anal gland-sniffing are usually seen. This is sometimes followed by mutual grooming. Individuals are recognised by scent and the areas sniffed

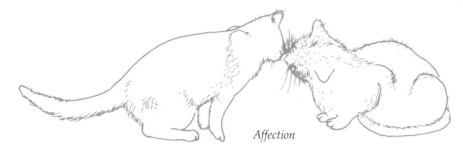

Affection

are where the scent glands are concentrated. Very friendly cats rub against each other, scent-marking their companion with their own smell for future recognition. Pet cats rub against their owners for the same reason.

An alert cat has a direct gaze with forward pointing ears and whiskers. The nostrils may quiver slightly as the cat tries to identify and recognise an intruder by smell as well as by sight and sound. If a cat senses a threat from a stranger it will freeze, all its muscles tensing. The pupils are constricted (into slits) and the cat will attempt to stare out the opponent. As the stranger approaches, the stance changes. The tip of the elevated tail points down, the chin is drawn in (to protect its throat), the ears flatten and the cat turns slowly to one side so it looks larger and more threatening. Gradually the hairs along the tail and body are erected. This is an aggressive posture in which the cat is trying to look as intimidating as possible. The hindlegs are tensed and ready to spring in attack or flight. The weight of the front of the body is supported on one foreleg while the other is prepared to strike. The lips may be drawn back so the teeth are displayed in a snarl and the cat growls fiercely. The pupils remain as slits and the tail wags aggressively from side to side. If the unwelcome visitor backs away, the cat may move forward smacking its lips, salivating and growling. When the threat has gone the cat will sniff at the invaded ground and then may spray urine, defaecate or claw at the ground before regaining its normal appearance and composure. Actual fighting may occur especially if two males are involved. Fighting is normally ritualised to bites and claw rakes being directed towards the shoulder and neck region. These areas are protected in the non-castrated male by thickened skin. The cheeks of the tom cat give him a fuller face, which help in display. The bigger looking the face, the more intimidating it would be to a rival. This is also why the lynx has fat cheeks and the lion has a mane.

When a cat is anxious or afraid the pupils dilate, the eyes dart rapidly from side to side looking for an escape route. It may adopt a submissive position crouching, with ears and whiskers flattened on head. Cats don't urinate in submission as dogs sometimes do. Submission may have the effect of appeasement if the aggressor is another cat who then withdraws without attacking. If the aggressor approaches, the cat may roll on its back but a paw will be raised and be used to defend itself if the need arises. Alternatively if a frightened cat can see an escape route it will flee. If the cat is cornered, it may become defensive (a combination of fear and aggression). The cat growls, hisses and spits. The back is arched and the cat stands side on to the stranger to make it look larger and more threatening.

Ultimately such a cat will attack if the stranger approaches to a distance less than one metre away. At this point the cat can no longer flee, so self defence is the only option.

A sick or wretched cat has a miserable facial expression, the tail is low and it spends a good deal of time hunched up, often not bothering to eat or wash.

Cats in an agony of indecision about how to behave in a perplexing or frightening situation may start to groom themselves in so called displacement activity. (Compare human biting fingernails.)

Fear – threat

Fear – submission

Submission

Aggression

Cats have a dislike of being looked at directly. If a cat being secretly observed suddenly becomes aware of the fact, it will stop whatever it is doing and then resume its activities in an obviously self-conscious and more hesitant manner.

VOCALISATION

Can cats talk to one another?
Cats don't actually form words, but they do appear to possess quite a vocabulary of meaningful sounds. Scientists have detected sixteen distinctive vocal sounds and believe there are many others that are inaudible to man. Some breeds are more vocal than others. Siamese are especially so, while Abyssinians tend to be quiet, but all cats are capable of a range of sounds. Many owners learn to tell from their cat's distinctive miaowing sounds whether it is happy or hungry, complaining, bewildered or just seeking attention. Cats may change their inflection to demand or merely to request. These different sounds are clear enough to an observant owner. Communication by sound between cats is probably much more extensive and subtle than we can appreciate.

Other distinct sounds we recognise in cats include the high-pitched mating yowl of the female on heat and the distinct call of the sexually excited tom. The queen miaows, cries, chirrups and croons to her kittens. They respond appropriately to these different calling signals.

Purring
Cats are able to purr from the age of about a week. They purr while sucking on a teat, pausing only to swallow. Purring is usually a sign of wellbeing and contentment, although an injured or frightened cat may purr loudly, perhaps as a pleading gesture.

All cats purr. Some purr for hours, self-inducing a euphoric state. Perhaps this is a regression to kittenhood as some cats not only purr, but also make all the other motions of suckling at a teat, and salivate while sucking and pawing at the imaginary mammary gland.

Kittens purr only in a monotone. Adults can purr very softly or build up to a loud vibrant roar. Veterinary surgeons attempting to listen with a stethoscope to the cat's chest are frequently frustrated because all that can be heard is a deep purring as the cat lies between the owner's hands. But purring can also work to a vet's advantage. In a patient suffering from breathing difficulties, for example

54

in a case of cat 'flu, if the cat can be induced to purr, then the breathing is greatly eased and the cat usually becomes much more settled and comfortable.

How do cats purr?
We do not know for certain. The most popular theory is that the purr is produced by a rhythmic vibration of the cat's vocal cords. These are situated in the larynx, at the entrance to the windpipe at the back of the cat's mouth. An electrical impulse flows through a nerve to stimulate the vocal cords briefly to contract. After a fractional pause, this electrical impulse is repeated. This causes the vocal cords alternatively to open and close as often as twenty or thirty times a second. The resultant intermittent air pressure changes in the larynx result in a purring sound.

SLEEPING

Cats spend about two thirds of their life in sleep. The actual number of hours slept each day varies with circumstances such as the weather, or whether the cat is hungry. During the mating season, toms find it difficult to relax at all and get very little sleep.

Cats do not have the same sleeping manners as man. We may sleep a solid eight hours. The cat spends more than half its day in a state called 'light sleep' or 'catnapping'. In light sleep, many of the cat's senses remain on guard. *Hearing* is especially acute, and the body muscles are only incompletely relaxed. The cat can revert virtually instantly to full alert. Catnaps usually last from ten to thirty minutes.

In 'deep sleep' the cat relaxes its body and muscles. Its senses are depressed and reactions slowed. The cat only needs three or four hours of this type of sleep per day. It is probable that cats dream during deep sleep as they have periods of 'rapid eye movement', a state that is associated with dreaming in humans. During these periods of rapid eye movement their ears, paws and nose will often twitch and tremble, and the cat may paw and scratch at phantom objects.

As cats get older they spend more time in deep sleep, and this muscle-twitching and jerking can get quite dramatic. This worries some owners, but it appears to be perfectly normal.

Kittens less than a month old only have two speeds. Stop or flat out. They indulge in deep sleep only. The state of light sleep is learned later.

BEHAVIOUR PROBLEMS

When you consider how much we have subjected cats to demands that they conform with our pattern of life, it is not surprising that we encounter behavioural problems. We have taken away their need to hunt by providing food. We prevent them from breeding by locking them up or neutering them or we go so far as to select *for* them what we consider a good breeding partner. We pamper, cosset and protect them. Domestication has brought great benefits to cats. Their expected life span has increased enormously. The life span of the wild male averages only three years. Wild females live only about a year longer.

By sublimating many of the cat's natural instincts and trying to curb those we perceive as undesirable, such as sharpening the claws, we have put new stresses on them. Sometimes this results in activities we label as 'problem' or 'nuisance' behaviour.

Aggressive behaviour in cats

Some aggression in cats is a natural and normal part of their inherited behaviour patterns. Cats will defend territory, protect their young, their food or themselves if they feel threatened. Some cats have an excessive tendency to aggression and become a problem for other animals or humans.

Fights between cats are best left for the cats to work out. These fights are often necessary to establish a decision over a territorial dispute or a place in the cat hierarchy.

Attacks on humans may occur over food. If a cat threatens or attacks you around mealtime it is essential not to feed the cat until it has settled down again. Feeding too soon after aggressive behaviour may only reinforce it.

In reprimanding an aggressive cat do not indulge in physical hurt. A firm command *'NO!'* backed up by a flick to the cat's nose is usually enough. If you attempt to slap or smack your cat you could end up badly scratched.

In recalcitrant cats, a 'NO!' plus a sharp squirt of water may be more successful. Some owners will pour a glass of water over the cat. Again, do not feed the cat after this reprimand. Wait until it has calmed and will accept petting before feeding it.

Some cats are not so much aggressive, as fearful of humans. Their behaviour is only self protective. Solving this problem requires patience and time to gain their trust. Some people have an affinity with cats and can win almost any cat over; but there are some cats that will never be tamed.

After I have been stroking my cat it suddenly attacks me. Why?

Worried owners sometimes report that their cat seems to have a Jekyll and Hyde personality. One moment it is lying docile being stroked and petted and the next it flies into an apparent rage, scratching and hissing then fleeing from the owner. This behaviour occurs usually when it is the underbelly or chest that is stroked. In the wild, the cat adopts a submissive posture by lying on its back, showing neck and underbelly to the dominant cat. In these 'Jekyll and Hyde' cats, stroking may simulate the sensation of being attacked and trigger a reflex 'fight and flight' response, where the cat lashes out at the apparent threat then bolts for safety.

Beware of the cat that is already frightened — perhaps by a thunderstorm, an unexpected loud noise or the presence of an unfamiliar dog. If the owner attempts to pick this cat up, or even stroke it, the state of tension may induce the cat to react aggressively. It is better to talk to the cat. Let it relax before attempting anything further. Certainly such reflex self protection behaviour does not warrant punishment.

MOVING HOUSE

Can I help my cat?

While a dog becomes primarily attached to people and is happy to go wherever they do, cats are often more concerned about territories. Consequently, moving house can be quite traumatic for a cat.

The cat usually becomes unsettled long before the actual move because of the atmosphere of discord and turmoil around him. It is common for owners to be unable to find their cat when the time comes finally to transport him to the new house. A prudent move may be to lock the cat in a spare room the night before the move, or even board him at a cattery for a few days.

On arrival at your new home keep the cat indoors for at least forty-eight hours. Then let him out only under supervision. Give him as many familiar items as you can, such as bedding, favourite toys or even a chair he is fond of. Keep the same litter trays, feeding bowls and scratching post. The fewer changes the better at this stage.

Give as much reassurance as you can. Some signs of anxiety should be expected, for example refusing to eat, becoming moody or hiding away. Some will temporarily start to defaecate or urinate inappropriately in the new home.

Drugs may help in some cases. Tranquillisers may be useful for the nervous traveller or very excitable cat. These are only available through your vet. Other medications your vet may discuss include megoestrol acetate — a hormone that apparently induces a feeling of wellbeing or euphoria in some cats, allowing them to adjust much faster and more smoothly to an otherwise traumatic change.

Many owners have tried the old trick of putting butter on the cat's paws when it arrives in the new house. Whether this works or not we are not sure, but many of our clients swear by it. We are throwing in the idea for good measure.

WOOL-SUCKING

Some cats love to suck, lick or chew wool. What at first seems an amusing habit can develop into a real problem for both the cat and its owner.

Why do these cats suck wool? The reason is obscure, although in some Siamese there is a strong inherited tendency. Perhaps some cats like the taste of the lanolin in the wool. In others the wool-sucking is probably a displaced suckling drive, similar to thumb-sucking in children. The odour of lanolin resembles the odour given off from the mother's nipple when she is nursing. This may account for the typical wool sucker's behaviour. Some of these cats induce in themselves an almost trance-like state, their eyes glazing over as they suck or chew, simultaneously kneading with their forepaws at a phantom breast.

Wool suckers can not only cause serious damage to expensive carpets or clothes, but can induce in themselves gastric upsets or even intestinal blockages.

Controlling this behaviour is difficult, and sometimes impossible.

Try dusting the woollen object with pepper. Covering the object with a scent that is unattractive to the cat may break the habit. Try carpet deodorant preparations or strong scents such as lavender. Naphthalene could be effective, but is less pleasant to have around. For example, stick moth balls to wallpaper or furniture. Not very decorative, but often effective!

Restrict access to wool as much as practicable. This helps, but the behaviour may return if wool is re-encountered in the future.

As wool-sucking can be an inherited trait it is unwise to get a kitten from a litter where one of the parents is a known 'wool sucker'.

EMOTIONAL UPSETS

The two most common signs of an upset cat are:
- Loss of appetite.
- Changes in toilet habits. They may start urinating or defaecating in the house.

The cause of the upset may not be obvious. It could be due to something we are not aware of, or to something that doesn't disturb *us* at all. Some of the more

common causes of behavioural or emotional upset are:
- New cat in the neighbourhood, especially if it is a tom.
- Changes in the household, such as one of the family moving out, or a new baby arriving.
- A new dog or other pet.
- Abnormal activities in or around the house, such as roadworks outside, a plumber calling or re-decorating.
- Thunderstorms.
- A cat comes into 'heat' nearby.

The reason for the upset is often not immediately apparent. Most of the factors listed above wouldn't disturb ourselves but could be quite distressing for the cat. Some cats are fairly tolerant of these stresses, others are severely affected.

Treatment
The best solution is to discover and eliminate the cause. This is often not possible or practicable. In time, many cats readjust and no specific treatment is necessary. Tranquillisers can be used in the short term, but are not a long term solution. Drugs such as megoestrol acetate (Ovarid, Ovoban etc.) can be used by a vet to help the cat if it is seriously upset. If the appetite remains jaded, try vitamin B supplements, or offer foods with a strong smell such as fish.

My cat occasionally runs madly round the house. Is this some form of fit?
No. Such behaviour is considered normal. Some cats do it frequently, perhaps even daily at around the same time. Individuals vary as to their exact behaviour, but a typical episode would be as follows: the cat suddenly fixes his gaze on a phantom object, then races madly around the house in apparent pursuit.

One possible explanation links this behaviour to the cat's hunting instincts which can be very strong. If not released in the natural manner then the cat is driven to release the pent-up nervous energy in pursuit of fantasy prey.

Why does my cat groom itself after being told off?
In times of embarrassment, humans may blush or become confused. Some people will loosen their collar or adjust their clothing, perhaps pull on a shirt sleeve or brush imaginary dust from a lapel. This serves to cover embarrassment. We believe the cat is doing the same when it sits down and starts to groom itself immediately after being chastised.

Similarly, some cats overgroom if subjected to uncomfortable or stressful situations such as moving house or if another cat is introduced into the home.

My cat behaves abominably if left home by himself. Why?
Although most cats are independent and enjoy periods of solitude, others seem to crave company. This is especially common with orphan kittens that have been hand reared, and may consequently have become over dependent on human contact. When left alone they fret and may become destructive, or exhibit neurotic behaviour such as urinating on the carpet. Others simply become bored with long periods of isolation, especially if they are in a restricted area such as an apartment.

A common expression of boredom or stress is for the cat to groom itself excessively, or begin self-sucking. This can lead to other problems such as skin damage. The licking or sucking inflames the skin, exciting the sensory nerves on the skin's surface. In time, a vicious cycle can establish itself as the licking causes the skin to be extremely itchy — lick — itch — lick — itch — the cat eventually cannot leave itself alone. The most commonly damaged areas are the tail tip, the paws and the skin over the wrist and hock.

Other expressions of boredom or resentment include tearing curtains, uprooting plants or pulling out all the washing.

Some measures that may help to reduce or even eliminate this behaviour:

● Feed the cat just before you leave rather than routinely when you arrive home.

● Leave the cat plenty of toys to play with.

● Allow the cat a window to look out of. Don't close all the curtains. If you leave only one open, select one where the cat gets a little sun.

● A radio left playing can fill the void. Select a station playing restrained music. Frenzied rock music does not have the desired soothing effect — this has been proved.

● A companion animal may help, although this is a bit unpredictable. Getting two kittens initially rather than one can prevent the problem arising. Introducing a new cat is a bit risky as your cat may not accept him (or her). The cat most likely to be accepted is a kitten of the opposite sex to the problem cat.

NUTRITION

Cats are true carnivores. Their natural food is small rodents. Cats require high levels of animal protein and some animal fats in their diet. Unlike dogs they cannot survive on substitutes of vegetable origin such as soy bean meal. Cats do not consume much of the intestinal and stomach contents of their prey, nor, in their natural state, do they eat other vegetables or cereals to supplement their diet. Because there are certain elements cats *must* have that can only be supplied from animal flesh it is not possible to raise a cat as a vegetarian.

The cat eats only until *energy* requirements have been met. This is, on average, 250 to 280 kcal a day for an adult cat. If the diet is well structured, or what nutritionalists term 'balanced', then by the time the cat has consumed his 250 calories he will also have consumed his daily requirements of protein, vitamins, minerals and fats. Unfortunately, many diets are not well balanced. If fed an unbalanced diet, the cat may consume his required energy needs and therefore stop eating *before* he has met his protein (and other) requirements. Diets excessively rich in fats and carbohydrates can therefore lead to protein deficiencies.

When choosing brands of food for your cat you might bear in mind the fact that fats and carbohydrates are cheaper than animal protein. Some manufactured cat foods contain a relatively high percentage of these fats and carbohydrates, so although they may be cheap, they are not necessarily good value. Other foods may claim a high protein content, but this protein content may be of poor biological quality, and be of only limited use to the cat because cats cannot adequately digest protein of low biological quality. Much of it passes undigested through the gut, and is wasted.

The majority of cats eat only to sustain themselves, and not for pleasure. Although they have a reputation for being finicky and choosy, it is more accurate to say that cats are very careful about what they eat. Some cats do become fussy. If you indulge your cat and pander to his every whim then you are liable to find it difficult or even impossible to change the diet if the need arises.

Cats can become virtually addicted to certain foods, such as liver

> BEWARE! Cats can become virtually addicted to certain foods, such as liver or meat.

A 'balanced' diet is essential.
Meat alone is not enough

It is essential to train your cat to eat a variety of foods right from the start. Cats which are allowed to eat nothing but liver or meat or a similarly non-balanced diet will eventually develop serious nutritional deficiency diseases. It is frustrating to have to treat these cats because, although the vet knows that the solution is to correct the diet, the cat may refuse any alternative to its habitual fare.

WHAT YOU SHOULD FEED YOUR CAT

You may choose to base your cat's diet on good quality commercial foods, or you may prefer to prepare the cat's meals yourself. Many owners choose to do a bit of both.

The aim is to provide all the cat's nutritional requirements, avoiding deficiencies or gross excesses.

A 'balanced' diet is formulated so that when a cat has eaten enough of the diet to satisfy his energy requirements, and therefore his hunger, he will also have consumed sufficient of all other required nutrients — vitamins, minerals, trace elements, protein, fats and carbohydrates.

Commercial foods
In most countries, pet food manufacturers are forbidden by law to misrepresent their product on the label. In other words, they cannot make false claims regarding their product's content. So if you read the packet label, it can tell you quite a lot.

Here are a few descriptive terms used by cat food manufacturers. Some commonly used terms include:

'Complete': This term means that this food supplies all the nutrients required by a cat, including protein, fats, vitamins, minerals and trace elements.

'Incomplete': (Most foods fall into this category.) These foods do not meet *all* of the cat's nutritional requirements, and should therefore not be fed as the sole food, even though the cat likes them, or because they are readily available or inexpensive.

'Varietal': A commercial food intended to provide variety in the cat's diet, but not formulated to be used as a staple food. Examples include sardines, pilchards in aspic and rabbit pieces. These varietals are usually highly palatable. Cats love them. Beware of letting the cat become too dependent on them — they are 'incomplete' foods.

'Treats': These are foods used as snacks or rewards. They may have little nutritional value but are always designed to be highly attractive. Examples in-

61

clude 'fishy treats'. They should be used as intended: as treats only, and not as an integral part of the diet.

Types of commercial food available

Dry food

Presented in a biscuit form, dry food contains a high concentration of energy sources and nutrients. Dry food contains three to four times the number of calories in a bowlful than the same bowl filled with canned food. Relatively small amounts are required to satisfy the cat's requirements. Dry foods have certain advantages: they are usually relatively inexpensive, are not as smelly or as messy as canned foods and yet can supply all of the cat's daily requirements (except for water) if they are formulated correctly.

Palatability varies with different brands. Don't write off all dry foods if your cat turns his nose up at one particular brand.

Remember: Read the label carefully to ensure the food is balanced and complete before relying on it as the basis of your cat's diet.

When feeding dry food, you must allow your cat free access to clean water.

Semi-moist or soft-moist foods

Semi-moist foods are about 65% dry matter, compared to dry foods which are around 90% dry matter, and canned foods which are only 25% – 30% dry matter. Surprising how much water there is in canned foods, isn't it? Semi-moist foods are presented usually as moist cubes, minces or chunks. They lack a strong odour, and are therefore not as attractive or tempting to cats as canned foods.

One advantage of semi-moist food is that it does not dry up and become unpalatable as quickly as canned food does.

Canned foods

Canned foods are usually formulated to be highly attractive and palatable to cats. A good quality canned food can provide a sound diet for your cat, but many do not. Read the label to find out what category the product falls into: does it provide a complete and balanced diet? There are two other provisos about canned foods — they usually do not adequately provide the following:

● Exercise for the teeth and gums. Exclusive feeding of canned foods will probably lead to dental disease. Some cats that have been raised on canned food don't learn to chew properly, and may subsequently refuse food that requires chewing.

● Good quality canned foods are expensive in comparison to most other types of cat food.

Whichever form of food you choose, it is best not to feed the same brand or flavour of cat food continually. The cat could become hooked on that brand. Any marginal deficiencies of vitamins or minerals will eventually show up. Also, a particular brand or flavour could become unavailable and it may prove difficult to get your cat to eat a substitute.

Feed your cat a variety of food types, brands and flavours.

PREPARING YOUR OWN RECIPES

If you choose to prepare your cat's meals yourself, you should know the essential components of a cat's diet.

Protein (e.g. eggs, meat, milk, fish, soy bean, yeast)
The cat has an extraordinarily high requirement for protein. Its diet must contain 34% – 40% protein. In fact, the cat may *refuse* to eat a diet containing less than 20% protein.

As an indication of just how much more protein cats require in comparison to other species, it has been calculated that kittens require about two and a half times the levels of protein required by puppies, while adult cats require nearly five times the amount required by adult dogs. A kitten could starve on dog food.

There are some essential dietary components that the cat cannot manufacture itself and which are only supplied in animal protein — for example the amino acid taurine. This is not the case in dogs or humans. Cats cannot survive on vegetable protein alone. (Dogs and humans can.)

Protein is required for the growth and maintenance and repair of all the body's tissues and the production of antibodies, enzymes and blood. Proteins are the body's basic building material. Even higher levels of dietary protein are needed during growth, pregnancy and lactation.

Sources of protein and how to prepare them
Eggs are better served cooked than raw. The white of the egg is more easily digested by the cat when cooked. Raw egg white contains avidin which interferes with the essential B vitamin biotin. Avidin is destroyed by heat.

Meat can be fed raw or cooked, although cats could pick up tapeworm infestation, toxoplasmosis and other conditions from raw meat. From a public health viewpoint, it is preferable to cook the meat.

Fish and fish meals are an excellent, palatable source of protein — but beware of feeding *raw* fish to excess. Diets that are comprised of more than 10% raw fish can become thiamine deficient (thiamine is an essential B vitamin). This is because some raw fish contain the enzyme thiaminase which destroys this vitamin, and a condition termed Chastek's Paralysis can result. This condition used to be seen quite commonly in cats living in fishing communities. (See 'Nerves', page 222).

Milk is an excellent source of protein plus calcium, phosphorous and various other minerals and vitamins. Unfortunately, some cats are intolerant of milk sugars, while others are allergic to the milk protein. Cow's milk can be a useful part of the cat's diet, but it is not essential. Some owners become concerned because their kitten will not drink milk. This is not necessary — cow's milk is no more a natural food for cats than cheese is for mice. There are plenty of other foods that supply all the nutrients contained in milk.

Fats
Cats must have some animal fats in their diet. They cannot survive on vegetable-based substitutes. Cats deprived of animal fats have poor growth rates, a harsh, dry coat, skin ulcers and sores. They are highly susceptible to disease and are usually infertile. The essential nutrients contained in fats are technically known as essential fatty acids. Most animals can manufacture all their own essential fatty acids, but the cat cannot.

Fats are a concentrated source of energy. A certain weight of fat contains double the calorie value of the same weight of protein. Fat is rich in vitamins A, D, E and K.

Cats can cope with a high level of fat in their diet. Like all other foods, the fat must be broken down in the digestive tract into its basic components before it can be absorbed into the body. It is a common misconception that if a cat is fed fat it will become fat. This is not so, unless you feed too much. Instead of trimming all the fat off the cat's meat, it is better to leave it on and simply don't give as much.

Some types of fat contain excessive amounts of components termed *unsaturated fatty acids*, or UFAs. There is a condition variously called yellow fat disease, steatitis or pansteatitis, which results from feeding cats excessive amounts of UFAs.

Cause: Usually, excessive feeding of fish oils that contain high levels of UFAs.

Signs of yellow fat disease: Hard, painful lumps form in the fat depots under the cat's skin. Cat becomes feverish, loses all appetite and becomes reluctant to move and extremely sensitive to touch.

Treatment: Change the diet and give high supplements of vitamin E.

Note: Used cooking fat should never be given to cats. It is likely to contain peroxides which are toxic to cats.

Carbohydrates

Cats do not need carbohydrates provided their diet contains sufficient protein and fat to satisfy their energy requirements. Nevertheless, carbohydrates can be a useful part of the cat's diet. Cats can use the carbohydrate as an energy source, thereby 'sparing' protein, which can be used instead for tissue building and repair.

Sources of carbohydrates include sugars, cereals, potatoes, pasta and rice. Cats can digest most carbohydrates more readily if they are cooked. They cannot digest cellulose, which is the carbohydrate that forms plant cell walls. These plant fibres are still a useful component of the cat's diet as they act as a 'bulking' agent and help the cat to form proper stools.

Carbohydrates can comprise up to one third of the cat's diet *provided* adequate levels of fat and protein are also present. If there is too high a level of carbohydrate, the cat will stop eating before all his essential daily protein and fat requirements have been met, because cats only eat until their *energy* requirements are satisfied.

Milk contains some carbohydrates, including the sugar lactose. Kittens have a greater ability to digest lactose than adult cats, but they can digest only a certain amount daily. Quantities in excess of this are liable to cause diarrhoea. Some individual kittens have a poor capacity for digesting milk sugars, and even small quantities result in diarrhoea. Siamese are especially likely to fall into this category.

> Milk, especially when fed in excess, is the single most common cause of diarrhoea in kittens.

Water

The amount of water any cat needs daily depends on a lot of factors including the ambient temperature, amount of exercise, nutritional state and so on. A very rough estimate of need is 50 mls per kg of body weight per day.

Most of the cat's daily water comes from the food. In many cases, cats extract *all* their daily requirements from their food. The feline kidneys are extremely efficient at retaining fluid, so the cat does not 'lose' as much fluid in the urine as most species do. Inevitably, some water is lost as the cat must flush away the normal waste products of body metabolism.

Cats which are fed dry or semi-moist foods *do* require additional water.

The easiest approach to water intake is simply to have plenty of clean water available at all times. Let the cat drink as much as he likes, when he likes.

Water is essential for life. If a cat is deprived of both food and water, it is dehydration that kills. If your cat stops eating for a few days he may become dehydrated and you may have to force him to drink fluids. Food is important, but it is not as critical as water.

Vegetables

Vegetables are not a natural food source for cats. Cats can only digest them after they have been cooked, and even then many cats refuse to eat them, presumably because they don't like the smell or taste.

Small amounts of cooked vegetables mixed with the rest of the cat's food are useful additional sources of vitamins and minerals.

Vitamins and minerals

Cats can synthesise most of their own vitamins, with the exception of vitamin A and niacin, both of which must be supplied in their diet. There are many minerals that must be supplied in the cat's diet. The following table outlines sources of vitamins and minerals. It also gives a brief description of the problems associated with deficiencies or excesses.

MINERAL	SOURCE	FUNCTION	DEFICIENCY	EXCESS
Calcium	Bones, milk, cheese.	Bone formation, nerve and muscle function.	Rickets, poor bone growth, convulsions.	Bone deformities.
Phosphorous	Bones, milk, meat.	Bone formation and energy utilisation.	Rickets.	Poor bone growth, convulsions (causes calcium deficiency).
Magnesium	Cereals, bones, green vegetables.	Bone formation, protein synthesis.	Anorexia, vomiting, muscle weakness.	Diarrhoea.
Iron	Eggs, meat, liver, green vegetables.	Part of oxygen transport system of red blood cells.	Anaemia.	
Copper	Meat, bones.	Part of oxygen transport system of red blood cells.	Anaemia.	
Zinc	Meat, cereals.	Used in digestion and tissue maintenance.	Hair loss, skin thickening, poor growth.	
Iodine	Fish, dairy products.	Part of thyroid hormone.	Hair loss, apathy, drowsiness.	
Vitamin A	Fish oils, liver, egg yolk, milk fat, kidneys.	Vision in dim-light. Maintains skin.	Night blindness, skin sores, behavioural changes, decreased reproductive performance.	Loss of appetite, pain on handling, bone malformation.

MINERAL	SOURCE	FUNCTION	DEFICIENCY	EXCESS
Vitamin D	Cod liver oil, eggs, animal products.	Calcium balance, bone growth.	Rickets, osteomalacia.	Anorexia, calcification of soft tissue. Pain on handling, bones fracture easily.
Vitamin E	Green vegetables vegetable oils, dairy products.	Reproduction. Utilisation of unsaturated fatty acids.	Infertility, anaemia, muscle weakness. If combined with excess unsaturated fats, steatitis results.	
Thiamin (Vit. B1)	Dairy products, brewer's yeast, offal.	Release of energy from carbohydrate.	Anorexia, vomiting, paralysis, ventroflexion of head.	
Riboflavin (Vit. B2)	Milk, animal tissue.	Utilisation of energy.	Weight loss, weakness, collapse coma.	
Niacin	Cereals, meats, liver, legumes.	Utilisation of energy.	Anorexia, mouth ulceration.	
Vitamin B12	Liver, meats, dairy products.	Division of cells in the bone marrow.	Anaemia, poor growth.	
Folic Acid	Offal, leafy vegetables.	Division of cells in the bone marrow.	Anaemia, poor growth.	

Common questions asked

Put simply, what should I feed my cat?
The golden rule is to vary the foods you give. If you feed a variety of good quality commercial cat foods your cat should thrive. Home recipes are liable to be deficient in some of the essential dietary elements. Snacks and treats should not form a major part of your cat's diet, although most cats enjoy and benefit from such treats, for example drinks of milk, scraps of meat and 'fishy treats.'

How often should I feed my cat?
Cat's prefer to eat a little at a time. They prefer several small meals to one or larger meals. Adult cats should be fed at least twice daily. Kittens should be fed from three to six times daily. Cats eat to satisfy their *energy* needs. When the cat has consumed enough to supply this energy requirement he will stop eating. If the diet is correctly balanced he will by this time have also consumed sufficient quantities of protein, fat, vitamins and minerals to meet his daily needs.

Ad-lib feeding, or free access to food, is a feeding method that works well with most cats. Some will become obese, but the majority of cats regulate themselves well. It is usually the cat which is confined indoors that becomes overweight as there is little opportunity or stimulus to exercise and therefore burn energy.

Exactly how much should I feed my cat?
There is no simple answer. The cat's needs vary with all sorts of factors such as age, the climate, amount of exercise and many other individual factors. The following table will give you some guidance, but you may discover that your cat eats considerably more or less than we indicate.

Note: Canned foods contain 70-80 kcal of metabolisable energy per 100 gm. Dry food contains 300-330 kcal/100 gm.

Weight of cat (kg)	Canned food (400 gm can)	Dry food (25 ml cup)
Young, growing cat		
1.0	⅔	⅔
1.5	1	1
2.0	1¼	1¼
2.5	1¼	1¼
3.0	1⅓	1⅓
Adult cat		
2.5	¾	¾
3.0	1	1
3.5	1	1
4.0	1¼	1¼
4.5	1⅓	1⅓
5.0	1½	1½
Lactating (peak)		
3.0	2½	2½
3.5	3	3
4.0	3½	3½

Should I give my pregnant queen more food?
Queens do not require any special feeding during pregnancy. It is during lactation that they need more food. Read chapter 7 on 'Reproduction', page 69 for more information.

Does a cat need any supplements?
Good quality commercial foods, whether dry, semi-moist or canned, will provide all the nutrients your cat requires. Under certain circumstances or in some disease states, your vet may recommend supplements. For example, extra calcium is indicated during lactation, and the B group vitamins are useful in tissue repair or in stimulating a waning appetite.

   If you are making up your own diet, there are good multivitamin and mineral supplements available from your vet that will cover any possible deficiencies.

   Cod liver oil has been a popular dietary supplement. If you do use it give half a teaspoonful *no more* than twice weekly. If given in excess, cod liver oil can cause diarrhoea, interfere with digestion and oversupply the cat with vitamins A and D. (Refer to the chart on page 65-6 for signs of excess.)

Can feeding liver cause any problems?
A little liver makes an excellent contribution to the cat's diet, but too much can be harmful. Liver is so palatable that some cats become virtually addicted to it, and it is these cats that will eventually develop problems. The major risk in feed-

ing excessive amounts of liver is that it contains excessive amounts of vitamin A, which is stored by the body and could gradually build up to a toxic level.

Signs of vitamin A poisoning
The first sign is usually that the cat has difficulty grooming. This is because, under the influence of excess vitamin A, changes are occurring in the spine, making it less flexible. The spinal ligaments, which are normally quite elastic, gradually become mineralised and hard. Movement of the spine becomes painful, and eventually impossible.

If this condition is detected early, treatment can be effective, but in many cases the condition is irreversible.

Vitamin A poisoning

My cat loves meat and won't eat anything else. Is this all right?
No. Meat alone is *not* enough. Meat does not contain enough calcium, iron, iodine, sodium, copper or magnesium. Kittens brought up on meat alone have poor bone development and growth. The bones bow, are fragile and easily fractured. The kitten may be weak and unco-ordinated. This condition is seen in all types of cats, although Siamese seem to be particularly prone. Perhaps this is because they can become very finicky eaters if allowed to get away with it early.

My cat constantly demands food. Does this indicate some disease?
If your cat is eating excessively but is still losing condition, or if this constant demand for food is unusual for that particular cat, then it is probable that the cat has a problem. A thorough veterinary examination is advisable. Heavy worm burdens, thyroid conditions and diseases such as diabetes or nephritis or even cancer could result in an abnormally voracious appetite. Fortunately, the explanation for constant food demands is usually much less sinister. Many cats simply prefer to eat something every hour or two. A change to 'ad lib' feeding could remedy the situation.

AD LIB FEEDING

Provide the cat with a large amount of dry or semi-moist food. Let him eat when he likes. Most cats will successfully self regulate their intake, and will not become obese. You should keep an eye on how much the cat consumes, because unfortunately *some* cats do become overweight. If this is the case, you will have to take charge again and control the cat's intake. Once you have decided on this limited amount, measure it out every morning and feed a little every few hours if possible. Even if you can only manage to divide it into thirds to be fed in the morning, when you return from work and late evening, this is preferable to feeding the cat only once or twice daily.

Should the cat's food be served warm?
Cats seem to prefer foods to be served at blood temperature. Palatability is reduced if the food is served straight out of the refrigerator.

My cat likes dog food. Is there any harm in feeding it?
Small amounts of dog food are all right. It will certainly not cause him to start barking, but dog foods are *not* a suitable base for a cat's diet. They have an insufficient protein content and the balance of nutrients is not correct for a cat's requirements. A kitten could starve if given only dog food.

REPRODUCTION

The sexual behaviour of cats is so vastly different from human sexual behaviour that comparisons can lead to confusion. While it is a natural inclination to interpret our pet's behaviour in terms of our own emotions or experience, such comparisons are not valid. Many of the problems that cat owners encounter stem from a failure to appreciate this.

Some terms used in this chapter:
- Queen — a breeding female.
- Stud — a breeding male.
- Tom — a male cat. The usage of 'tom' is fairly loose, and is sometimes applied to neutered males as well as entire males.
- Heat — that phase of the female's sexual cycle where she is attractive to the stud and will mate.
- In season — synonym for being on heat.
- On call — synonym for being on heat.
- Queening — giving birth to kittens.
- A Castrate — desexed male cat.
- A Neuter — desexed male or female cat.
- Entire — not neutered.

To breed or not to breed?
Domestic cats are extremely fertile. They reach puberty early and have a long

breeding life. Queens are excellent mothers. They can produce and rear up to three litters a year. This results in far too many kittens being born for the homes available.

Animal welfare organisations are faced with the melancholy task of destroying an alarming number of cats every week. Up to 80% of all stray cats entering shelters have to be euthanised despite vigorous efforts to find them homes. Some organisations have better success rates, but all are aware that a cat population explosion can occur with alarming speed.

> Before you breed, be certain you have homes for the kittens.

There are several misconceptions regarding breeding that could unfortunately lead to owners allowing their cats to have litters unnecessarily. For example, it may be thought that the experience of coming into heat or of having a litter will improve the cat's personality and character. This is not so. Having a litter has no long term effect.

Sometimes owners wish to allow their cat to have kittens so that the children can have the experience of watching birth. This is certainly a moving and worthwhile experience, but there are alternatives. In most cases, the queen prefers solitude, and the birth often occurs in the early morning, so for either or both of these reasons, the children may miss the event. It is usually possible instead to arrange a viewing of a breeder's queen giving birth, or of a friend's bitch whelping, or even of a mare foaling or a cow calving.

> In summary, unless you have an excellent reason for breeding, have your cat desexed.

PREVENTING PREGNANCY

Females: the available methods
- Surgery: The most common method of preventing pregnancy is to spay the cat. This means the surgical removal of the reproductive organs.
- Drugs: In some countries there are drugs available to prevent the queen from coming into heat or to stop heat once it has started. Your vet should be consulted regarding the correct dosage and timing of administration of these drugs.
- Postponing heat with drugs: Heat can be postponed by either a long acting 'depot' injection or by tablets. If an injection is used, a drug such as proligestone is given *before* the cat is due to come into season. Tablets can also be given. These can be started during the breeding season if necessary.
- Dose of megoestrol acetate: Can be used for up to two months beginning treatment in the breeding season (early spring) but *not* when the cat has actually started calling. Or dose once a week for extended periods beginning in the non-breeding season.
- Artificial induction of ovulation (see page 79).

Note: Dosage of drugs should be under the control of your vet. Some cats do not tolerate them as well as others. Try to avoid extended periods of time on drugs.

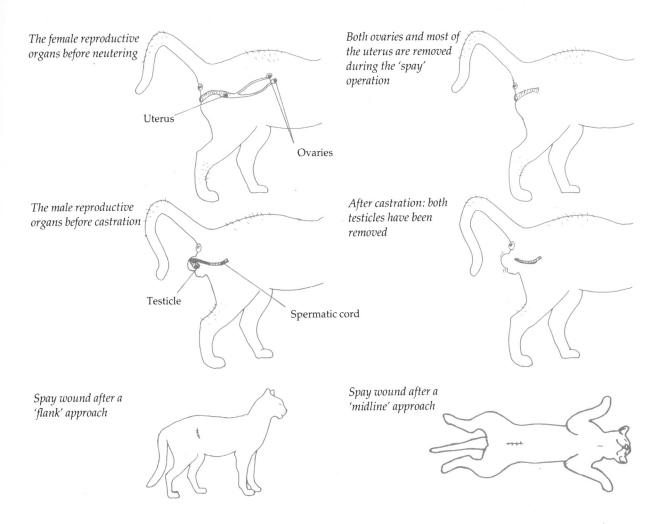

The female reproductive organs before neutering

Uterus

Ovaries

Both ovaries and most of the uterus are removed during the 'spay' operation

The male reproductive organs before castration

Testicle

Spermatic cord

After castration: both testicles have been removed

Spay wound after a 'flank' approach

Spay wound after a 'midline' approach

THE SPAY OPERATION

The female cat is sterilised, or neutered, in an operation commonly called a 'spay.' Most veterinary surgeons remove not only both ovaries, but also most of the uterus.

The operation is performed with the cat deeply asleep under the influence of a general anaesthetic. She feels nothing. After clipping the fur from the incision site, the nurse cleans and sterilises the skin. The surgeon, using sterile instruments, opens the abdomen either on one flank or in the mid-line near the belly button, according to the surgeon's particular technique.

The two ovaries and the uterus are removed, and any blood vessels and stumps remaining are carefully tied off ('ligated'). The opening in the muscles is usually closed with sutures (stitches) that will eventually 'dissolve' or be absorbed by the body. The skin is usually closed with 'non absorbable' sutures. These are removed, usually about ten days after the operation.

What precautions should I take after the spay operation?
The cat is usually hospitalised for twelve to twenty-four hours after the operation. When she is allowed home you should keep her confined indoors until you are certain she is mentally alert and physically capable of walking freely. This usually takes less than a day. Cats recover from surgery quickly and are soon right back to normal.

After an anaesthetic, offer the cat a small drink. If she accepts this and does not vomit, further small amounts can be offered. Do not give food for at least twelve hours after the anaesthetic. Don't overfuss. Give her a little reassurance and a lot of peace and quiet.

The most common complication to occur is if the cat removes her sutures or has them removed for her by another pet. If the wound gapes open, it may have to be re-sutured. Bandaging the wound is not practicable, and you cannot watch the cat for twenty-four hours a day. An Elizabethan collar may be necessary. Often the wound will not gape open, even if the sutures are removed after only twenty-four hours. If this is the case, then confine the patient to a cage or small room. This will minimise movement and therefore strain on the wound. If there is any doubt as to whether the wound should be re-sutured, revisit your vet for an assessment of the situation.

An Elizabethan collar can be fashioned from firm plastic or cardboard. This collar must fit snugly, or the cat will remove it. Once it is in place, leave it on – 24 hours a day – until it is no longer necessary

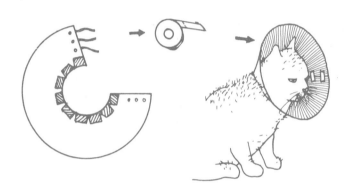

After being spayed, will my cat still attract male cats?
The neutered female no longer comes 'on heat' and therefore this powerful, almost irresistible attraction to males is lost. The male still recognises her as female, so there is still a vague attraction for the tom, however his attention is usually transient.

Will she become fat and lazy?
Not necessarily. Because she is no longer functioning as nature intended, there are not the constant demands and physiological drains of rearing kittens. As a result, the cat could put on weight. If you are careful, watch her diet and encourage exercise, then obesity can usually be avoided.

Will spaying alter her character? Wouldn't it be better to have a litter first or at least a period on heat?
No. The cat returns to her pre-heat personality whether she goes off naturally or is spayed. Having a litter is not believed to change her character permanently.

Why not just 'tie her tubes' (tubal ligation) as in the operation often performed in women?
Because the cat would continue to come into heat, (the ovaries would still be active) with all disadvantages of attracting toms, fighting and wandering. Certainly, she would not become pregnant, so there are certain advantages to the operation. Most people want to avoid all the associated nuisances of a queen on heat as well as just avoiding unwanted kittens.

ACCIDENTAL BREEDING (MISMATING)

If you find your cat has an unplanned pregnancy, there are several alternatives open. The easiest solution is to go ahead and have her spayed. If she is less than four or five weeks pregnant the surgical risks are only slightly greater than for a normal spay. However, if she is a queen you want to breed with later, your problem is more complex. You could let the pregnancy proceed, and then find homes for the kittens or, if necessary, have them humanely destroyed at birth. There will be no effect on the purity of future litters, despite the common misconception that she will be somehow 'tainted'. If you know that the queen has been mated, and take action within the first twenty-four hours, your vet may be able to short-circuit the pregnancy with an injection of a drug that prevents the implantation of the fertilised eggs, and therefore prevents the continuation of pregnancy. If you wait for longer than twenty-four hours after the mating, the chances of such an injection succeeding are reduced.

Therapeutic abortions, such as are practised in human medicine, are not feasible in cats. (The anatomy of the cat's reproductive tract makes it unsuitable for a curette).

Drugs have been developed that cause the resorption of a developing foetus. These may be of use even up to the fortieth day of pregnancy. Your vet will advise you regarding these drugs if necessary.

THE MALE: *neutering (castration)*

While the female cat's personality is unaffected by being spayed, the male's is dramatically changed by castration. Male cats are dominated by their sex drive, and will wander, fight and mate whenever there is a queen on heat.

Entire toms can be unpleasant in other ways. They mark out their territory with urine. This urine has a penetrating, offensive and persistent smell. Toms fight ferociously and are often responsible for serious wounds and abscesses in other cats. Entire males should not be allowed to roam free — they are a menace.

The neutered male, on the other hand, can make an excellent pet. Castration, especially if performed before puberty, results in the loss of the sex drive and all its undesirable consequences.

Castration is a simple surgical procedure. It is painless when performed under a short, general anaesthetic. Both testicles are removed. This removes the cat's ability to produce sperm and also removes the major source of the hormone testosterone, which is responsible for the fiery sexual drive of the tom.

There is occasionally some confusion with the vasectomy operation, which is used as a contraceptive method in humans. In a vasectomy, the testicles are not removed. Instead, the spermatic cord is tied so that sperm can no longer be ejaculated during intercourse. Because the testicles are left intact, the production of testosterone is not halted, so the sex drive is not inhibited. Nor is there any change in the human's 'secondary' sex characteristics such as pubic hair patterns, muscle development and body hair.

In the tom cat, it is eminently desirable that the sex drive *does* cease, and with it the highly undesirable secondary sex characteristics of urine spraying, aggression and fighting.

A vasectomised cat does have some uses. A stud owner may use one to terminate heat in a queen if she is not ready to have a litter. After being mated by a vasectomised male, the queen will cease to call, but does not become pregnant.

Vasectomised males could also play a big role in reducing the excessive cat

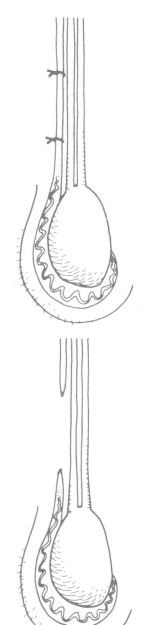

The vasectomy operation: a part of the spermatic cord is cut out so that sperm cannot be ejaculated. A vasectomised cat is sterile, but retains his sex drive

population. If they were released into the wild, or into areas where the cat population was expanding too quickly, then sterile matings would reduce the number of kittens produced.

Is it fair to castrate toms? Castration seems such a mutilation — it isn't natural. Why do it?

The argument *for* castration is overwhelming. There are tens of thousands of homeless cats in every major city. These cats prey on native birds and animals, and can wreak havoc with domestic pets. They are noisy and they smell. The entire tom is dominated by his sex drive — he will mate whenever possible. He leaves a pungent urine trail to mark his passage, plus sundry victims of fights, left with wounds and abscesses. Entire toms do not make suitable pets. The neutering operation is painless. The tom has no idea what has happened — he simply loses his sex drive. It is not a matter of 'missing out'. The neutered male has no desire to mate. There are no psychological scars, as there could be in a castrated human.

CRYPTORCHISM (retained testicles)

There should be two testicles present in the scrotum. In some toms, one or both testicles fails to descend to their normal position in the scrotum. If only one is absent, the cat is termed a monorchid. If both are absent, he is a cryptorchid.

During the development of the male foetus, the testicles form near the kidney. They gradually migrate backwards through the abdomen into the pelvis and eventually into the scrotal sac. If the testicle fails to follow this path, or to complete its journey, the testicle is said to be 'retained.'

The testicle must be positioned *outside* the body cavity if it is to produce viable sperm. Sperm are produced at temperatures below body temperature. A retained testicle can still produce hormones (so the cat behaves like a male), but produces only sterile sperm.

Monorchid cats should not be used for breeding, as this condition could be hereditary.

Treatment

It is debatable whether treatment should be contemplated, other than to castrate the cat. Castration of these cats is not as straightforward as for normal males. An exploratory abdominal operation may have to be performed to find the missing testicle(s).

Various drugs and surgical techniques have been promoted as possible treatments for retained testicles. We do not support their use.

INHERITED DISEASES

For thousands of years, the cat bred according to the rules of natural selection. These were hard and uncompromising. The fittest, strongest and best adapted animals survived. As a result, the cat is extremely well suited to its biological niche as a hunter of small rodents and mammals. The wild cat is tough, cunning and resourceful. When humans began to take an interest in cats, they initially encouraged them as a means of controlling vermin. Gradually, the cat became partly domesticated and humans started to select those they preferred, and bred only with these. The criterion for selection was no longer the bitterly fought battle for survival. Instead, selection was based on more mundane characteristics such as temperament, coat colour, body conformation and even eye colour. Inevitably, the inherent resistance of the domestic cat declined. We have certainly achieved a more manageable cat, but breeders should be aware of the enormous potential for selecting for the wrong reasons. Fortunately, selective breeding has not yet made disastrous inroads to the basic health and viability of the cat, as has already occurred with some breeds of dog, such as the bulldog, the Pekinese and the Chihuahua.

Inherited defects not only detract from the cat's overall health, they are also usually responsible for pain or discomfort which can generally only be controlled, not cured.

The 'Scottish fold' cat is a concern. If the gene that produces the folded ear is present in only one parent, then (on average) half of their kittens will have not only folded ears, but skeletal abnormalities of the tail and lower limbs as well. If the gene is present in both parents, then (on average) half the potential kittens will be lost because of a lethal genetic effect. Surely this is too high a price to pay for a breeder's whim.

The Scottish Fold

Some inherited defects are quite well known, for example deafness of blue-eyed, white cats, cleft palates, hare lips and umbilical hernias.

In the Siamese breed there was a trend to accept inherited defects, and even to include mention of them in the breed standards. So squint eyes and a kink in the tail were deemed to be 'acceptable'. Reason has prevailed, and these characteristics are being bred out again — fortunately for Siamese cats.

The Manx (tail-less) gene has an influence over the entire vertebral column, not just the tail. If a kitten inherits the dominant Manx gene from *both* parents, this is lethal. The kitten dies before birth. If it inherits only one Manx gene, it will be tail-less, but many also suffer from maldevelopment and partial fusion of the spine.

Other inherited defects which breeders should be aware of are included in the chart on page 76. Genetics is a fascinating subject, but can be complex. It is not within the scope of this book to cover it adequately. If you want to know more, ask your vet to recommend or lend you a suitable book.

FASHION AND DISEASE

Breeding for fashionable whims, and not for efficient function, can cost the unfortunate cats involved in terms of discomfort or even pain. The short-nosed, longhaired breeds have a tendency to suffer from breathing difficulties, crowded mouths (and therefore dental disease), overshot jaws, tear duct malformation, intolerance of heat, an increased tendency to dermatitis and a general deterioration in temperament that makes them more inclined to be shy or aggressive. We may admire their looks, but has it been worth it?

The shortnosed breeds may suffer unnecessary discomfort due to fashionable breeding whims

BREEDING

Assuming you have carefully considered the situation and have decided to breed, there are many things you should know and do.

First things first: Prepare the queen for pregnancy:

Vaccinations
The queen passes important protective antibodies to her kittens. Some of these antibodies are transferred while the kittens are still in her uterus, but most are given with the first milk, or 'colostrum'. This immunity conferred by these an-

INHERITED FEATURE	CHARACTERISTICS & COMMENTS
Inherited hydrocephalus	Kitten has large, bloated head. Often also has hare-lip and cleft palate. (Cause: recessive gene.)
Hairlessness	Majority of body hairless. May be a fine down or fuzz on muzzle and feet. As kittens grow, condition deteriorates and skin becomes thick and wrinkled. (Cause: recessive gene.)
Luxating patella (slipping kneecap)	Especially in the Devon Rex. Causes intermittent hind leg lameness that could progress to arthritis. (Cause: probably a recessive gene or genes.)
Retained testicles, also called cryptorchism (two testicles retained)	Both testicles should be present in the scrotum by six months of age.
Umbilical hernia	Defect in correct closure of muscles around the umbilical cord. This is associated with protrusion of umbilicus ('belly button') probably due to recessive gene in some cases.
Tear duct malformation	The result of breeding for a short face. Results in facial staining, facial dermatitis and perhaps eye disease.

tibodies is strong but temporary, and the antibody level in the kittens gradually falls to below protective levels a few weeks after birth. You can ensure the kittens get the maximum protection by correctly vaccinating the queen. Recommended vaccination times are either before mating or during the last three weeks of pregnancy. It is *not* recommended that the queen be vaccinated during early pregnancy, as the kittens could be adversely affected.

You should vaccinate against feline infectious enteritis and, preferably, the feline respiratory diseases. There may be other vaccinations recommended by your vet, such as rabies or leptospirosis. Consult him for details.

Worming the queen
The queen should be wormed before mating to help ensure she is in good physical condition for pregnancy. You could take a sample of her faeces to your vet for analysis to determine what parasites she is carrying, or simply use a product the vet recommends to control possible roundworm, hookworm and tapeworm infestations.

Treat the queen again for roundworm either a few days before the expected delivery, or a day or so after. Use a mild, safe drug such as Piperazine. It is not essential to use a powerful, '100% kill' drug. Piperazine is not as effective as some drugs, but it does have a good safety margin and not only will it kill most roundworms, it will at least stop the others from laying eggs for a while. This reduces contamination of the environment with roundworm eggs around the critical birth period.

Note: Around queening, you should wash the queen's nipples to remove any worm eggs stuck to the skin. There can be huge numbers of these which the kittens might otherwise ingest while sucking.

At what age should a queen be bred?
If nature equips the queen to breed from about six months of age onwards, then who are we to deny that this is the correct time to mate and breed? Nevertheless, experience suggests that the queen is better able to cope with the stress of pregnancy if you wait until she is over ten months and preferably twelve months old. She will be stronger and more physically mature and therefore better able to channel her resources into the developing kittens.

What about the male?
Any age after puberty is theoretically all right. A calm, experienced queen will accept him without much fuss, but he may need either age or experience before he can successfully be used at stud with flighty, nervous females.

HEAT — the breeding cycle

What is meant by 'heat'?
The expressions being 'on heat', or 'on call' or 'in season' are all euphemisms for that stage in the queen's sexual cycle when she is attractive to toms and ready to mate. Her ovaries are active and have produced a crop of eggs that are nearly ready to be released ('ovulation') for possible fertilisation by sperm from the tom. The ovaries also produce hormones which are responsible for the various behavioural and physical changes that occur in the queen at this time.

At what age does the queen first come into heat?
The age a queen comes into heat is usually given as seven to nine months. This varies according to factors such as the queen's breed and nutritional state, the time of the year, the presence of other cats, housing and even sudden changes in the weather.

Some cats come into heat as early as four months old. The longhaired breeds tend to achieve sexual maturity later than most — at ten months or older.

Factors influencing when a queen comes into heat

Length of daylight
This is probably the most important factor. Queens usually come into heat as the daylight hours lengthen in spring, then continue to cycle until the short winter days set in. While there are peaks of sexual activity in autumn and late spring, most cats cycle more or less continually throughout the longer daylight period — unless the cycle is interrupted by pregnancy, as it usually is.

Weather
Sudden changes in the weather can put queens off heat, or alternatively bring non-cycling queens into heat.

A queen in 'heat' will crouch, lift her pelvis and hold her tail to one side

Socialisation
Indoor cats that have little contact with the other cats come into call less frequently, less vocally and for shorter periods than do outdoor cats.

The signs of a queen on heat (in season/on call/in oestrous)
The first sign is a slight swelling of the vulva, which also becomes slightly moist. This change is easily missed.

Changes in behaviour are more obvious. The queen crouches, lifting her pelvis and holding her tail to one side. She may tread with her hind feet. The queen's miaow becomes lower pitched and much more frequent — hence the expression 'calling' or 'on call'. She usually becomes restless and more affectionate, rubbing up against legs and rolling in front of you.

To determine if your cat is on heat, stroke her firmly down her back with the side of your forefinger. If she is on heat she will respond by crouching down and thrusting her pelvis up, will twitch her tail to one side and miaow intermittently.

As the mating urge becomes stronger, the cries become intense. Inexperienced owners may believe their cat is in pain as she rolls about, kneads the carpet and howls.

The 'calling' phase usually lasts five to ten days with two-to three-week intervals between, but there is great individual variation. Once a particular queen has established a pattern, this pattern normally repeats itself each season. After the cat has been mated she will go off call within a few days. If she is not mated, calling can continue for around ten to fourteen days.

Queens living in groups call more often and for longer than do solitary queens. If she has had more than one litter, a queen tends to stay on call for a long time if she is not mated.

Cats return to call after only two or three weeks, and this cycle continues unless the queen becomes pregnant or until the shorter days and cooler weather return.

OVULATION

Cats are different
Unlike most animals, cats do not spontaneously release eggs from the ovary. It is the mating act that stimulates the final development of the eggs in the ovary and their subsequent release about twenty-four to thirty hours later. The eggs then go via the fallopian tubes (where fertilisation usually takes place) to the uterus. In most animals and in man, the eggs are released spontaneously as part

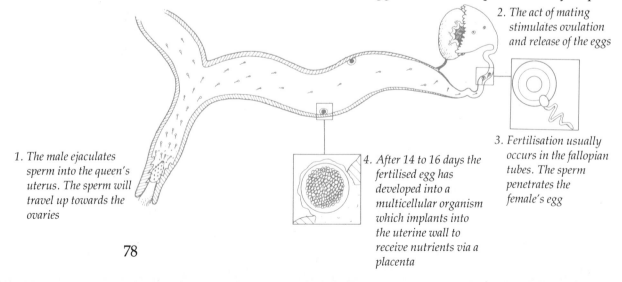

2. *The act of mating stimulates ovulation and release of the eggs*

3. *Fertilisation usually occurs in the fallopian tubes. The sperm penetrates the female's egg*

1. *The male ejaculates sperm into the queen's uterus. The sperm will travel up towards the ovaries*

4. *After 14 to 16 days the fertilised egg has developed into a multicellular organism which implants into the uterine wall to receive nutrients via a placenta*

of the sexual cycle. Timing of mating in cats is therefore of little consequence, in contrast to the situation in bitches where mistiming of mating is one of the most common causes of infertility.

Usually four eggs are released for possible fertilisation, although it could only be one or two, and a dozen or more have been known to be simultaneously ovulated. Not all the eggs necesarily become fertilised, nor do all fertilised eggs develop to result ultimately in a kitten born sixty-plus days later.

Artificial induction of ovulation
The artificial induction of ovulation is sometimes used as a method of taking the queen off heat. A glass rod (such as a rectal thermometer) or a cotton bud ('Q' tip) is introduced into the vulva and gently twirled around. This action mimics the insertion of the male penis, and usually stimulates ovulation. The queen will then go off call. A state of 'false pregnancy' then ensues which can delay the return to heat by a month and sometimes longer. Some breeders have a vasectomised tom (see page 73) to perform the same function: a sterile mating that takes the queen off call until a more convenient time for mating with a fertile stud.

TAKE GREAT CARE!

MATING

Mating is more likely to be successful if the queen is taken to the male, rather than vice versa.

Once signs of heat are established, take the female to the stud fairly soon so that she becomes accustomed to the different environment. Long journeys should be avoided as they can stress the queen and put her off heat.

Place the queen in a pen adjacent to the male's run. After she has settled, allow her to come out and wander about in her own time. Keep the male confined. The queen will gradually become conditioned to her new environment. When she approaches his pen and begins to show interest, the stud's gate may be opened.

If the queen is receptive, she will allow the stud to approach her, then to sniff, touch and lick. This foreplay is important to many queens, and essential for a successful mating with them. The absence of this foreplay may be one reason why artificial insemination has not been as successful in cats as in some other species.

The queen will adopt the mating position when she is ready. She crouches down, with pelvis raised and tail held to one side. The male will straddle the queen, holding her between his forelegs and seizing the skin over the back of her neck.

The male's penis normally points backwards. On erection this changes. As the penis engorges with blood and swells to erection it curves under and between the male's thighs to be directed forwards.

The male introduces his penis into the queen's vagina, simultaneously thrusting with his pelvis. Ejaculation of sperm usually occurs within five to fifteen seconds. The male usually emits a deep growl during ejaculation.

The receptive female will allow the male to approach

(A) When she is ready, she crouches in the mating position. The male straddles the female;
(B) As the male withdraws the Queen screams and may lash out at the retreating male

A   B

79

The male's penis has numerous barbs or spikes at its tip

The queen screams stridently. As the male dismounts, she may turn and lash out at him. This is common and not cause for concern. It may be caused by pain on the withdrawal of the penis, as it has numerous barbs or spikes at the tip. (However the same scream and paw slash sometimes occurs when a smooth glass rod is introduced then withdrawn instead of the penis.)

The queen usually relaxes quite quickly after mating and commences a typical post-mating sequence of rolling and grooming herself.

What part do you play in all this?
It is prudent to have an observer present during this sequence in case the pair do not accept each other. The queen may not be quite ready, or the male may become too aggressive. Some queens simply won't tolerate some males, yet will accept others with ready compliance. In these situations, an ugly confrontation may develop and one or both cats may be hurt unless they are separated.

Beware when approaching cats in a mating situation. You could be badly scratched or bitten, even by your own cat.

Cats usually mate several times over one to three days, and maybe even three or four times within an hour. Most stud owners like to ensure that at least two matings occur.

Too much human interference is likely to reduce the chances of a successful mating.

Some problems that may interfere with mating
- *Queen not ready*

The most common cause of failure to mate is that the queen is not ready. The owner may have introduced her to the stud too early, or the stress of entering an unfamiliar environment may temporarily put her off heat. The queen must be given a chance to settle down and become comfortable with her new surroundings. If she refuses to mate, or gives no sign of being receptive, be prepared to wait. Try again in one or two days.

- *Male aggression*

The stud may be too aggressive, and reluctant to let the female near. Or he may frighten her with his aggression. Tranquillisers may be useful here, but the correct choice of drug is important. Many tranquillisers reduce male fertility. Seek veterinary advice here.

- *Inexperience*

A very young, inexperienced or exceptionally quiet male may lack the vigour to achieve a successful mating. Some sexual aggressiveness is necessary, especially if the queen has a dominant character. These restrained stud toms should be mated with an experienced and compliant queen. This usually improves subsequent performance.

- *Abnormalities*

Occasionally there may be a physical problem or defect preventing the male from copulating. A possibilty is that hair becomes wrapped around the penis. Or the presence of crystals in the bladder and penis may cause obstruction to sperm or pain on erection. A complete physical examination is warranted, with special attention being paid to the penis and testicles.

ARTIFICIAL INSEMINATION

Artificial insemination is possible in cats. It has not been widely used. Basically, in this technique, semen is collected from the male then injected into the vagina of the queen.

One method sometimes used is to allow the male to mate with another queen, then to harvest the sperm by syringing it from her vagina, and subsequently injecting it into the queen you wish to be fertilised. There are a few situations where this procedure could be useful — for example, it could be used if it was impracticable to take the queen to the stud for reasons of distance or temperament. If you are interested in knowing more, then you should consult your vet. Correct techniques and proper handling of the delicate sperm are essential to maximise your chances of success.

INFERTILITY PROBLEMS

In general, cats are an extremely fertile species. Few problems are encountered, especially in comparison to the difficulties that arise in other species. Most of the troubles arise because we try to breed cats under artificially contrived circumstances. If we left them to it, cats would ordinarily mate and reproduce very efficiently, although occasionally an individual cat would be infertile.

Infertility problems require some thought and deduction, but in many cases they can be overcome.

Note: In this section there is reference to the queen 'cycling' or 'coming in' to heat. The activity within the queen's ovary is thought of as a continual, cyclic process:

Situation one
Queen is not coming into heat at all, or there are prolonged periods when she does not come on.

Possible factors:
- Nutritional deficiencies
- Light hours
- Isolation
- Pregnancy
- Hormone upsets

- *Nutritional deficiencies*
A poor diet, lacking in a proper balance of nutrients, vitamins and minerals can cause infertility. Two relatively common deficiencies are:

Vitamin A: Cats need a lot of vitamin A (1600 to 2000 international units (IU daily). Many commonly used cat foods are low in vitamin A. Liver is an excellent source, or you could use a commercial multi-vitamin supplement. *Beware:* it is possible to oversupply vitamin A (see 'Nutrition', page 60).

Iodine: One telltale sign of iodine deficiency is that in cats which normally have black coats, the hair lacks pigment and instead of looking black, appears to be rust-coloured.

If the queen is in a poor nutritional state she may not come into season when expected. This could occur, for example, if she has lost a lot of condition while rearing her previous litter. Such a delay is a natural safety valve, designed to protect the mother and to maximise the chances of a healthy litter being produced.

Supplementation: Iodised salt, one pinch daily.
- *Light hours*
The length of daylight is a critical factor in triggering the ovaries into cycling. The active, sexually fertile season normally coincides with long daylight — twelve to fourteen hours per day is usually necessary. Outside pens and runs are an advantage.

Heat
(oestrous)

Prooestrous   Metoestrous

Rest
(dioestrous)
often short
or non-existent

Pregnancy or false pregnancy can break the cycle here

If the female is not cycling, all the male's efforts will be in vain

81

- *Isolation*

Queens who are kept isolated from other queens or from males may fail to start cycling. Pheromones are chemicals found especially in the urine that have a role in triggering ovarian activity, as well as their role increasing sexual attraction between male and female. When a queen is not exposed to pheromones, the onset of heat can be delayed. There is also a condition that is variously called 'concealed heat' or 'silent heat'. A queen experiencing a silent heat does not show the normal overt signs of being on heat, so the owner is usually unaware that she is cycling. This condition is mainly associated with isolated queens. Silent heats are responsible for many of the situations when an owner brings a pregnant cat to the vet complaining she never even knew she had been on heat. Alternatively, the owner of a stud queen could be anxiously awaiting the onset of heat so that she can be taken for mating, when in fact the queen has been cycling quietly for some time. If in doubt, have your vet take a swab of the vaginal cells (although this procedure can put the cat off again (see 'Artificial induction of ovulation', page 79).

- *Pregnancy*

You may miss the signs of your queen being on heat, but the local toms will not. They are not only efficient at heat detection, they are extremely persistent, and frequently also successful, in their efforts to mate. If you intend to breed your queen to a specific stud tom you have to be absolutely certain of her security. Do not let her out 'just for a minute' if there is any likelihood at all of her being in season.

- *Hormone upsets*

The precise mechanisms by which the ovaries are stimulated into activity are complex and incompletely understood. If you have a problem queen and you have exhausted other possibilities, then you may decide to consult with your vet regarding induction of heat using hormone therapy. In certain cases this treatment can be successful.

Inducing heat

One of the most successful ploys to bring a quiescent cat into heat is to use natural hormone stimulation. Allow her to cohabit with queens which *are* cycling. There is a powerful influence from pheromones excreted by these queens into the environment that often triggers a non-cycling queen into activity.

Injections of follicle stimulating hormone (FSH) daily for several days may start ovarian activity.

Injection of oestrogens will produce the signs of heat. This heat is artificial, and the external signs do not reflect activity in the ovary. No eggs are produced, therefore pregnancy cannot occur. However, the injection may start the ball rolling and the queen may come in herself after the effect of the injection has worn off, and have a fertile heat where eggs are produced. *Note:* Oestrogens are potentially toxic. Great care must be exercised with the dose when treating cats.

Situation two

Queen is coming into heat but fails to become pregnant. Possible factors:

- *Infertile male* — aggression
            — inexperience
            — abnormalities
- *Infertile queen* — ill health
            — intolerance of male
            — wrong timing
            — lack of proper courtship
            — uterus infection
            — endometrial hyperplasia

Infertile male
- *Aggression*

An over-aggressive male can frighten and cower a queen, especially one who is inexperienced or of a nervous disposition. Sometimes tranquillisers help, but the drug used should be selected carefully. Antihistamines such as trimeprazine (vallergan) can be effective in some males, without having a detrimental effect on the sperm.

- *Inexperience*

Many males will not mate until they are over twelve months old. In some long-haired breeds it could take until eighteen months of age before they are ready. If possible, provide the virgin or reluctant male with a placid and experienced queen. After he has mated with her several times his future performance is likely to be more confident and enthusiastic.

Hormones such as luteinising hormone have been used to stimulate the testicles to produce sperm and the hormone testosterone. Increased blood levels of testosterone stimulate the tom's sexual ardour.

- *Abnormalities*

A general physical check of the male is an obvious starting place. If his general health is apparently good, then examine his genitals carefully. The testicles should be firm — the consistency of a pencil eraser. Extrude his penis by pressing just below it with your finger. Look for signs of bruising, or the presence of crystals or a discharge at the tip that might indicate urinary tract disease. Occasionally a cuff of hair will wrap around the penis, making it difficult to extrude, and therefore painful on erection.

In theory, an examination of the tom's sperm would be very useful. In practice, a sample may be difficult to obtain. Two possible methods sometimes used by your vet are either to wipe a slide over the vulva of a queen who has just been mated, (as some of the ejaculate is likely to have spilled out there) or, preferably, syringe out a sample of ejaculate from the vagina of a recently mated queen.

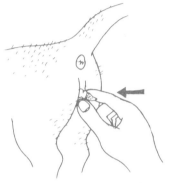

To examine the male's penis, push the foreskin backwards and slightly upwards

Infertile queen
- *Ill health*

Before looking for specifics, a thorough physical check should be performed to determine whether the queen is fit, and a check of her diet should be made with attention to possible nutritional deficiencies.

- *Intolerance of male*

Some queens are dominant and as a result are intolerant of other cats. In most cases, this behaviour abates under the influence of the sex hormone oestrogen. The desire to mate predominates over other drives. In the case of the queen that refuses to accept the presence of a male, tranquillisers such as trimeprazine (vallergan) may work.

- *Wrong timing*

(This is the most common cause in other species such as dogs.) Queens should be mated three days into call, but it may be the fifth day before she accepts the tom. Queens that will not accept the male's advances may not be quite ready, or — more often — are already past their peak. Your vet may choose to take vaginal swabs to determine the stage of heat, but this procedure can put the queen off heat as it mimics copulation (see page 79, on induction of ovulation).

- *Lack of proper courtship*

There is a complex pattern of courtship during a natural mating that is rarely allowed for by breeders. This courtship ritual is thought to aid in the ripening of the egg-bearing follicles in the ovary. Under natural mating conditions, copulation stimulates the follicles to rupture about twenty-four to thirty hours after

mating. This does not always happen with a planned mating where the queen is artificially introduced to the male. Although copulation occurs, the follicles may not have reached a sufficient stage of development or 'ripening' to respond.

The failure to ovulate (that is, to release eggs from the developed follicle) can be diagnosed by a rapid return to call after mating — usually within only a few days, or up to ten days later. If ovulation *had* occurred, the return to call would not be for at least thirty days.

Treatment
Your vet could give an injection of luteinising hormone (LH). This can be given to the queen on the way home from the stud cat. LH is the hormone that should be produced naturally. It is responsible for rupturing the ripe follicle to release the eggs for potential fertilisation by the male's sperm.

- *Uterus infection*
Many bacteria and some viruses have been implicated in feline infertility. (These include streptococci, E. coli, pseudomonas, salmonella, some 'amoerobes' and feline leukemia virus.)

Diagnosis
By vaginal swab, preferably taken when the queen is in season. Your vet will have this specimen 'cultured' (or grown) in a laboratory. If significant bacteria are grown, these are tested against a range of antibiotics to determine which drugs are most likely to control the infection.

Treatment
An appropriate antibiotic can be used if a bacterial infection is present. Treatment of a viral infection is difficult, but the infection may be self limiting anyway.

Treatment is most effective if given when the queen is on heat as the blood supply to the uterus is better, and the cervix is open to allow better drainage of pus from the uterus. Some cases of uterine infection respond better if the uterus is also irrigated with an antibiotic or antiseptic solution, or even 'curetted' with a vaginal swab. This is done under a general anaesthetic.

- *Endometrial hyperplasia*
This is a pathological condition of the uterus. Many breeders delay mating for example because they want to show the queen, or because it is not convenient to breed at certain times. It is now known that if you allow continual cycling without pregnancy, this can result in reduced fertility because the uterus lining gradually changes. It becomes thicker and is less suitable for the implantation and subsequent growth of fertilised eggs. This condition is called endometrial hyperplasia.

Diagnosis
The diagnosis is suspected if there is a history of prolonged cycling without pregnancy prior to the first attempt to breed. The problem of infertility becomes apparent when the breeder eventually tries to mate the queen. Usually the mating seems to have gone well, but no kittens result. A positive diagnosis of endometrial hyperplasia is made on biopsy of the uterus, or by sectioning the uterus after spaying the queen. Treatment is unrewarding.

Prevention
It is preferable to breed on the second or third call. Prolonged postponement of breeding is likely to result in infertility. Many successful breeders believe all queens should be 'pregnant, lactating or both', until they have finished their breeding life.

84

Situation three

Queen is persistently on call, but fails to conceive and never really goes 'off'.

This condition of nymphomania may be due to the formation of hormone-producing cysts on the ovary. Normally, the developing follicles eventually rupture to release the egg for potential fertilisation. In the nymphomaniac queen the follicle fails to rupture, and instead goes on producing oestrogen, the hormone responsible for the overt signs of heat. In some cases these cystic follicles are present, but do not produce hormones. Under these circumstances, the affected queen does not appear to be on heat, but fails to cycle at all. The presence of unruptured follicles on the ovary prevents the normal cycle from proceeding. She is therefore infertile.

Treatment

In either case — whether the cystic follicle is producing hormones or not, the treatment is the same. An exploratory operation is performed to examine the ovaries. If it is discovered that there is only one large cyst, then this is lanced (ruptured) and an injection of LH given simultaneously to mimic the natural situation and therefore to get the cycle going again. The prognosis for future breeding is reasonably good. If, however, it is discovered that there are multiple small cysts on the ovary, the prognosis for future breeding is so poor that it is probably better to spay the queen.

Sometimes injections of LH alone are sufficient to rupture the cyst without the necessity of an operation. If the condition is long-standing the chances of hormones alone working are poor.

It has been observed that cats which have formed a large cyst on the ovary are frequently very nervous or vicious, and are liable to hysteria or even convulsions when excited. After treatment of the cyst, their behaviour usually improves dramatically.

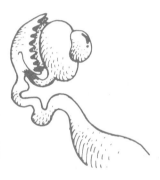

A cyst may form on the ovary, causing infertility. There may be one large cyst, as above, or numerous small cysts

ABORTION (spontaneous miscarriage)

'Abortion' means the premature expulsion of dead kittens from the uterus. Abortion of kittens is more common in pure bred cats. Quite often the cat's owners are not aware of the abortion because the queen, being fastidiously clean, eats the aborted foetus and cleans the discharges so they are not observed. The possible causes of abortion are as follows.

Hormone deficiencies

The hormone progesterone is produced in the ovary of the pregnant queen. If the supply of progesterone dries up prematurely, the pregnancy might not proceed. The most typical time for this to occur is between the fortieth and fiftieth days of pregnancy.

A diagnosis of progesterone deficiency is made from a history of repeated spontaneous abortion at this time. The queen may be observed to have a thick, reddish discharge from the vulva.

This particular condition can usually be controlled by giving injections of the hormone progesterone. Repeat injections, probably at least every tenth day, are necessary. If the interval between injections is longer, the kittens might not be retained. *Note:* There are various preparations of progesterone, and some types must be repeated every three to five days to maintain the pregnancy. Your vet will advise you.

VET TREATMENT
URGENT

Infections
Bacterial: The uterus can be infected in a variety of ways. Some infections spread from a generalised body infection, or from a urinary tract infection, or infection could ascend from the vagina. Diagnosis is made by culturing some of the aborted material in a laboratory.
Viral: Feline leukemia virus (Fe.LV) is said to be the most common cause of abortion in cats in the USA. It is known that 80% of Fe.LV carriers will either abort or resorb the foetus, or give birth to weak or dead kittens. Any surviving kittens become lifetime carriers of Fe.LV themselves.

If you are faced with an impending abortion — for example you see a dark red to bloody discharge from the queen's vulva — then take IMMEDIATE action. You may save the kittens. Your vet may elect to give hormone injections (progesterone) and perhaps antibiotics. If the queen is becoming very ill and has lost her appetite you might have to consider having a total ovariohysterectomy (spay) in order to save her life.

DETERMINING PREGNANCY

The length of a cat's pregnancy (the gestation period) is usually between sixty-three and seventy days. The average is sixty-five to sixty-six days. Some cats give birth to normal, healthy kittens a little earlier or later than this range.

day 16   *day 18*   *day 28*   *day 42*

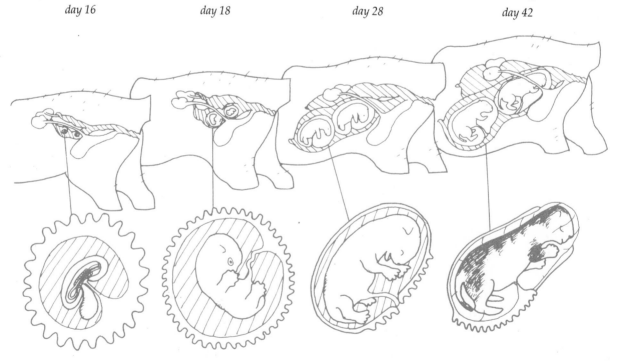

By twenty-eight days the kittens can be felt in the abdomen as discrete, round lumps in the uterus. They are about the size of a child's glass marble. An experienced breeder or vet will palpate the uterus gently and not harm the kittens. If you decide to have a feel, be careful not to exert too much pressure or upset the queen.

TAKE
GREAT
CARE!

At thirty-five days a distinct rosy halo develops around the nipples. The breasts begin to develop, starting with the nipples which enlarge and become more prominent.

From thirty-five days onwards until term there is a detectable increase in the size of the abdomen.

By fifty days the kittens can be seen or felt to move. By this stage the mass in the uterus is sausage-shaped and the heads can be palpated.

If there is doubt as to whether the cat is pregnant and it is important to know, then X-rays could be taken. You will have to wait until after the thirty-ninth day as the kittens' bones do not show up well until then.

FALSE PREGNANCY (pseudopregnancy)

Following an unsuccessful or sterile mating, or following artificial induction of ovulation (see page 79) the queen may show some of the early signs of pregnancy, such as enlargement of the nipples. Usually these misleading signs last only to the fortieth or forty-fifth day, then they terminate spontaneously.

CARE OF THE PREGNANT QUEEN

The queen does not require a lot of extra attention during pregnancy. Excessive feeding or overfussing can produce unnecessary problems. Do not increase the queen's ration until the last two or three weeks of pregnancy. The main drain on her reserves will occur when she is feeding the kittens, not during pregnancy itself.

Overfeeding can produce problems. A fat queen with a 'lazy' uterus may be capable of only weak and perhaps ineffectual muscle contractions. Excessive fat around the pelvic canal and oversized kittens can add to the obese queen's difficulty in expelling the kittens at term, so that veterinary assistance may be required. If you are feeding a good, balanced diet (see 'Nutrition', page 60) there is no need for extra supplements of vitamins or minerals.

Do not be surprised or concerned if, in late pregnancy, the queen eats only a little at a time, or seems to be only 'picking' at her food. Her abdomen is crowded with kittens. This makes it uncomfortable to fill up with large meals. By eating little but often she will usually consume her normal daily intake.

Some queens are eating about twice their normal ration by the end of pregnancy. This is all right so long as you do not start the increase too early. Be certain that the queen is not putting on fat. It is usually possible to offer food on an 'ad lib' basis from late pregnancy through to the weaning of the kittens. Most queens will not overeat. Have the food freely available and the queen will help herself. Dry foods are especially suitable for this style of feeding.

Exercise: Within reason, normal exercise and activities should be allowed. Jumping from heights should be discouraged, especially in the last two weeks.

Beware of using powerful insecticides or harsh worming preparations during pregnancy. Check with your vet to see if the product you contemplate using is safe. If you take your cat to the vet for any reason be certain to tell him/her

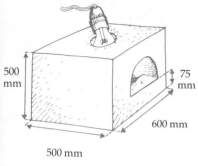

500 mm

75 mm

600 mm

500 mm

A home made kittening box

your cat is pregnant — or could be pregnant. There are many drugs and vaccines that are safe for the mother but which could seriously harm the developing kittens, especially if given in early pregnancy.

Ideally, you should accustom the expectant queen to a suitable kittening area well before the due date. She will prefer somewhere quiet and dark. If you can, accustom her to a 'kittening box'. This may be made from cardboard or wood.

A wooden box has the advantage that shelves or ledges can be fitted to allow the kittens to shelter away from the queen when she rolls over.

The kittening box can be lined with newspaper or towels or anything clean and absorbent that can be disposed of or easily washed.

The queen may show a preference for kittening inside a wardrobe or cupboard, or under a bed. If feasible, put the kittening box into this preferred area (although obviously it will not fit under a bed). If she is showing a strong attraction to an area you definitely *don't* want her to kitten in, for example in the airing cupboard, then you may have to block off that area.

The critical factors in determining the suitability of a place for kittening are that it is warm, dry and draught free. If the queen has a suitable bed then that will usually make a perfectly satisfactory 'labour ward' for her.

It is preferable for her to have the kittens at home where she is most likely to be relaxed in a familiar environment.

Keep a discreet eye on proceedings during delivery, but don't constantly hover over the queen. Your anxiety is infectious and only serves to upset the mother.

SIGNS THAT BIRTH IS IMMINENT

A few days prior to the birth the queen usually becomes restless. She will pace the room, then fuss about, grooming herself frequently, with special attention being paid to her genitals and breasts. She may eat less, or even stop eating.

Sixty-five days is only the average term of pregnancy. There is a variation from sixty to seventy-one days which could still be normal for that particular queen.

About twelve to twenty-four hours before labour starts there is a transient drop in her temperature from the normal 38.5°C (101.3°F) to around 37.5°C (99.5°F). We doubt that there is much to be achieved by continually sticking a thermometer in the poor cat's rectum just so that you are better informed and know when to prepare for the actual event. However, it is up to you.

Keep an eye on the queen to ensure she does not disappear into some dark and inacessible place to give birth.

THE BIRTH

Most cats have their kittens without the need of the slightest help from you. Stand back, observe quietly from a distance and interfere only if necessary.

The strength and range of the maternal instincts are remarkable. Even inexperienced queens perform as if they have read a manual. However, nervous queens may not, and there is always the possibility of a hitch so be prepared just in case.

If the cat refuses to use the kittening box, it is better to let her have the kittens where she chooses (within reason) and move the lot to your preferred area only after the birth is complete — all the kittens having been presented and now contentedly suckling.

88

Labour in a cat is not the traumatic, long, drawn-out process it can be in humans. Most queens deliver the kittens quickly and quietly. They will have them cleaned and feeding while you are still getting ready for the anticipated drama.

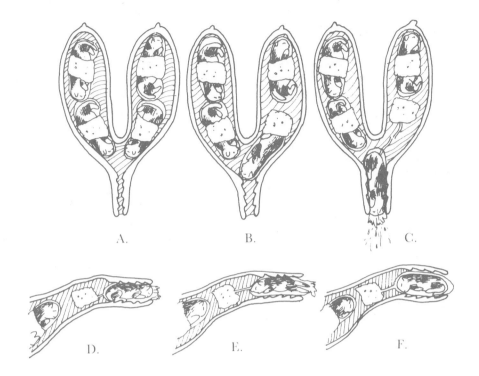

A. Prior to delivery.
B. The cervix opens. The first kitten is forced into the pelvis;
C. The membranes usually rupture as the kitten passes through the pelvic canal;
D. E. Both head first and feet first presentations are considered normal;
F. Sometimes the membranes fail to rupture. Note the placenta following, attached to the membranes

The first stage: preparation for delivery

Internally, the cervix dilates (opens wide). The ligaments of the pelvis have already relaxed to produce a relatively spacious passage for the kittens to pass through. The kittens are moved towards the pelvis by rhythmic muscular contractions of the uterus until the first in line is lying ready to be passed through the pelvis and out into the world.

The first stage lasts about twelve hours. It may take much longer. On the other hand, many queens start to produce within an hour of the *apparent* onset of labour. You may be able to observe the uterine contractions as the kittens are moved into position. The queen's breathing gradually becomes shorter and more rapid. Purring may be quite loud. Some tremble and become restless, looking around tentatively at their flank. Others may cry out. A nervous queen may become distressed and apparently confused. In such a case, some quiet, calm reassurance is needed. Speak soothingly to her, stroke her and try to induce purring. In some cases — fortunately quite rare — tranquillisers are indicated. Use these only on veterinary advice.

The second stage: delivery

The queen usually lies over on one side or sits forward on her chest. The contractions of the uterus become strong and rapid, pushing the first kitten out through the pelvic canal, into the vagina and through the lips of the vulva. Contraction of the abdominal muscles and diaphragm help in these expulsive efforts. As the kitten is squeezed through the narrowest part of the birth canal (the pelvis), the membranes surrounding the kitten usually burst, releasing the thick, yellowish fluids which have bathed the kitten in the uterus and which now aid in lubricating the birth passage for its final few inches to life. In some cases, the fluid sac can be observed bulging through the lips of the vulva before bursting.

The kitten may be presented head first or feet first. Both presentations are considered normal. The queen rarely has trouble expelling a kitten. If more than ten minutes pass after the first appearance of the nose or legs of the kitten without the delivery being completed, then the queen needs help (see pages 92-3).

Once the kitten has been delivered, the queen instinctively licks away the membranes surrounding the kitten. Her rough tongue serves to stimulate the kitten to breathe. Each kitten is thoroughly cleaned and the umbilical cord is sheared off. (The umbilical cord joins the kitten to the membranes. It has been the kitten's lifeline for the past two months.) The umbilical cord is usually broken during the passage through the pelvis. If not, and if the queen fails to cut it or if it is bleeding, then you should tie it off.

The third stage: expelling the placenta
The third stage involves the expulsion of the placenta followed by a period of rest for the uterus before the next kitten is delivered.

The placenta is usually passed with the kitten or immediately after. The queen may eat the placenta. This does not appear to do her any harm. Some believe there are hormones or nutrients within the placenta that are helpful to the queen. Most breeders prefer the queen to eat only one placenta. Too many can produce indigestion or vomiting.

A common interval between kittens is fifteen to thirty minutes. This varies, and can be much longer especially if the queen is overweight, old, or if there are many kittens and the uterus is becoming tired.

All the kittens are usually delivered within two to four hours. Occasionally it may take up to twenty-four hours.

YOUR ROLE

Don't interfere unless you have to. The birth and immediate aftercare provided by the mother is not only efficient and natural, but it is important to the formation of a bond between mother and kittens.

If the queen becomes preoccupied with one kitten, or a bit nervous or confused and fails to break the membranes around her kitten, then you should do it for her. Don't rush in — give her a minute to adjust. If she takes too long then you must clear the membranes from the kitten's face. After clearing the membranes, present the kitten back to the mother to be licked and cleaned. If she will not do this, you should rub the kitten dry with a rough towel. Be gentle, but thorough. This action dries the kitten thus reducing the chance of chilling and also stimulates the kitten to breathe.

As each kitten arrives, watch for the delivery of the placenta. Make sure that there is one placenta passed for each kitten born. If a placenta is retained in the uterus it could lead to infection. If in doubt, have your vet check her about twelve hours after the last kitten has been delivered.

Other problems that could arise

Narrow pelvis
The kittens must pass through the pelvis. If this passage is too narrow, a caesarian section may be required. There are several conditions which can lead to a narrowing or deformity of the pelvic canal. The two most likely are:
● Motor car accidents, where the pelvis has been fractured (this is surprisingly common).
● 'Rickets' — a calcium imbalance or deficiency suffered when the queen was a kitten. This can result in spinal and/or pelvic deformity.

Bleeding cords
If the kitten is bleeding from the umbilical cord you must stop the blood flow quickly. This is not a common problem but could occur if, for example, the queen nips off the cords too short. Tie the cord off with dental floss or thread — preferably some that has been soaked in antiseptic first, but don't delay if this is not available.

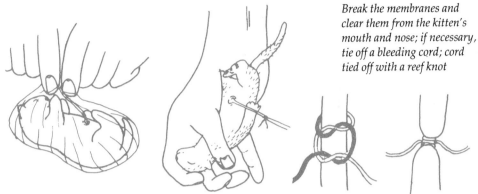

Break the membranes and clear them from the kitten's mouth and nose; if necessary, tie off a bleeding cord; cord tied off with a reef knot

If the kitten fails to breathe, rub it with a piece of rough towelling.

Kitten not breathing
● Clear any membranes from the mouth.
● Rub the kitten vigorously with a piece of towelling. *Be gentle* — don't press down too hard and squash the kitten.
● If that does not succeed, then hold the kitten between your hands and stretch your arms out in front of your body. Swing the kitten down toward the floor, stopping abruptly with the nose pointing down at the floor. Any mucous in the breathing passage should be expelled by this procedure. Repeat two or three times if necessary.
● If still no success, mouth to mouth resuscitation may be necessary.

When to call the vet
● Queen passes a green, yellow or bloody discharge *before* kittens are born. (This could indicate premature separation from the placenta or a uterus infection.)
● Queen is straining for one hour without success.
● Kitten's feet or nose presented but birth is not complete within ten to fifteen minutes. (Also read section on assisting birth.)
● Queen is anxious and upset and the birth is not progressing.
● Too long an interval passes between delivery of kittens. More than three hours is abnormal. *Note:* Sometimes a queen will have one or two kittens, appear perfectly normal, will suckle the kittens and be comfortable and content, but will then go back into labour next day to produce more healthy kittens. This particular situation does not require intervention on your part. A situation that *should* trigger your anxiety is if the queen is unsettled, uncomfortable and does not seem able to produce the next kitten. This is most likely to occur in overweight queens, or in queens that are debilitated or weakened for some reason.

AFTER THE BIRTH

To clear the breathing passages, it may be necessary to swing the kitten downwards, thus forcing the fluids out.

It is worthwhile having a veterinary check of the mother and kittens. The queen will be examined to see that there are no kittens or membranes remaining and you will be given whatever advice is necessary.

Some vets give postnatal injections of oxytocin. This is a hormone that causes the uterus to contract. This injection may help to clear any remaining debris from the uterus.

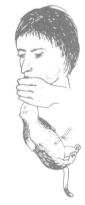

Mouth to mouth resuscitation may be necessary

Oversized kittens
Occasionally an extremely large kitten is presented. This is especially likely if the queen is carrying only one or two kittens. The presenting history and signs are usually that the queen started labour normally, straining for a while, but since then has done nothing. Sometimes the kitten's legs will show then disappear again.

  The treatment depends on many factors, but mainly on just how large the kitten is. A caesarian section is usually performed. Some vets may prefer an episiotomy under some circumstances (minor surgical procedure in which the vulva opening is enlarged by means of cutting the tissue on either side).

DIFFICULTIES AND HOW TO DEAL WITH THEM

This section is designed to help you in an emergency. Obstetrics is not a field for amateur treatments. Whenever possible, get experienced or professional help. If this is not feasible, then hopefully the information below will help you to make the right decision when a little assistance can ease a potentially awkward situation.

Abnormal presentation
The classical birth position is head first with the forepaws alongside the head. In about 40% of feline deliveries the hind feet come first, and this is also considered normal for the cat.

  If the rump or tail comes first, with the hind legs tucked back under the kitten, this is termed a breech presentation. Kittens presented in this way are usually passed without much difficulty, but occasionally there is a physical or mechanical blockage.

  Other presentations which might similarly obstruct the birth canal are: head back, or head and neck back.

What to do (where professional help is not available)

TAKE
GREAT
CARE!

  ● Wash your hands thoroughly.
  ● Lubricate your forefinger, preferably with surgical lubricant gel, but white petroleum jelly will do.
  ● Gently introduce the finger into the queen's vulva. The angle of entry is not straight in, but slightly upwards. Take your time. Try to determine exactly what part of the kitten you can feel.
  ● If a leg is back, try to push the whole kitten slightly back into the uterus, then hook the offending leg forwards. You may require one finger to hold the kitten back, and one finger of the other hand to do the hooking.

Before trying to reposition a kitten, first push it backwards. This takes pressure off the kitten and gives you room to manoeuvre the limbs

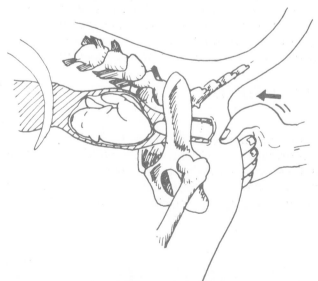

- Proceed similarly for a head back. Do not try to realign the kitten until *after* you have pushed it back a little. This gives you room to manipulate.
- If the kitten is normally placed (head and forefeet in pelvis *or* hind feet in pelvis) but the queen is having difficulty expelling it, then lubrication of the birth canal may help.
- A sterile lubricating jelly is ideal. You should use a greaseless, non irritant lubricant. These are available from veterinary suppliers or pharmacists. In an emergency, white petroleum jelly will do.
- Push the lips of the vulva back to enlarge the opening for the emerging kitten. If the head is presented, you may be able to work the lips of the vulva over the kitten's head.
- Try to grasp as much of the kitten as possible, preferably with a piece of clean towelling. Never pull on one single limb — you risk seriously damaging it. Time your pulls to coincide with the mother's uterine contractions. Exert the pressure of your pull on the kitten *downwards* as well as *outwards* from the vulva.
- By slightly rocking or rotating the kitten you may find the kitten slips out more readily.

Retained placenta blocks the passage
Hook the placenta with a cleaned finger. If possible, grasp it with a piece of clean towelling or gauze. Exerting gentle pressure, *slowly* pull it out. DON'T jerk as you may break it or — worse — cause bleeding.

No contractions
If the muscles of the uterus have become exhausted, whether from straining against an obstructed kitten or because the mother is in a poor or weakened condition, then there is little you can do. Your vet may be able to induce contractions with an injection of oxytocin. If not, a caesarian may be indicated. If there are no signs of contractions but you know, or suspect, that more kittens are still in the uterus, it is always a problem to know how long to wait. This guide may be helpful:

Queen bright, alert, comfortable, previous kittens content, suckling.	Wait at least two hours. No real cause for concern.
Queen exhausted, lies on side occasionally. Panting. Neglecting kittens.	Wait no more than two hours. Less if queen's condition deteriorating.
Part of kitten presented — perhaps feet or tail, which subsequently either disappears back or there is no further progress.	Wait no more than twenty minutes. Less if queen is distressed.
Fluids expelled, but no kitten presented.	Wait no more than twenty minutes.

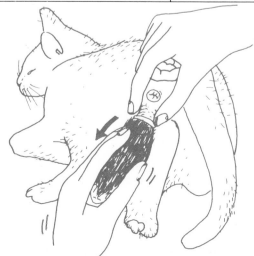

Pull gently outwards and downwards

THE CAESARIAN OPERATION

This operation is usually performed with the queen under a general anaesthetic, although it is theoretically possible to do it under local anaesthetic. Using sterile techniques to avoid infection or contamination, the surgeon opens the abdomen and brings the uterus up to the incision site. The uterus is then opened and the kittens removed. While an assistant attends to the kittens, the surgeon carefully stitches up the uterus and then the abdomen.

In most cases the queen is awake enough to suckle the kittens within one to two hours. If the operation is performed while the queen is still quite strong, the prognosis for a successful outcome is usually excellent. Unfortunately, many owners wait too long and fail to present the queen for examination until she is already exhausted. The kittens may already be dead, and the risks for the queen become much higher than they should be.

> Undue delay in opting for a caesarian can put mother and kittens at risk.

CARE OF THE QUEEN AFTER THE BIRTH

Feeding
The queen's food requirements increase dramatically once she starts feeding the kittens. Although at first she may not eat much at all, soon she should be consuming at least double her normal ration. By the time the kittens are four to five weeks old, she may be eating three times her normal ration.

> It is difficult to *overfeed* a nursing queen.

Feed a balanced diet (see 'Nutrition', page 60). A good multi-vitamin/mineral supplement seems to help, in our experience at least.

Allow free access to clean water. Beware of giving too much milk as this could precipitate diarrhoea, with potentially serious results.

Mastitis
Mastitis is infection or inflammation of one or more of the mammary glands (the breasts).

Possible causes of mastitis include:
- Infection by bacteria.
- Physical knock or blow.
- Blocked teats, due to inverted nipples, damaged nipples or infection of skin involving the nipples.

Signs
- Queen refuses to feed kittens. Instead she gets up and moves away when they nuzzle in because of the pain.
- Affected gland(s) swollen, tense and painful, may be hot to the touch.
- Kittens usually refuse to suckle, even if queen would let them.
- Secretion from gland — watery (usually),
  — or blood-stained,
  — or thick, foul smelling,
  — or normal in appearance, but smells sour.

- Queen may be feverish.
- Sometimes the first sign is diarrhoea and/or colic in the kittens.

Treatment

The treatment depends on the cause. Seek veterinary advice.

Antibiotics are usually indicated. Relief of pain may be achieved by bathing the affected gland with a flannel soaked in a warm salt solution and by gently expressing a little of the milk, to relieve the build-up of pressure in the gland.

The queen may resent treatment of the gland itself. Do not persist if she is becoming distressed by your efforts.

Vulva discharge

Some discharge from the vulva is normal for up to a week following the birth. Initially there is a copious, thick, brownish-red fluid passed. This gradually clears to a yellowish or clear mucoid discharge. There should not be an offensive smell. Be concerned if:
- The discharge smells strongly.
- The discharge is persistent, bloody or a dark red or green colour.
- The queen is lethargic, off her food, or otherwise unwell.

An abnormal discharge is usually due to an infection in the uterus, perhaps resulting from a retained foetal membrane.

Infected uterus

An infection of the uterus is serious.

Infections can start with a retained placenta, a dead kitten or by an infection spreading from the vulva and vagina, for example following contamination around the time of delivery. Wet and soiled bedding or similar unsanitary conditions are especially conducive to uterine infections (and mastitis).

Signs

- Fever (39.5°C (103°F) plus).
- General malaise: lack of appetite, listlessness, dull coat.
- Discharge from vulva: instead of a normal post-natal discharge (which is light reddish and not foul smelling), the discharge is thicker, smells strongly and may be greenish, yellow, or a deep red colour.

Treatment

Veterinary treatment is essential.

You may have to wean the kittens if the queen's condition is poor, as she will be unable to feed them properly and the stress of feeding them will further weaken her.

It may be necessary to spay the queen.

VET TREATMENT URGENT

Viral infections of queen and kittens

A potentially awkward situation can develop, especially in a cattery or breeding establishment if a queen is carrying a latent (sub-clinical) viral infection. This is termed the carrier state. The stress of birth and of lactation can allow multiplication of virus particles within the queen. She then sheds virus into her immediate environment. Susceptible cats can then become infected. The kittens may initially have a temporary protection conferred on them by antibodies from the queen. This protection wanes with time. Once the level of protective antibodies falls below a critical level, the kittens themselves become infected. This usually occurs when they are between four and eight weeks of age. Kittens can be weaned, and already have gone to new homes before they come down with a viral infection. They had actually contracted the infection from their mother but the infection had been 'incubating' for a few days. The stress of weaning or moving to a new home can be enough to allow the infection to flare up. Apparently healthy kittens can quickly become severely affected.

The most common virus involved is a Herpes virus — causing feline viral rhinotrachertis (see feline respiratory disease, page 107).

An extensive survey in the UK showed one in every three show cats to be a carrier.

If you are in a situation where a carrier cat is present, eradication is difficult. Ideally, you should stop breeding, clear the premises of all cats for one to two years, then repopulate with fully vaccinated cats from a stud known to be clear of the problem. Understandably such a programme is rarely feasible.

Research has shown that up to 80% of cats in an infected cattery are carriers of FVR. It is not usually feasible to cull them all. In any case it is difficult to identify the carriers or to be certain that apparently healthy cats are not harbouring hidden (sub-clinical) infections.

An alternative programme for control of respiratory disease (FVR) in infected catteries

Transmission of this virus is almost exclusively over very short distances that is by 'nose to nose' contact, or by contamination with nasal discharges. Separation of an infected cat from susceptible cats by even short distances can virtually eliminate infection.

The size of the exposure dose is important. A high infecting dose is likely to result in a short incubation period and then severe clinical signs. If the infecting dose is low, the incubation period before signs start is much longer, and the disease is usually less severe.

The aim of this control programme is to prevent the transmission of virus between the carrier and susceptible cats.

Breeding queens are allowed to mix with the other cat until two weeks prior to their due date. They are unlikely to shed the virus prior to this.

The queen is then put into an individual kittening pen that has been thoroughly disinfected with hypochlorite. The walls of this pen must be impervious and must be of a material capable of being thoroughly cleaned. Wire mesh is *not* suitable on either count.

The kittening pen must be separated by at least a metre from any other pen.

Proper ventilation is important. Plenty of air should circulate but draughts must be avoided.

Any feeding bowls, litter trays, etc. used by the queen should be kept exclusively for her use. Or use disposables.

If possible, use disposable plastic gloves when cleaning. Wearing rubber boots that can be disinfected in a hypochlorite foot bath is strongly recommended.

All queens should be vaccinated against the feline respiratory disease immediately prior to mating or every six months.

Kittens should be weaned early. The kittens have a temporary immunity to infection, but this protection wanes quickly and they become susceptible soon after four weeks of age.

Wean the kittens at four weeks and transfer them to a kitten quarantine pen and keep them under conditions of strict isolation and cleanliness, similar to those under which their mother was kept.

If the kittens show no signs of respiratory disease within ten days they can be put into a less strictly controlled nursery to be eventually either sold or to join the other cats.

Eclampsia (milk fever)
Eclampsia is not supposed to be a common problem in cats. It may be more common than is recorded, especially in pure bred cats fed a predominantly meat diet.

Cause
A certain amount of calcium must be present in the cat's bloodstream for normal function of muscle and other tissue. The calcium level can fall due to the abnormally high demands for calcium in production of the queen's milk, and — to a lesser extent — prior to the kitten's birth in the formation of bone and other foetal tissues. If the blood calcium levels fall below a critical level, eclampsia, or 'milk fever', results.

Signs
- Nervousness, anxiety.
- Rapid, shallow breathing.
- Muscle spasms.
- Apparent unco-ordination, possibly developing into collapse or convulsions.

Treatment
Calcium is required. In critical situations it must be given intravenously. Intravenous treatment can be dangerous. Your veterinary surgeon will carefully monitor the cat while giving the calcium.

It may be necessary to wean the kittens as continuing drains of calcium are likely to result in recurring attacks.

If this condition occurs in a queen the diet should be rectified so that it does not happen again.

CARE OF THE NEWBORN KITTEN

Normal palate

Usually you can leave the care of the kittens entirely to the queen. For the first few days after their birth the queen will spend almost all her time with them. If the kittens suck vigorously and sleep soundly then there is no cause for your concern.

Excessive handling of the kittens can create unnecessary problems. You might, for example, make the queen anxious and unsettled. Very young kittens are quite delicate and can be hurt, expecially by children who could inadvertently be excessively rough with them. Kittens are easily chilled, so too much time spent away from the protection of the queen's body warmth can be very stressful to the kitten.

Signs that there might be a problem
The first indication of trouble is often constant crying by the kittens. This means they are hungry, cold or both. If an individual kitten is rejected by the mother you should examine it carefully for any obvious defects, such as cleft palate, a severe hernia or lack of eyelids. Or the kitten may be poorly developed and undersized in comparison to its littermates. If the kitten is malformed or grossly abnormal it is probably better to destroy it quickly and humanely. The mother will usually abandon a weak kitten. This may seem cruel to us, but it is a strong and natural instinct. Perhaps this natural culling of the weak is harsh, but it is also sensible.

If the queen rejects a kitten, but on examination it seems healthy, and especially if the mother is inexperienced or upset, then remove the kitten temporarily. Keep it warm, dry and draught free.

After the mother has settled down, try to return the kitten to her. If she still refuses to accept it, you should milk a little colostrum (the first milk) from the queen and give it to the kitten.

The colostrum contains antibodies which are vital because they give the kitten a degree of protection against many diseases for the first few weeks of life. These antibodies can only be absorbed into the kitten's system during the first day of life.

If the kittens are unsettled and crying, or have diarrhoea, or seem to be weak and unresponsive, and the cause is not obvious, consult your vet for advice. (See also 'Fading kittens', page 101).

The kitten's eyes should be closed for the first week of life. If the eyes are open, examine them carefully. If the kitten lacks normal eyelids, it should be humanely destroyed. If lids are present, the future outlook is better but you must keep the eyes lubricated or they may become dried out and ulcerated. Artificial tears and other eye ointments are available from your vet.

Cleft palate – they are sometimes less severe than this. In others, virtually the entire roof of the mouth is absent

98

If the kittens lack hair, but the skin is reddish, it may be that the hair has been licked off by the mother. If so, it will grow back by the time they are weaned. If the kitten is born without hair, other than a fine down on the muzzle (the skin in these cases is *not* red) then the kitten could have an inherited alopecia (lack of hair) which is sometimes caused by a recessive gene. This condition does not improve with age. There is no treatment. Affected kittens should be euthanised and the mating programme carefully examined to eliminate this fault in future litters.

On some occasions, fortunately rare, the queen may kill and perhaps even eat the kittens as they are born. This may be a form of hysteria. Or it is sometimes associated with ripped umbilical cords. In this latter case, the mother makes the haemorrhage worse by licking or chewing at the bleeding stump. Eventually the kitten dies from the shock and blood loss.

If the queen tries to kill the kittens, you must remove them immediately they are born. Attempt to return them when the queen has calmed. If she is still aggressive, or refuses to mother them, it may be necessary to foster the kittens.

Umbilical hernia

ABANDONED OR ORPHAN KITTENS

In many cases it is possible to find a foster mother. In a large cattery this is particularly easy as most queens are cycling simultaneously, and therefore several litters may be born at the same time. Nursing queens usually readily accept new kittens. Try to mix the orphans in with a litter of the same age, otherwise small kittens may be bundled out of the way by bigger kittens and not be able to compete for a fair share of the milk.

If a foster mother is not available, you may decide to rear the kitten yourself. *Be warned:* it will require a lot of your time, patience and effort. Sometimes the kittens die despite the best endeavours. On the other hand, success can be extraordinarily rewarding.

Nursing queens will usually readily accept another kitten

HAND-REARING ORPHAN KITTENS

Orphan kittens must be kept in a warm, draught-free environment. They have no ability either to lose or gain heat, so you must control their body temperature for them. Normally, this precise temperature control is achieved by snuggling against the mother and amongst the other kittens. For the first week of their lives, the temperature should be kept about 30-33°C (85-90°F). You can then gradually lower the temperature every few days so that by the time the kittens are a month old the temperature in their box is down to 21-25°C (70-75°F).

Heating can be provided by an overhead light or heating coil, but it is better to use a heating pad. Do not cover the entire floor of their box with the pad. Allow them about half the area for cooling off if they become overheated.

The bedding material will become soiled and wet and should be changed frequently. Something that is washable or disposable is indicated. We prefer towelling, but you could use newspaper, old sheets, even a lambskin if you like.

Give the kittens a source of warmth that will substitute for the mother and that they can snuggle against — for example a well wrapped hot water bottle. This has to be replaced every three hours during the night.

FEEDING THE ORPHAN KITTEN

The first twenty-four hours

Feed as much of the queen's 'first milk' or colostrum as possible. This could be milked from the queen's nipples then fed to the kittens with an eye dropper. As this colostrum contains antibodies that are vital to the kittens' defenses in their first weeks of life, every effort should be made to ensure that the kittens get at least some colostrum. The colostrum can be supplemented by making up a solution of glucose in water: Dissolve four teaspoons of glucose in a cup of boiled water. Feed one to two mls to the orphan kittens every three to four hours. An eyedropper or nursing bottle is usually adequate.

Cow's milk does not adequately replace queen's milk, as it is deficient in both protein and energy content. A suitable replacement formula may be available from your vet in the form of a commercially produced artificial queen's milk replacer.

Or you could make up one of the following recipes after the first day:

Recipe 1

Make up powdered whole cow's milk to double the strength recommended for human babies. To this mixture add vitamins A and D. These are available from a pharmacist as children's vitamin drops.

Recipe 2

1 cup full cream evaporated milk diluted to double the strength recommended for human babies using boiled water.
Add 1 egg yolk
    ¼ teaspoon Calcium Carbonate
    5 drops of a liquid children's multi-vitamin preparation
    2 teaspoons glucose
Store in refrigerator.
Warm to body temperature before use.

How often to give

Second to fifth day — five times daily.
Sixth to fourteenth day — four times daily.
Fourteenth to twenty-first day — three times daily.

Feed the kitten only until it is comfortably full — not until the stomach is tight and distended. A kitten that is doing well will put on about 10g weight per day in the first week, then gradually increase this rate of gain to about 20g a day by the third week. Do not be surprised or concerned if there is a small *loss* in weight the first day.

Do not overfeed

Progressive weights and feeding quantities should be recorded.

The replacement formula should be warmed to body temperature — about 38°C (100°F). Most kittens will suck from a doll's bottle or a specifically designed nursing bottle. These are available from most vets or pet shops.

When feeding a very young kitten, first wrap it in towelling, with the paws restrained. Hold it firmly and gently. Put the rubber teat into the mouth. If the kitten does not automatically suck at the bottle, you may have to show it how. Using thumb and forefingers, gently move the kitten's lips up and down over the teat, mimicking or simulating the action of sucking lips. The kittens usually catch on quickly.

If the kitten will not suck, a stomach tube can be used. This is not difficult if you are careful. You must ensure the tube is passed down the correct length, and must make certain it is down into the stomach and NOT into the lungs before pouring in the formula.

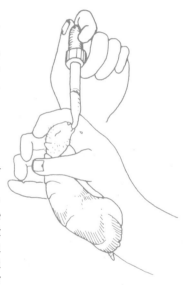

TAKE GREAT CARE!

After feeding the kitten, clean the area under the kitten's tail with a piece of rough towelling that has been dampened with warm water. This mimics and substitutes for the mother's tongue and stimulates the kitten to urinate and defaecate — both very necessary functions, albeit unpleasant for you.

The consistency of the kitten's stools will give you a guide to whether you are feeding the right strength of replacement formula. Normal stools are putty-like in consistency and a yellow colour. If diarrhoea develops you should dilute the formula. If the diarrhoea is persistent or severe, immediately consult with your vet. Diarrhoea in the young kitten can be serious and should be controlled as quickly as possible.

WEANING THE KITTENS

Most kittens can be weaned from the queen or the replacement formula onto solids by three or four weeks of age. The weaning procedure is not difficult. The method is to offer foods of gradually increasing consistency and complexity. At first, the kittens will puddle in amongst the food, feet and all, but they soon learn to lap and then to eat. Initially, offer the kittens normal replacement formula in a shallow dish instead of in a bottle. Let them suck your finger, then gradually lower the finger into the dish of milk. Start to add a little mashed egg, homogenised cooked meat or baby food. Other foods that can be gradually introduced include cottage cheese, yoghurt and commercial kitten foods.

It is essential to wean the kitten on to a variety of foods, otherwise the kitten could become 'hooked' on a certain type of food for life. Just like babies, kittens should experience a range of tastes and textures early in life.

'FADING KITTENS'

A 'fading kitten' is one that is not gaining weight properly, and may be constantly crying out or abnormally passive and unresponsive.

In approximate order of incidence, the possible causes include:

Inadequate milk supply
Kittens weigh, on average, between 90g and 140g at birth. If the queen's milk supply is adequate they should gain about 10g per day, although they sometimes lose weight for the first one or two days, and this is within normal expectations.

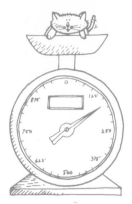

Weigh the kitten daily

The *only* way to be certain whether the kittens are developing satisfactorily is to weigh them daily. If there is any doubt, start a diary and chart their progress.

The queen's milk supply is often scanty immediately after the birth, but should improve rapidly. You can determine whether the supply is good by gently squeezing a nipple between thumb and forefinger. You should readily be able to express a few drops of milk.

An inadequate milk supply may only be temporary. By improving the queen's nutrition and perhaps by resolving any possible stresses on the queen, the milk production will often improve dramatically.

If the queen is not able to produce enough milk it may be necessary to supplement their food, or to foster one or more of the kittens, or even to raise the kittens as orphans.

COLD STRESS

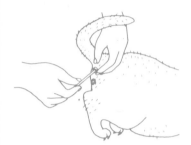

Taking a cat's temperature
You will need someone to hold the cat still. Dip an ordinary round-ended clinical thermometer in vegetable oil. Make sure the mercury is shaken down. Raise the cat's tail and gently insert the mercury end of the thermometer into the anus until about 2 cms is inside the cat. After about a minute, remove it and check the reading.

Kittens are extremely sensitive to cold. They are unable to warm themselves if they become chilled. Undetected draughts, inadequate housing or damp bedding can lead to cold stress and loss of kittens.

Cold kittens are sluggish, and usually cry only weakly. They attempt to suckle, but desist after a short time.

Diagnosis: Take their temperature. Make sure you shake the thermometer right down first. Normal temperature is around 38.5°C (101.3°F). (See page 26.)

Cold kittens should be slowly, gently re-warmed. Rapid heating can lead to shock or even to burns. Wrap them in a warm, dry blanket (see page 27).

INFECTION OF THE NAVEL (umbilical cord)

Signs
Bluish tinge around stump of umbilical cord (navel, belly button). If left untreated, this could develop a pus discharge. Newborn kittens have little resistance and a cord infection could flare into a serious condition very quickly. These cord infections are especially likely if the bedding is soiled or wet.

Treatment
Paint the stump with an antiseptic such as acriflavine or mercurichrome. If the kitten is not suckling you may have to give it supplementary food. Seek veterinary assistance early if the discoloured area is enlarging or if pus develops. The kitten will probably need antibiotics.

VIRAL INFECTIONS

Navel infection ('navel ill')

The queen may be a carrier of various viral infections. The stresses of late pregnancy are usually enough to allow the virus within the queen to multiply resulting in a period of virus shedding at, or just after, the birth of the kittens.

The most commonly involved viruses are those of the feline respiratory disease complex. The kittens usually have some immunity to these viruses, but it may be overcome, resulting in respiratory problems or even an overwhelming infection that will probably kill the kitten. Other viruses that could be similarly involved include feline panleukopeaenia (FIE) and feline leukaemia virus (FeLv). For more detail, refer to the chapter on 'Infectious Diseases' (page 104).

One of the herpes viruses may be an important factor. The newborn kitten's temperature is below that of the mother, and this slightly lower temperature is ideal for this virus to thrive. So a herpes virus infection contracted from the mother could flare in a kitten, even though it has caused no apparent problem in the mother. The kitten may develop a range of possible conditions from diarrhoea to pneumonia or even septicaemia.

MASTITIS OR METRITIS IN THE QUEEN

Bacterial infections of the queen are most likely to involve either the mammary glands (mastitis) or the uterus (metritis). The kittens could also become infected, resulting in a range of possible conditions from diarrhoea to pneumonia or even septicaemia.

SOUR MILK (sometimes called toxic milk)

Cause
If the mother has mastitis or metritis, toxins may build up in the milk.

Signs
Kittens cry, are bloated, with rough coats and raw, inflamed anuses.

Treatment
Kittens must be hand-reared until the mother's milk returns to normal. If the queen takes some days to recover, she may not return to full milk production, so the kittens might have to have some supplementary food.

Kittens usually refuse to suck from a queen with sour milk

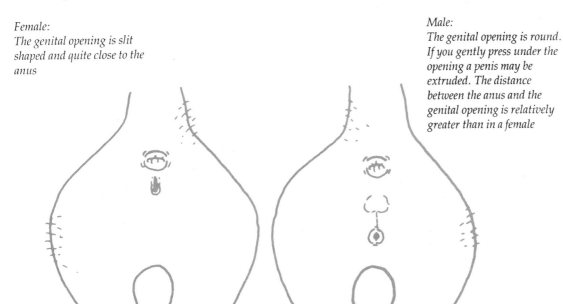

Female:
The genital opening is slit shaped and quite close to the anus

Male:
The genital opening is round. If you gently press under the opening a penis may be extruded. The distance between the anus and the genital opening is relatively greater than in a female

How to tell a kitten's sex

INFECTIOUS DISEASES

FELINE INFECTIOUS ENTERITIS (FIE)

Also called panleukopaenia and incorrectly called cat distemper.

Feline infectious enteritis (FIE) is a major cat disease. It is caused by a very resistant and easily transmitted virus, and was for years the scourge of the cat population. Fortunately, an effective vaccine is available and outbreaks are now relatively uncommon.

Signs of FIE
Not all cats that contract the virus causing FIE are affected in the same way. There are four syndromes associated with FIE, although not all cases fit neatly into one category or the other.

Syndrome 1: sudden death
In this, the most severe form, the virus multiplies and spreads so rapidly that the victim becomes ill and dies in less than a day — often before any warning signs appear. The owner may mistakenly think the cat has been poisoned.

Kittens under six months are more likely to be the victims of this form than adult cats.

Syndrome 2: severe illness — may be fatal
In this syndrome, the course of feline infectious enteritis runs three to seven days. The signs shown are described below, but note that most cats show only some, not *all* of these signs.

Vomiting
This is often the first sign, and can be severe. It is often frothy and foul smelling.

Diarrhoea
The virus attacks the lining of the bowel, damaging it and this results in diarrhoea. The damage to the gut lining may be so severe that some recovered cats are prone to recurrent bouts of diarrhoea for life.

Other signs
Affected cats are profoundly physically depressed. They usually refuse to eat but develop an apparent desire for water, often hovering over a water bowl but seldom drinking. Abdominal pain can be severe, causing the cat to adopt a hunched stance.

The cat becomes dehydrated, the coat assumes a rough feel and the skin becomes inelastic. You can test for this: pull up a generous pinch of skin over the back or neck. When released, this skin should immediately slide back into place. In the dehydrated cat it only slowly ebbs back into place.

A cat with feline enteritis might hover over its water bowl

Syndrome 3: few or no signs
Many cats exposed to the virus develop few or *no* apparent signs. After the virus has invaded the body, the cat's natural defenses can be sufficient to prevent it from multiplying. This is termed a 'sub clinical' form, and it is a common form especially in adult cats.

Syndrome 4: wobbly kittens
If a kitten is infected just before or after birth, damage can occur in the part of the brain responsible for balance (the cerebellum). Affected kittens lack co-ordination and balance and this causes them to stagger and tumble. Some kittens also develop chronic diarrhoea, probably due to severe damage to the developing gut lining. Inco-ordination may not be noticed until the kittens are several weeks old as prior to that *all* kittens are a bit wobbly. There is no treatment for kittens with this brain damage. The inco-ordination is permanent and euthanasia is recommended if the kitten is unable to cope with basic activities such as eating or turning around.

How does the infection spread?
Affected cats shed vast numbers of the feline enteritis virus in all body secretions — urine, saliva, droppings and vomit. The virus is very tough and can persist in the environment for up to twelve months.

Why does the virus cause these signs?
The FIE virus attacks all rapidly dividing body cells — and is especially attracted to the lining of the bowel (resulting in vomiting and diarrhoea) and to the white blood cell producing tissue. A blood test from an affected cat shows a dramatic reduction in the number of white blood cells — hence the alternative name 'panleukopaenia', which translated means 'a general lack of white cells'.

White blood cells are essential in combating infection by bacteria and other invaders, so the course of FIE is often complicated by other (secondary) infections.

Treatment: what can be done?
Treatment of any viral disease is limited because an effective anti-viral drug is not available. Antibiotics kill or control bacteria, but they have no effect against a virus. Prevention, and not treatment, is the best way to control viral infections.

Treatment should be under the supervision of your vet. He/she may give fluids intravenously or under the skin to counter dehydration. Injections of hyperimmune serum can be useful although this can be expensive and often not rewarding. Antibiotics are often given to prevent the invasion of bacteria. Drugs to reduce vomiting, diarrhoea and pain may also be indicated. We have found vitamins (especially the B group) very helpful.

Good nursing cannot be overvalued. Owners who are willing to apply time and effort to give fluids, medicine and tender loving care can make an enormous difference to the outcome. Feline enteritis is a serious disease and the outlook is

NURSING

always 'guarded'. If the cat survives the first three days, the chances of ultimate survival are reasonable. Some cats have a strong will to fight the disease, others just seem to give up. The personality of your cat is a significant factor in determining the final outcome.

PREVENTING FIE: VACCINATION

VACCINATION

BOOSTER

| Vaccination against FIE is strongly recommended. |

Kittens
Can be given a temporary vaccination from as early as six weeks but usually at eight or nine weeks of age. 'Permanent' vaccination at twelve to fourteen weeks. Usually annual revaccination is recommended, but ask your vet. In high risk situations, such as following an outbreak, vaccination can be repeated as often as fortnightly from two weeks of age to sixteen weeks.

Adults
Cats of any age can be vaccinated. Booster vaccinations are usually given annually.

Queens
It is not recommended that 'live' vaccines be used in pregnant cats. It is better to vaccinate queens prior to mating, or to use a 'killed' vaccine in the last three weeks of pregnancy. By vaccinating the queen, a strong temporary immunity is passed to the kittens — 99% of this immunity is passed in the first milk (the colostrum) so it is important that kittens suckle soon after birth to gain this protection.

How long after the cat is infected do signs of disease occur?
The virus incubates in the body for between two to ten days before signs start.

For how long after it has recovered is the cat dangerous to other cats?
The affected cat sheds the virus in large numbers even *before* clinical signs develop and this continues for about a week. After that, the cat may shed the virus intermittently even after recovery — maybe for months.

How long are soiled properties dangerous to new cats entering?
The virus causing FIE is a 'parvo' virus and is very resistant. It may persist for up to a year. It is resistant to heating but is killed by boiling. It is resistant to disinfection by chloroform, ether, phenols and acids or alkalis, but 0.2% formalin will inactivate the virus in twenty-four hours. Aldehydes and hypochlorite bleaches are also effective.

Is FIE contagious to children or adults?
No, nor to dogs or other animals except for other members of the cat family.

Does vaccination give instant immunity?
No. It takes ten to fourteen days after the first vaccination for a protective level of immunity to develop. The response to 'booster' vaccination is much quicker, taking only a few days.

FELINE RESPIRATORY DISEASE (FRD)

Also called cat 'flu or snuffles. Feline respiratory disease is a common viral infection of cats that resembles the head cold of humans. It is often incorrectly called cat 'flu (short for the 'influenza' virus). It is not caused by the influenza virus. More than 80% of cases are caused by one of two agents:
- Feline viral rhinotracheitis (FVR) or
- Feline calicivirus (FCV).

A vaccine is available which gives good protection against these viruses. Correct vaccination can save your cat from unnecessary discomfort.

Signs of FRD

Signs appear within ten days of infection, usually within only two to six days. The effects of these viral infections vary from case to case and range from mild to extremely severe and potentially fatal. The course varies from one to three weeks. Siamese and Burmese seem particularly prone to the severe form.

VACCINATION

Feline viral rhinotracheitis (FVR) infections are generally more severe than the other form (FCV), although mixed infections occur. The first sign is usually sneezing, then a watery eye discharge which gradually becomes thicker and yellow. Crusts form around the eye. In severe cases, the eyes become swollen and puffy and can become ulcerated. It is important that these cases are treated by your vet as permanent damage can occur. There is frequent sneezing. The discharge from the nose changes from watery to thick and purulent. Because the cat's sense of smell is affected, the cat will often stop eating because food odours are necessary to stimulate the cat's appetite. Other signs may include coughing, drooling saliva and mouth ulcers.

Improvement usually starts five to seven days after the onset of signs, but severely affected cats may continue to deteriorate.

> Siamese and Burmese usually suffer severely, and should be correctly vaccinated against the feline respiratory diseases.

The pain in the cat's mouth and throat, gummed up eyes and nose, plus the loss of sense of smell and taste can seriously reduce the cat's willpower. Some appear to give up the will to live. Good nursing is particularly important in these cases (see *Treatment*).

After recovery some cats can be left with residual damage to the sinuses. This is most common if the cat is less than six months old when infected, and in Siamese and Burmese. These cats may have recurring bouts of sneezing and persistent nasal discharge.

Feline Calicivirus Infection (FCV). There are different strains of calicivirus and the severity of the attack varies according to the strain.

> A frequent sign of calicivirus is ulceration of the tongue.

Some calicivirus attacks produce virtually no signs. Others are almost as severe as FVR. In general the course is more moderate and lasts only seven to ten days.

Ulcers may also appear on the paws, so the disease has been called 'paw and mouth disease'. (There is no connection with the more serious Foot and Mouth Disease of farm animals).

Ulcers on tongue of a cat with feline respiratory disease

107

Other effects of FRD (FVR, FCV and other agents)
Abortion
Pregnant queens may abort (or 'miscarry') one or two weeks after exposure to the virus. Live virus vaccination of pregnant queens is not recommended.
Pneumonia
The virus attacks the upper respiratory system (nose and throat) but it can predispose the cat to infections of the lower areas, especially in young cats. Bronchitis (infection of the bronchi) and pneumonia (infection of the lungs) are serious conditions. The cat should be put under veterinary care if there is any suspicion of chest involvement.
Eye problems
If kittens are affected before weaning there is a high risk of eye damage. If the eyes have not yet opened (that is, kittens under two weeks old) they should be taken to the vet to be checked.

Treatment of FRD
As with FIE, the best approach is not treatment, but prevention by vaccination. Once cats have contracted the disease vaccination is too late.

Treatment is aimed at reducing the severity of the disease's effects and maintaining the cat in the best condition possible until natural immunity to the virus develops.

Antibiotics are often used to control the serious and potentially fatal secondary bacterial infection.

Eye ointments or drops may be prescribed. During treatment the eye should be kept free of discharge and any crusts that form can be gently soaked and removed with damp cotton wool.

Fluids can be given by mouth if the cat will accept them. Broths are excellent and may stimulate the cat to drink. Glucose (not sugar) and water gives an easily assimilated energy source or your vet may supply an electrolyte (body salt) replacement solution.

If the cat is severely dehydrated the vet may inject fluids intravenously or subcutaneously (under the skin).

NURSING

Nursing
As with FIE the capacity for good nursing to improve the outlook is enormous. The patient should be kept in a warm, draught-free but well ventilated area. Gently clean away the eye and nose discharge using damp cotton wool balls. A thin smear of petroleum jelly below the eyes prevents the discharge sticking to the hair.

Try to keep the cat eating. Highly flavoured foods are not as stimulating as strong *smelling* foods. Try fish or cheese, and warm the food a little to increase the aroma. Force feeding is successful in some cats, but do not persist if it causes distress and resentment.

Groom the cat. This increases his sense of wellbeing.

Vitamins help — especially the B group and vitamin C. Getting the cat to take these can be difficult, although highly palatable tablets and gels are available. Your vet may give vitamin injections.

Most of the treatment may have to be done by you, as many veterinary hospitals are reluctant to hospitalise these cats due to the highly infectious nature of the disease.

Purring
If you can induce your cat to purr this can ease breathing dramatically. Several purring sessions daily — a few minutes at a time is enough — can relieve distressed breathing and can greatly improve the cat's comfort.

108

Inhalation therapy

The aim of inhalation therapy is to loosen thick mucous from the nasal passages. Some cats co-operate well and seem to enjoy it, but if the cat appears distressed, *do not persist.*

One simple treatment is to put the cat in a cage and take him into the bathroom with you while you have a shower or bath. A slightly more elaborate method is to use a bowl of hot water with an inhalation preparation such as eucalyptus oil or Friars Balsam added. (Not too much! The cat has sensitive air passages and too much is irritating.)

The cat is unlikely to sit over a steaming bowl, so put him in an open mesh basket or cage and suspend him over the bowl. A blanket thrown over the basket will prevent the vapours from dissipating.

PREVENTING FRD: VACCINATION

A vaccine injection against FVR and FCV can be given from nine to ten weeks of age. A second injection is needed three or four weeks later and an annual booster is recommended. After the vaccination you *may* see mild signs of feline respiratory disease but these are usually transient and not cause for alarm.

Kittens in high risk areas, such as catteries, can be given intranasal vaccines from six weeks of age. After this intranasal vaccine some cats develop runny eyes and nose and this may persist for a week or two. These kittens still require injection of vaccine to maintain their immunity. Commence when they are twelve to fourteen weeks.

VACCINATION

Is the vaccine effective?
The protection derived from this vaccination may not be complete, especially if the cat is challenged by a high dose of virus as could occur during an outbreak or during a visit to a cattery. Vaccination decreases the severity of the disease and a vaccinated cat is unlikely to suffer a fatal outcome.

BOOSTER

Is the virus very persistent? How long before infected premises are safe again?
In contrast to the FIE virus, the respiratory disease viruses are fragile and can be destroyed by most common disinfectants and bleaches.

FVR virus only survives about a day away from the cat. FCV may survive up to a week.

Where is a cat likely to pick up feline respiratory disease?
The spread of FRD is mainly from direct or indirect contact with infected cats. Cat shows, catteries and breeding establishments are areas of potentially high risk, as many cats are brought together, often under stress. Stress can trigger off virus shedding in 'carrier' cats. Infection comes from sneezing infected droplets and direct nose to nose contact in neighbouring cats.

Carrier cats may show no signs of illness. When many cats are brought together, at catteries, shows or breeding centres, the risk of infection is greatest

What is a 'carrier' cat?
Over 80% of cats that have recovered from FVR infection will intermittently shed the virus for up to a year and in some cases for a lifetime. So a cat may appear healthy but, especially when stressed, can shed virus and therefore infect susceptible cats in its immediate vicinity. Cats that have recovered from FCV infection are not quite so dangerous. About 50% shed virus for at least a month. Others can shed it for two or more years after apparent recovery.

Most carrier cats may show no symptoms of the disease. Others show chronic signs such as runny nose or eyes.

My cat has recovered from FVR. For how long is he immune against reinfection?
Only three to four months.

How do I prevent infection in a group of cats, such as in a cattery?
Make sure all cats are vaccinated before entering the cattery.

Adequate ventilation is essential and overcrowding must be avoided, not only to reduce contact but because overcrowding causes stress, which may in turn cause carrier cats to start shedding virus.

Direct nose to nose spread is the main route of transmission, so individual cages should be separated by at least a metre. Adjacent cages should have solid partitioning to eliminate direct nose to nose contact. Airborne transmission is also important. Viruses can travel several feet — more with moving air.

In a breeding establishment all new animals should be isolated for two weeks before being allowed to mix. This is important for control of other diseases as well, such as feline leukemia virus (see page 111).

If cat 'flu is a persistent problem in a cattery, vacating all cats from the premises for several weeks to allow disinfection may be the only solution.

Can the cat catch 'flu from people?
No. The virus cannot develop in a cat. But when we have a heavy cold we also shed large numbers of bacteria when we cough or sneeze and the cat could develop a respiratory infection from these bacteria.

In the terminal stages of FIP, the cat may develop a bloated, fluid-filled abdomen

FELINE INFECTIOUS PERITONITIS (FIP)

Feline infectious peritonitis, or FIP, is at present an uncommon viral disease in cats, but it is increasing in incidence. Only about 20% of cats exposed to the FIP virus develop signs of the disease. However, once signs do develop the course is almost invariably fatal, irrespective of treatment. Fortunately, many cats have a natural resistance to infection by the FIP virus while others develop an immunity after exposure and infection without developing any clinical signs of disease.

There is no vaccine against FIP.

Signs of FIP
There are two forms of the disease — the 'wet' form from which the disease gets its name and the less spectacular but equally fatal 'dry' form.

The virus may be present in the cat's system for several weeks or months before signs appear. Young or debilitated cats, or cats suffering from some injury to their immune system are most likely to be affected.

The wet form of FIP
The peritoneum is the membrane which lines the abdominal cavity and covers the abdominal organs. This peritoneum becomes inflamed and produces a discharge that slowly builds up in the abdomen, giving the cat a swollen, bloated appearance. Meanwhile, the cat loses appetite, becomes lethargic and is intermittently feverish. Sometimes the cat develops diarrhoea, vomiting and jaundice (yellowing of the gums and the whites of the eye).

The dry form of FIP
There is no fluid accumulation in this form. Instead, individual organs are attacked, such as the kidney, liver or pancreas. Signs depend on which organ(s) is affected. Diagnosis can be difficult as FIP can mimic other diseases. Blood tests may be necessary for definite diagnosis.

Some signs that can be associated with the dry form include vomiting, diarrhoea, abdominal pain, abortion, stillbirth or weak kittens and infertility. The colour of the cat's eyes may change.

Once the disease has been in the household, can it be eliminated so that other cats are not at risk?
Yes. The virus is easily killed by most disinfectants and does not persist for long outside the cat's body. If you have lost a cat through FIP you could safely introduce another after a few weeks.

Why are some cats so severely affected and others unaffected?
We are not sure. One factor that is important is that in many cases of FIP, the cat's immune system had been suppressed by some other condition, most commonly by the feline leukemia virus (see below).

FIP is more common in young cats (under three years old) and is more likely to occur in cat-colonies than in individually housed cats. This is presumably because the virus is fragile and cannot survive away from the cat for long, so it persists better if there are many potential victims in the one area.

Treatment of FIP
There is no effective treatment at present. 'Supportive' treatment such as fluids, multi-vitamins, force feeding and antibiotics may prolong life, but usually the cat will die in six weeks or less.

No preventive vaccine is yet available.

FATAL

ENTERIC CORONAVIRUS INFECTION

This is a recently reported condition, confirmed in the USA and suspected in other countries. It is related to FIP but the course is mild and only rarely severe or fatal.

The usual signs are a mild fever and perhaps vomiting and diarrhoea.

Like FIP, the causative virus is readily destroyed by most disinfectants and is not long-lived away from the host cat.

FELINE LEUKEMIA VIRUS

The feline leukemia virus (or Fe.LV) can produce severe illness leading to death and may lead to cancer of the lymphatic tissue.

> Most cats exposed to Fe.LV do not develop any signs of illness.

Signs of Fe.LV
The majority of cats show no signs at all. Tests show that in various countries from 30% up to 70% of the adult cat population has been exposed to Fe.LV. Of

these, a few (about 2% or 3%) become carriers and will shed the virus intermittently for years, or until their own deaths from the disease.

In the minority of cats that do become ill, the signs are variable, but may include:

- Fever.
- Malaise (lethargy, weakness, physical depression).
- Swollen glands.
- Blood changes — a drop in the number of red and white blood cells.

Death may occur at this stage, although most cats *appear* to make a recovery. Some cats do in fact make a complete recovery. This is more likely if the signs of illness were only mild.

The sinister aspect of Fe.LV is that some cats remain persistently infected. The presence of the virus predisposes them to seemingly unrelated diseases, or the cat may experience a recurrence of the original signs. Of persistently infected cats, 70% die within eighteen months.

THE FELINE LEUKEMIA VIRUS RELATED DISEASES

Cancer

In the cat the feline leukemia virus can cause leukemia. (In man and the dog, the cause of leukemia is not known.) *Lymphosarcoma* is the most common type of cancer seen in cats, and is caused by Fe.LV. Lymphosarcoma is a malignant tumour affecting the lymph nodes, which are located throughout the body. Lymph nodes act as filters of the body fluids. The best known lymph nodes in humans are the tonsils and adenoids, but there are lymph nodes in all strategic sites throughout the body such as in the neck, armpits, groin and behind the knee. The spleen, the thymus and the walls of the intestine are other common sites of lymphosarcoma. The thymic form is especially common in young Siamese cats. For more on lymphosarcoma *see* page 237.

Bone marrow suppression

Fe.LV depresses the bone marrow's production of new blood cells. This leads to anaemia and decreased resistance to disease.

Infertility

About 80% of infected queens become infertile. There may also be abortion, stillbirths or weak kittens. Kittens that survive have a very high chance of developing Fe.LV-related diseases as adults.

Susceptibility to other diseases

Fe.LV virus affects the lymphoid tissue which is vital in the body's defensive response to invasion by other viruses, bacteria or other organisms. In the affected cat this immune response is suppressed so that other diseases are more likely to overcome the cat's weakened defences.

In a cat suffering from lymphosarcoma the superficial lymph nodes may swell and can be felt in the positions marked. The spleen also swells

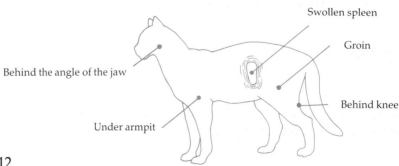

Swollen spleen

Groin

Behind the angle of the jaw

Behind knee

Under armpit

112

Lung conditions and mouth infections are the most common. Other conditions such as feline infectious peritonitis (see page 110) and feline infectious anaemia (see page 119) which are otherwise usually very mild, may instead be severe — possibly fatal.

The treatment of Fe.LV
There is no effective treatment currently available.

How do cats become infected?
The feline leukemia virus is fortunately not highly contagious and it may take many months for a cat carrying and shedding the virus to infect other cats in the household. The virus can be transmitted in saliva, urine and faeces, so infection can occur via grooming equipment, contaminated dishes or other utensils, or cat bites. Infected queens can pass the virus to the kittens in the uterus or through her milk.

Are any breeds more susceptible to Fe.LV than others?
Siamese and Burmese are more susceptible than most breeds.

Is there a risk to humans?
For a time it was suspected that the virus might be transmitted to humans. A virus that causes cancer is worrying. A lot of research has been done to answer this question. The evidence is now strongly indicative that Fe.LV is *not* transmissible to humans. This has not been conclusively proven. However, it seems likely that eventually the virus will be classified as being 'no risk' to humans.

Is a vaccine available?
A vaccine has been developed. Ask your vet regarding local availability.

Are there tests for the disease?
Yes. There are specific tests to determine whether your cat has, or has had, Fe.LV. Ask your vet for details of the test in current use.

A single test is helpful, but the test is usually repeated about three months after the first because:
• If the test was negative the cat could have been incubating the virus at the time of testing, so a second test might be positive.
• If the test was positive the cat may recover and get rid of the virus, so the next test may be negative, or lower than the first test.
So two tests give a more accurate assessment of the cat's infection status.

What should you do if your cat is positive for the Fe.LV test?
If you have only one cat the situation is more straightforward than for households with several cats. In the past, when considering the single cat situation, the biggest concern was that we did not know if the disease was transmissible to humans; this worry now appears unnecessary.

There is no treatment for Fe.LV. Of chronically infected cats, 70% will die in one or two years, usually with one of the Fe.LV-related diseases such as lymphosarcoma. If your cat develops one of these conditions and is starting to suffer you should consider euthanasia.

Remember — one positive test is not enough to be sure your cat is seriously affected. A second should be taken because many cats will recover from a subclinical or mild infection. If the second test is negative, the outlook for your cat is excellent. If it is still positive, the cat has only a small chance of recovery.

In the multiple-cat situation, the infected cat is a great risk to the other cats. Once a positive test is obtained, the infected cat must be isolated from the others. This may not be possible and in these cases euthanasia must be considered. Talk it over with your vet — if the cat is not 'clinically' ill and a second test has not yet been taken, there is a chance the cat will not become a chronic carrier of the virus and therefore in time will cease to be a risk to the other cats.

How soon after an infected cat has left the premises is it safe to get another cat?
The Fe.LV virus is susceptible to most disinfectants and bleaches. You should thoroughly clean and disinfect all utensils, trays or other items the infected cat has been in contact with, and bedding should be destroyed.

Even after thorough cleaning and disinfection, wait at least a month before introducing a new cat.

In cat colonies, any new cat should be tested and certified free of Fe.LV before being allowed in. When a vaccine becomes available new animals should be vaccinated *before* they arrive and time allowed for immunity to develop.

RABIES

FATAL

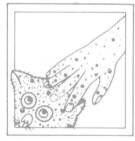

TRANSMITTED
TO HUMANS

Rabies is the most feared disease of cats as it can affect man. Once signs develop it is invariably fatal.

Rabies is a viral disease that can affect any warm blooded animal, but it is most common in carnivores (meat eaters) such as wolves, foxes, skunks and bats.

How is rabies caught?
The saliva of an infected animal is loaded with the virus and infection can occur through broken skin or on open wounds or by inhalation of the virus, for example in a cave infested with rabid bats. Most infections occur through bites. One of the sinister effects of the virus is to produce in many of its victims the desire to attack and bite. When another animal is bitten by the rabid animal the virus is injected into the victim's body where it seeks out the nervous system.

Signs
After the infecting bite, the virus 'incubates' in the cat's body for up to six months. Normally only two to eight weeks pass before signs of the disease start. There are then three further stages.

The first sign is often a personality change — the timid cat may become very affectionate, or the normally placid and affectionate cat become irritable or shy.

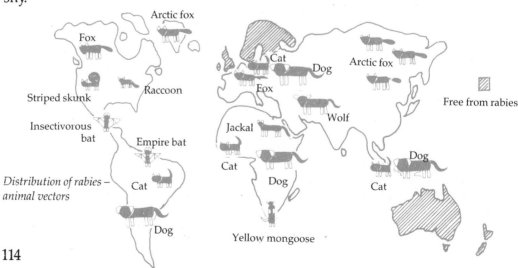

*Distribution of rabies –
animal vectors*

114

Usually the cat becomes apprehensive and hides away, often showing a dislike of bright light and noise.

In two days or less the cat's condition progresses to the next two stages — firstly one of increased excitability (the 'furious' form) followed by the last stage, a state of developing paralysis (the 'dumb' form).

The furious form can last up to four days and the cat is extremely dangerous during this period. Most hide away but if disturbed will attack viciously and persistently. Attacks may be triggered by sudden movements or noise.

The 'dumb' form follows. The cat becomes progressively paralysed. Paralysis starts in the hind legs and gradually ascends towards the head.

Death is inevitable and usually occurs within five days of the first signs. It is rare for cats to survive more than ten days. Some cats do not appear to undergo the 'furious' stage and go directly into the 'dumb' phase.

Treatment

Immediate treatment of a cat known or suspected to have been exposed to rabies will give a good chance of survival. However, once signs have developed the cat has *no* chance — death is inevitable. Any treatment must be carried out by a vet and it will probably include antiserum and vaccination.

The World Health Organisation strongly recommends that all unvaccinated cats with rabies be destroyed immediately because of the extreme risk to humans and other animals.

In areas presently free of rabies any cat suspected of having rabies would be taken into isolation by the authorities and stringent tests carried out.

Vaccination

Some countries are free from rabies due to strict quarantine laws, aided by geographical isolation from infected areas. Britain, Australia, Hawaii, New Zealand and parts of Scandinavia are at present free. In these areas vaccination is usually illegal as vaccination can interfere with testing for the disease in the event of an outbreak.

VACCINATION

Where rabies *is* present (most of the world) vaccination gives good protection. In some countries vaccination is mandatory. Vaccination can be started at three months of age and an annual booster is recommended.

When is an infected cat first dangerous to humans or other animals?

The cat's saliva is infectious even *before* signs start — usually for twenty-four hours. The cat is then infectious until its death.

What to do if a person is bitten by a rabid animal

BOOSTER

Any person bitten or scratched by an animal known to have rabies, or bitten by *any* animal in an area where rabies is known to exist, should seek *immediate* medical attention, but first:

● Flush the wound thoroughly — use plenty of soap and liberally flush and rinse afterwards.

● Then apply an antiseptic to the wound — e.g. tincture of iodine or cetrimide.

TOXOPLASMOSIS

Toxoplasmosis is extremely common in cats and in man.

TRANSMITTED
TO HUMANS

> Toxoplasmosis is transmissible to humans.
> Pregnant women especially should *beware.*

It is estimated that at least one-third of all cats in the USA and UK have been infected at some stage of their lives. In the vast majority of cases infection results in *no* apparent disease. It is only rarely that toxoplasmosis causes illness in cats. Its major significance is as a health hazard to humans.

Toxoplasmosis is caused by a minute parasite called toxoplasma gondii (a protozoan). The cat is the key to its life cycle, but it can infect any warm blooded animal.

By far the most common form in the cat is 'asymptomatic' (that is, there is infection, but no apparent sign of disease). These asymptomatic cats also present a hazard to humans as they still pass out millions of toxoplasma 'oocysts' in the droppings over a period of one to two weeks. After only one or two days these oocysts become capable of infecting other animals or humans.

The less common forms of toxoplasmosis in the cat are the following two syndromes:

1. *Acute generalised infection*
This form is more common in young cats and can even be acquired before birth if the queen is infected during pregnancy. The course is short; only about two weeks. If a vital organ is severely damaged the cat may die.

Signs may include:
- Fever, loss of appetite, breathing difficulty.
- Jaundice.
- Occasionally diarrhoea and vomiting.
- The heart may be damaged.

2. *Chronic, generalised infection*
This form is more likely to affect older cats and the course may take many months. Firstly the cat has an intermittent fever. May be vomiting, have diarrhoea and breathing difficulty. Other signs develop slowly and depend on which organs become involved. They include:
- Nervous signs: If the brain is affected there may be signs such as loss of balance, convulsions, blindness.
- Eye disease: Permanent damage, even blindness, can result from damage to the retina, iris or cornea.
- Heart disease: Including irregular beat or even heart failure.
- Anaemia: Cat tires easily. May have pale gums.
- Abortion of kittens or birth of weak or dying kittens.

Treatment of cats with clinical signs of toxoplasmosis
Treatment is not always advisable due to the public health aspects (see later). If treatment is commenced it can be quite successful although it only inhibits or controls the disease until the cat develops its own immunity. Any brain or eye damage that occurs before treatment is commenced will be permanent.

Your vet may use drugs such as sulphonamides and pyrimethamine in combination to control the toxoplasma infection.

Toxoplasma infection of humans
Toxoplasmosis is one of the most common infections found in man throughout the world. In countries like USA, UK and Australia, 40% to 50% of the population have been infected. In parts of France the figure is 95%. Only Antarctica is free.

116

Toxoplasmosis is especially common in:
- People who eat raw or undercooked meat.
- People who handle meat, e.g. butchers.
- Persons in contact with soil, such as gardeners.
- Children playing in inadequately covered sandpits.
- Persons who fail to empty their cat's litter trays frequently enough.

Signs of toxoplasmosis in humans
Most infections result in no signs at all, or in only mild signs of disease. The usual symptoms of patients who do present themselves to a doctor are tiredness, a low grade fever, swollen lymph nodes and muscle pains. In one study in Great Britain 7% of all patients with swollen lymph nodes had toxoplasmosis. That is a surprisingly large number.

The most serious form of toxoplasmosis in humans occurs when a mother is infected during pregnancy. One sad statistic is that in Europe 1% to 6% of all babies born are affected by toxoplasmosis.

If a mother is infected during pregnancy there is about a 40% chance that the baby will become infected. Of these babies about 15% will be seriously affected.

Infection during pregnancy can cause spontaneous abortion (miscarriage), stillbirth or deformities in the child, including mild to severe mental retardation and blindness.

> Care must be taken to avoid toxoplasma infection during pregnancy.

Diagnosis
In the cat: By examination of the faeces to find the microscopic oocysts. Blood tests can be performed (similar to humans).
In humans: A paired blood test is used. One blood test is not enough, as many people have positive tests due to mild infections contracted up to some years previously. Similarly, one negative test may miss an infection that is only just developing. If the second test shows a rise in the test levels compared to the first test, then the diagnosis is 'positive'.

Preventing toxoplasmosis in cats
These recommendations will require some effort on your part, but when the risks of acquiring toxoplasmosis are high, for example during early pregnancy, then they should be adhered to:
- Only feed your cat with canned food, dry food or food that has been frozen at -20°C for several days.
- Any meat fed to your cat (that has not been frozen) should be cooked well. Cut the meat prior to cooking to allow better heat penetration.
- Cats should not be allowed to hunt or scavenge. This is not always possible. At least vigorously control vermin such as mice and rats as they are a potent source of infection.

Preventing toxoplasmosis in humans

> All women of childbearing age should know these recommendations.

It is worth repeating here that most toxoplasma infections cause no problems. But the unborn child is especially at risk.

Litter trays should be cleaned out daily to minimise the danger of toxoplasmosis

• Pregnant women should avoid eating raw or undercooked meat. They should be careful of even *handling* raw meat: better to wear gloves or at least wash your hands thoroughly afterwards.

• Avoid introducing a new cat, especially a young one, to a household where a pregnant woman is present.

• Cat litter trays can be dangerous but are safe if cleaned daily as toxoplasma oocysts do not become infective for at least a day after being passed. To be safe, litter boxes can then be disinfected with hydrogen peroxide, ammonia, sodium hydroxide or strong acid. Flushing with boiling water is adequate if done thoroughly. Preferably, someone other than the pregnant woman should clean the litter tray.

• Wear gloves when gardening. Once the soil is infected the toxoplasma oocysts can remain potent for up to a year.

• Children's sandboxes should be covered when not in use as they are a favourite spot for cats to use as a toilet.

The life cycle of toxoplasma
(Understanding this will make it clear why the recommendations above are made.) The cat is the key to the life cycle of toxoplasma gondii. Although any animal can be infected, it is only in the cat that sexual reproduction of the parasite takes place.

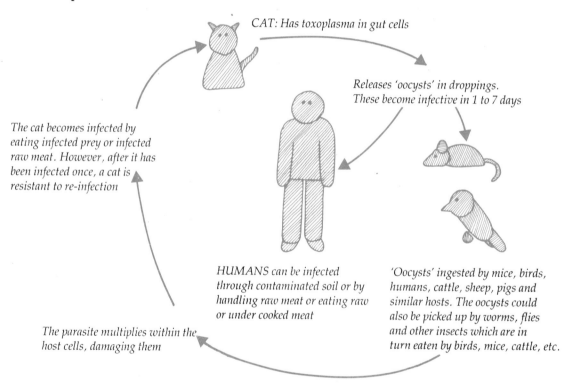

CAT: Has toxoplasma in gut cells

Releases 'oocysts' in droppings. These become infective in 1 to 7 days

The cat becomes infected by eating infected prey or infected raw meat. However, after it has been infected once, a cat is resistant to re-infection

HUMANS can be infected through contaminated soil or by handling raw meat or eating raw or under cooked meat

'Oocysts' ingested by mice, birds, humans, cattle, sheep, pigs and similar hosts. The oocysts could also be picked up by worms, flies and other insects which are in turn eaten by birds, mice, cattle, etc.

The parasite multiplies within the host cells, damaging them

Interesting facts about the life cycle of toxoplasma:

• Young cats (four to six months old) are the main source of contamination of the environment, as most older cats are immune to toxoplasma infection.

• The infected cat can pass twenty million oocysts (the infective stage of toxoplasma) per day. These cats continue to pass oocysts for seven to twenty-one days, so up to 400 million oocysts could be passed by a single cat.

• Once passed, the oocysts take one to seven days to become infective and can remain infective for up to a year if conditions are right.

118

FELINE LEPROSY

Feline leprosy is not common. It occurs in most countries. It is caused by a bacteria called *mycobacterium lepraemurium* and is transmitted mainly through rat bites.

Signs
There are multiple firm lumps or nodules under the cat's skin, mainly on the head and legs. The skin over these lumps may ulcerate. The nodules usually do not appear to bother the cat unless ulcerated.

Treatment
Human antileprosy drugs can be used, for example diaminodiphenylsulphine. Surgical treatment to remove troublesome nodules may be indicated.

TETANUS

Cats are about 1500 times more resistant to tetanus than horses, so cases are rare. Tetanus is caused by a bacteria called *clostridium tetani* that lives in the soil. Infection occurs when animals suffer a deep puncture wound that is contaminated by soil, faeces or putrefying matter that is harbouring the tetanus bacteria.

Signs
After infection it takes from four to twenty days for the signs to appear, so any wound or even any recollection of a wound may have disappeared.

The earliest sign is often a general muscle stiffness, then prolapse of the third eyelids (the 'skin' at the inside corner of each eye moves across to cover part of the eye). The cat often appears to have an 'anxious' expression or a 'sardonic grin' due to spasm of the facial muscles. The brow may be furrowed and the ears pulled close together. Muscle spasms can be triggered by noise, touch or even light. Without treatment death results. Even with treatment recovery can take up to a month.

Treatment
Tetanus antitoxin and antibiotics given early can be an effective treatment. In certain animals where tetanus is a high risk, notably horses, tetanus antitoxin is given whenever a deep wound is suffered. Because cats are so resistant to tetanus, the antitoxin is not usually a routine part of wound treatment.

Once signs of tetanus develop, muscle relaxants and sedatives may be needed.

If the cat recovers there is usually no residual nerve damage. The cat returns to normal.

Can the cat be vaccinated against tetanus?
Yes, but routine vaccination is not usually recommended as the cat has such a high natural resistance. If vaccination is required your vet can use tetanus toxoid. Three injections are needed: one initially, one a month later and a third after a year.

FELINE INFECTIOUS ANAEMIA

Feline infectious anaemia is a disease that occurs worldwide. It is caused by a tiny parasite that lives on the surface of the cat's red blood cells. This parasite multiplies on the cell and causes blood cells either to rupture or to be destroyed by the cat's spleen, resulting in anaemia. In the USA feline infectious anaemia is responsible for about 10% of all feline anaemia cases treated.

The disease: what happens in the cat
A small rickettsia called *haemobartonella felis* is responsible. It is not completely understood how it spreads from cat to cat but biting insects such as fleas are responsible for some cases and others are spread via cat bites. It is common in young, male cats, probably due to their fighting tendencies. It can also spread to the unborn kittens of an infected queen.

Signs
In two-thirds of the cases, only a mild anaemia results, but then these cats are prone to relapses if stressed (for example by another disease or by such events as moving house, a new pet in the family, boarding and so on). Such a state is called 'latent infection'. Infection can flare up as a result of one of these stresses to cause severe anaemia.

In about one-third of cases the cat develops a severe anaemia without going through any 'latent infection' stage. In these cats clinical signs may include lethargy and physical depression, loss of appetite, pale gums, weight loss, a weak pulse and sometimes a fever. Your vet may detect a swollen spleen.

These signs take time to develop, as the tiny blood parasite builds up in cycles or waves — disappearing for a few days at a time, then reappearing in ever increasing numbers and gradually destroying more and more red blood cells. The course may take months.

Treatment
Treatment is successful in about 50% of cases. In severely affected cats whole blood transfusions may be needed. Long courses of antibiotics may eliminate the infection. Multi-vitamins, iron and other blood production stimulants may be useful.

COCCIDIOSIS

Coccidiosis is a condition seen mainly in cats kept in crowded, unhygienic conditions such as may occur in some pet shops, markets or catteries. It is caused by the microscopic parasites *isospora felis* or *isospora rivolta*. Rats and mice can be a source of infection, but most transmission is due to contamination of the cat's coat, feet or even food with faeces containing the parasite. When the cat grooms itself or eats, the parasite is then ingested.

Signs
Loss of appetite, diarrhoea and weight loss. A faecal test performed by your vet will be needed for a definite diagnosis.

Control of infection is achieved by raising the standard of hygiene and reducing overcrowding. Soiled areas and utensils such as feeding bowls should be disinfected with alkaline cleansers such as sodium hydroxide or ammonia.

THE SYSTEMIC MYCOSES, OR FUNGAL DISEASES

Fungi occur naturally in soil and organic waste. Infection of cats with fungi is not common, but when it does occur, treatment is often difficult. The development of fungal disease is slow and insidious.

Cryptococcosis (cause: cryptococcus neoformans)
This fungus is widely distributed. It is a soil organism that finds pigeon droppings especially suitable for growth. Infections are uncommon.

Signs
The signs depend on the location of the fungal infection.
- Upper respiratory tract: Invasion of the nasal passages produces a thick discharge and partial airway blockages resulting in noisy or difficult breathing.
- The infection may break through bone into the area around the brain and cause a meningitis.
- In the skin form, cryptococcus produces multiple lumps or nodules on the face or body. These may ulcerate and resemble skin tumours or abscesses.
- In other forms the eyes or the abdominal organs may be infected.

Treatment
Treatment is difficult and can be expensive. Usually by the time it is diagnosed the infection is firmly established. There may be apparent improvement, but relapses are common. Euthanasia is often recommended.

The disease *is* transmissible to man but this transmission is highly unlikely, unless the person in contact is very old, very young or is highly susceptible to infections.

Nocardiosis (cause: nocardia asteroides)
Nocardia is a common soil organism.

Signs
The usual form affects the chest cavity of the cat, producing large quantities of a characteristic brown pus which causes the cat to have great difficulty breathing. There may also be involvement of the skin, with multiple swellings that ooze fluid.

Treatment
The outlook is not good, but draining the chest of pus and vigorous treatment with antibiotics may eliminate the infection after several weeks of treatment. Even with treatment relapses are common.

Other rare fungal diseases requiring vet treatment:

Actinomycoses (cause: actinomyces bovis)
This is a rare infection of cats that may occur after a physical trauma to the nose, plus contamination with soil. Actinomyces causes large irregularly shaped swellings in, or just under, the skin. Large pockets of pus may form.

Histoplasmosis (cause: histoplasma capsulatum)
Seen in the central river basins of North America, it is transmitted mainly through starlings' droppings. Spores can be ingested or inhaled. It can cause problems in the lungs (cough, difficult breathing) or the gut (diarrhoea, weight loss), or both.

Blastomycoses (cause: blastomyces dermatides)
Found in central parts of North America. Causes a lung infection. In some cats

it may progress to a generalised disease with abscesses under the skin which rupture and discharge. Lameness and blindness may occur.

Coccidiomycosis (cause: coccidiomycosis immitis)
Found in south west USA. The main significance of coccidiomycosis is as a respiratory disease of man. The cat can be infected by its owner, producing a mild condition of the lungs which may be complicated by bacterial infection. It usually causes the cat little or no distress.

Tuberculosis
Tuberculosis can affect man and all domestic animals. Fortunately its incidence is rapidly diminishing, but it is still found worldwide.
Cats are usually infected by drinking milk from an infected cow.

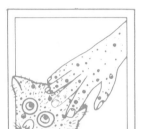

TRANSMITTED
TO HUMANS

Signs
In the early stages there are no signs but the causative bacteria take an insidious hold. Later there is gradual weight loss and intermittent fever. In man, it is the lungs that are mainly affected, but in cats the abdomen is the usual site. In some forms there are open skin ulcers that do not heal.

Treatment
Treatment is not usually attempted because the cat is a risk to other animals and man. Treatment, if contemplated, will be prolonged and expensive and is often unrewarding.

Leptospirosis (cause: leptospira icterohaemorrhagia or leptospira canicola)
Leptospirosis is an uncommon disease in cats. It is believed that cats possess a species immunity against leptospiral infections.
Leptospirosis is a disease that can infect man. The main source of infection is via urine contamination from rats, mice and other animals. Dogs can be a source of infection for man.

Rats are a potent vector of Leptospirosis

TEETH AND MOUTH

The cat is a predator. Its teeth have gradually evolved to suit that role. The cat uses its teeth to hold and kill prey, and then to shear meat into pieces small enough to allow swallowing. The cat's food requires little or no chewing to make it digestible. The cat can eat large meals very quickly, gulping it all down — scales, feathers, hair and all.

Cats bite with a chopping up and down action. They are unable to use the side to side grinding action that the human jaw is designed to make.

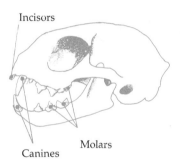

THE NORMAL TEETH

Kittens have twenty-six teeth. Adult cats have thirty. The mouth is dominated by the four huge canines, designed to hold and kill prey and for defence. The back teeth, or molars, have cusps, or cutting edges, to allow the cat to shear the food into manageable pieces.

Teething in kittens

The kitten is born without teeth. The first of the temporary or 'milk' teeth emerge at about two weeks of age. By the fifth or sixth week the kitten has twenty-six teeth. The permanent teeth start to emerge at around four months of age, or a little later. It takes another two months for all the teeth to emerge. The roots of the temporary teeth break down and the tooth is pushed out by the emerging permanent tooth. During this period of change the kitten may experience occasional episodes of tenderness around the gums, and may therefore be reluctant to eat. This discomfort is transient. There is no need for concern or medication. Nor should you try to tempt the kitten with tasty treats. This could lead to trouble later. The kitten is quick to realise that if it refuses one type of food, something even better will be produced. These cats can develop into fussy, picky eaters. A day or two without food will not harm a healthy kitten.

Teething is a far less traumatic experience for the kitten than it is for many human babies.

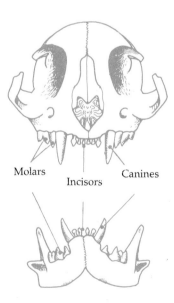

123

Retained temporary teeth

The adult teeth grow under the temporary teeth, displacing them as they emerge. Temporary teeth may fall out when the kitten is eating or playing and this can cause unnecessary alarm especially if a few drops of blood also appear. Similarly, if a temporary tooth is swallowed by a kitten, there is no cause for concern.

Sometimes the permanent tooth will grow up next to the temporary tooth and fail to dislodge it. These retained teeth can interfere with the correct alignment of the permanent teeth, therefore it is best to allow your vet to inspect the mouth. The vet may decide to remove the offending temporary teeth because food and debris can be trapped alongside retained teeth, causing foul breath, sore gums and a reluctance to eat on the tender side.

The most commonly retained teeth are the canines.

Above: Undershot jaw ('parrot' mouth)
Top: Overshot jaw ('sow' mouth)

Overcrowding of teeth

Some short-nosed breeds such as the Persian, Colour Point or Himalayan have too short a jaw to fit in all the teeth comfortably. The resultant overcrowding can cause difficulty eating or rapid build up of tartar with consequent gum disease (see page 126). In severe cases, your vet may have to remove some teeth to allow the cat to close its mouth comfortably. Cats with badly overcrowded mouths should definitely not be used for breeding.

The lower jaw of some cats, notably the Persian, may be overlong ('sow' mouth) or too short ('parrot' mouth). The upper and lower teeth of these cats do not meet correctly. This results in abnormal wear, especially of the incisors.

If you intend to buy a Persian kitten you should inspect its 'bite' before purchase and so avoid the dental problems associated with an abnormal jaw.

Signs of mouth pain or disease

Affected cats may show some of the following signs:
- Drooling of saliva.
- Bad breath.
- Reluctance or inability to eat.
- Lip smacking.
- Pawing at mouth.
- Open mouth (the tongue may protrude a little as a result).

Bad breath can be a sign of dental disease

MOUTH ULCERS

The most common cause of mouth ulcers is feline respiratory disease (see page 107). The tongue is the most common site of the ulcers but the gums and throat can also be involved.

Kidney disease can lead to mouth ulcers. In a cat suffering from advanced kidney disease the saliva changes composition. The body is trying to eliminate the waste products that are building up in the cat's bloodstream because of the kidneys' inability to eliminate them efficiently. One alternative route of excretion is through the saliva. Levels of the waste product urea build up in the saliva favouring bacterial growth. This in turn results in the production of ammonia. Ammonia irritates the sensitive membrane lining the mouth. In time this can lead to ulceration.

Corrosive chemicals such as alkalis and strong acids will burn and ulcerate the mouth. Cats almost never sample such chemicals willingly, but they may pick them up while grooming themselves or when licking contaminated paws.

124

Treatment
The ulcers themselves heal rapidly once the underlying cause has been remedied. When the ulcer is fresh, the mouth will be sensitive, and the cat will probably be reluctant to eat or drink. After one to three days the cat will usually start to accept a little food. Offer small chunks of meat or little boluses of food. These can be quickly swallowed without much effort. Food and drink is less irritating to a sensitive mouth if served warm — at about blood temperature.

Multi-vitamins help to stimulate the appetite and to speed up healing. Vitamin C and the B group are especially recommended.

A large mouth ulcer

BROKEN TEETH

Car accidents or fights can result in broken or chipped teeth. Unless the root is exposed, these teeth rarely cause the cat any concern and no treatment is needed. If the tooth is broken flush with the gum line or if it is worrying the cat, it is probable that the sensitive inner part of the tooth has been exposed. Infection may enter. Let your vet inspect the damaged tooth. It may be necessary to remove the remaining tooth and root under a general anaesthetic.

An overambitious leap may result in a fall and broken teeth or jaw

OLD CATS AND WORN TEETH

As cats age, their teeth wear down. Some may be lost through gum disease or through deterioration of the jaw bone. In some disease states — for example, chronic kidney disease — calcium is leached from the bones, the teeth become unstable in their sockets and may fall out.

Cats with only a few teeth or even no teeth can cope quite happily as long as you feed them soft foods, small chunks or balls of food that are small enough to be swallowed without chewing.

Can you tell a cat's age by the teeth?
Not accurately. Once a cat's permanent teeth have erupted they do not have a consistent variation with age, unlike the horse's teeth where changes occur at fairly predictable intervals.

JAW FRACTURES

Jaw fractures can result from knocks, kicks, car accidents or similar traumas. The most frequent cause is a fall from a height. The cat's lower jaw thumps onto the ground and may break — usually in the middle of the mandible.

Treatment
Most jaw fractures respond well to wiring or pinning. The patient will usually be able to eat and drink comfortably with these pieces of hardware in place while healing progresses. See chapter on 'Bones and Joints', page 216.

FOREIGN BODIES IN THE MOUTH

Pieces of bone, fish hooks, needles and other foreign bodies can become accidentally lodged in the cat's mouth.

The cat's tongue is covered with small horny barbs or 'papillae'. These project back towards the throat and turn the cat's tongue into an efficient rasp which can be used to remove flesh from bones when eating and to remove loose hair from the coat while grooming.

If a cat is playing with a thread, these barbs may catch the thread and the cat may be unable to disentangle it. By gulping and moving the tongue, the papillae gradually move the thread back down the throat and it is swallowed. Complications can arise if there is a needle on the other end of the thread. Fortunately, the needle usually enters blunt-end first. Many small needles will pass through the cat's bowel without causing harm. Others get caught and severe discomfort and illness may result if the needle penetrates the throat, gullet (oesophagus) or the bowel.

Fish hooks may become caught in the cat's mouth, especially if hooks are unwisely left still baited. If the barb has gone through the lip it is possible to cut the hook in two and remove it relatively painlessly (see page 27).

TARTAR

In the wild, cats *use* their teeth and this keeps them clean and healthy. As the cat eats, the biting, tearing and cutting actions have a natural abrasive and cleansing effect on the teeth. Cats which are fed foods that encourage this mouth exercise rarely have problems with tartar formation. Unfortunately many cats are fed mainly on soft processed foods that require little or no chewing. As a result these cats frequently develop a heavy build-up of tartar on their teeth.

What is tartar? How does it form?
Tartar, or dental calculus, starts as little more than an apparent stain on the teeth but it can gradually build into huge masses covering the teeth, exposing the roots and loosening the teeth. Bacteria proliferate at the gum margin.

Tartar begins as dental 'plaque' — an invisible film on the teeth. It always starts at the gum margins where the tooth is rubbed least. Food debris trapped between the teeth provides a medium in which oral bacteria can multiply. The bacteria invade between the tooth and the gum, making the gum red, swollen and painful.

Salts and minerals in the cat's saliva gradually precipitate on to the plaque, building up a hard concretion on the sides of the teeth. Once tartar formation has

Some of the possible ways of repairing a fractured jaw. The wires and/or pins are removed after the fracture has healed

126

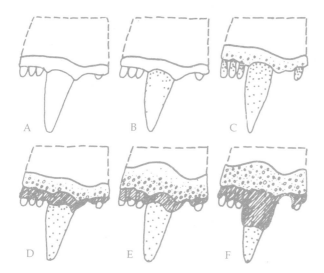

The stages of tartar formation. A. Dental 'plaque' is initially little more than an invisible film; B.C. gradually the plaque is stained and a mineral deposit starts; D.E.F. salts and minerals precipitate and gradually a solid mass forms. The gum is pushed back. Bacterial infections can become established between the tartar mass and the gums

started, there is a snowballing effect as more and more salts and minerals are deposited on to the tartar mass.

In time the tooth can loosen in its socket due to erosion by bacteria, and may be lost.

Signs of tartar build-up
- Foul breath.
- Excessive salivation, perhaps occasionally blood flecked.
- Pain on eating, or reluctance to chew.
- Pawing at the mouth.
- Sudden dropping of food from the mouth.

If you lift your cat's lips back to expose the molars you can readily see if tartar is forming. If the gum margins are reddened and inflamed, the cat is probably experiencing some discomfort. Although the build up of tartar is very gradual, taking months or years, the onset of signs of discomfort can be quite sudden.

Treatment
If the tartar has built to a formidable mass it is best to have your vet thoroughly clean the teeth under a general anaesthetic. An ultrasonic scaler, similar to the ones dentists use, may be used. Damaged teeth can be removed at the same time. Although cats rarely develop cavities in their teeth, damage to the tooth roots may be so extensive that removal of the teeth is necessary. However, cats with few or even no teeth survive quite happily. If tartar formation is only in the early stages, preventive measures may slow or even reverse the process.

Preventing tartar formation
Prevention is the best approach to dental disease. A sensible diet is the key. If the cat is fed only soft canned or minced foods, there is little natural cleaning of the teeth. Instead, food debris accumulates and bacteria can flourish. By feeding chunks or strips of meat and occasionally some hard, dry foods you will promote the natural abrasion of the tooth surfaces and stimulate a good flow of saliva. Both these actions aid in removing debris.

Provide your cat with something to chew on. Teeth and gums need exercise to remain healthy

Some cats will even allow their owner to clean their teeth. Use a soft, child's toothbrush or a damp piece of flannel plus a mild abrasive paste. (A mixture of equal parts bicarbonate of soda and table salt is suitable.) An unflavoured tooth powder may be tolerated, but do not use toothpaste as cats appear to object strongly to both the taste and the foaming action. It is better to clean only one or two teeth at a session until you have the teeth clean. Later you can keep any new tartar formation under control with a short weekly session encompassing all the teeth. Concentrate on the gum margins of the molars, premolars and canines, as this is where the problem starts.

Can cats taste sweet foods?
Probably not. There are no 'sweetness' receptors in the cat's mouth. Read more in the chapter on 'The Senses'.

SALIVARY CYSTS

There are several salivary glands situated in and around the mouth. If these glands, or the salivary ducts which deliver the saliva into the mouth, are damaged, the result can be the formation of a salivary cyst, or *ranula*.

Salivary cysts are usually not painful. They can become quite large, and may interfere with normal eating, especially if they form under the tongue. They are soft, usually either round or oval in shape, and fluctuate like a jelly when prodded.

Treatment
The cysts can be difficult to eliminate. In some cases simply draining the cyst is enough to result in a cure. However, in most cases the cyst re-forms. It may then be necessary to dissect out the cyst and perhaps also to remove the damaged salivary gland that spawned its formation.

RODENT ULCER *(eosinophilic granuloma)*

Rodent ulcers are open sores found primarily on the inside of the cat's upper lip, adjacent to the canine tooth. They sometimes develop in other sites — on the tongue, lips, roof of the mouth or on the skin of the abdomen or inner thigh.

The term 'rodent' ulcer is misleading. It originated because it was thought these sores were due to infections contracted from mice or rats. Their real cause is still uncertain, but it is generally believed they are the result of constant irritation from the cat's rough tongue. The reason why only some cats develop them is not understood.

The sores are usually oval in shape, with a raised edge or border. The affected area is gradually eroded, or 'eaten away.' It becomes red and inflamed and may bleed intermittently especially if knocked.

Early in its course, the ulcer is small and causes little concern to the cat. As it progresses, eating can become uncomfortable, and the cat may lose its appetite, salivate and paw at the mouth.

Treatment
Some cases respond to treatment with drugs such as corticosteroids (cortisone) or hormones (megoestrol acetate). In advanced cases, surgical removal may be contemplated although this can be deforming. X-ray treatment, cryosurgery (deep cold treatment) and injections into and around the sore have been successful in some selected cases.

Treatment is not always successful and recurrence is common.

A rodent ulcer is easier to see if you lift the lip back

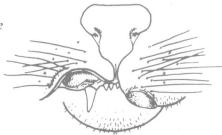

THE COUGHING CAT

A cough is a defensive reflex designed to clear irritants from the throat or chest. The cough is produced by the violent contraction of the chest and diaphragm, resulting in a blast of air through the windpipe and throat.

Could there be a foreign body stuck?

The manner in which a cat coughs can present a worrying sight to an owner. A cat cough is less subtle than a human cough, and it appears to come right from the throat. As one cough leads to another, a paroxysm of coughing can develop, inducing many owners to believe erroneously that their cat has something lodged in the throat. Not infrequently, the cat appears to be on the point of vomiting.

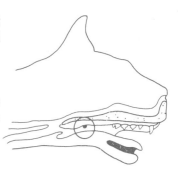

A cat that really *does* have an object caught in the throat that is large enough potentially to obstruct breathing will usually exhibit the following signs:
- Mouth open, drooling saliva.
- Gagging.
- Head down, neck extended.
- Pawing at mouth.
- Perhaps blood flecking of saliva.
- Violent expulsive effects with chest.

When the foreign matter is small, such as a fish bone, it can be very difficult to detect. If such an object is suspected and the cat is distressed it may be necessary to examine the cat under a general anaesthetic.

Causes of a cat's cough

Many conditions can lead to a cough. The most common include:

Matter caught in the back of the throat

Hair is a common cause. While grooming, the cat may get a small hairball caught in the pharynx or behind the soft palate. Other matter that might be involved includes grass, pieces of dry food and fish bones.

Tonsilitis

Infection of the tonsils leads to swelling and inflammation, and in some cases to pus formation. Tonsilitis can be one part of a more generalised disease, such as feline respiratory disease (see page 107).

Lungworm
See page 212.

The tonsils are situated out of sight at the back of the throat

Roundworm (especially in kittens)

The roundworm larvae track through the lungs, causing irritation. The cough is an essential part of their life cycle as the larvae must be coughed up from the lungs, then swallowed, to get back into the digestive tract. Refer also to page 192.

Lung infections

If mucus or other debris is building up in the chest the cat will cough it up in an attempt to clear the airways.

Heart disease

Heart disease is not common in cats but if present can lead to fluids building up in the chest, resulting in congestion. The cat coughs to bring up this fluid as it pools in the air passages.

Irritating fumes or dust

Some cats like to sit near heating vents or fan heaters and may breathe in considerable amounts of dust particles blown up from the floor. Other cats may be housed incorrectly where fumes form — for example, a garage. These fumes can irritate the throat and lungs.

Growths in the mouth

Cysts, polyps or even cancerous growths can form in the mouth. If these encroach towards the back of the cat's mouth or throat they may cause coughing.

Allergies

Coughing is not a common sign of allergy in a cat. This contrasts to the situation in man where allergic rhinitis, hay fever and asthma quite often have an associated cough.

Treatment for the coughing cat

Because there are so many possible causes of the cough, it is undesirable to try home remedies if the cough is persistent or severe.

Fortunately, in most cases, the cough is merely a reflex-clearing mechanism. Even if the cough develops into a short spasm there is usually little cause for concern nor need for treatment. However, if the cough is repeated and is distressing the cat, you may be able to relieve it with a little warm mineral oil (2 to 5 mls) given by mouth. This breaks up any matter trapped in the back of the cat's throat and helps to flush it down to the stomach. Also read the 'First Aid' section on how to give medicine and how to give relief to the congested, stuffed up cat (*see* 'Infectious Diseases', page 104).

It is important to try to determine the cause of the cough and to eliminate it. For example, your vet may prescribe antiparasitic drugs for lungworm infestations, antibiotics for bacterial infections, or anti-inflammatory drugs for chronic bronchitis.

THE EAR

A cat's ears are normally held erect and alert, but they can be directionally aligned to gather sound, or flattened in a show of anger. Unlike dogs, most cats have the same basic ear shape, with the exception of the Scottish Fold, which wears its ears folded forward on its head.

CLEANING EARS AND ROUTINE TREATMENTS

The cat is sensitive about its ears, and may resent excessive attention or handling of them. However, it may become necessary to clean or treat the cat's ear, for example to remove dirt or wax accumulation or to treat an infection.

Your vet will supply you with a solution designed specifically to clean a cat's ears, or you can use a wax solvent preparation designed for humans. Some owners find that warm mineral oil is satisfactory. If you can get someone to help hold the cat, the whole procedure is much easier.

A few words of caution: the cat is likely to flick its head and ears, throwing oil and wax about. Be careful this does not stain valuable clothes or furniture.

- Hold the cat's head slightly to one side.
- Instill a few drops of the cleaning or medication preparation into the ear canal.
- Massage the preparation down the ear canal deep into the ear.
- Wipe away any excess with damp cotton wool. (*Do not* use cotton buds. They are liable to damage the ear.)

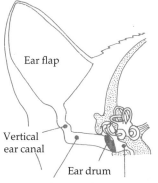

The cat's ear has a long, deep canal where infections or infestation could become established

Ear flap

Vertical ear canal

Ear drum

Horizontal ear canal   Middle ear

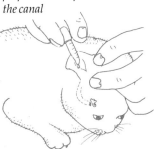

When applying medications, gently massage the preparation deep down into the canal

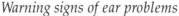

Warning signs of ear problems
Some of the following signs may indicate that your cat has an ear problem:
- Head shaking.
- Head tilted to one side.
- Twitching ear.
- Pawing or scratching at or near the ear.
- Strong or foul smell from the ear.
- Discharge from ear — may be pus, wax or dark discharge.
- Rubbing ear along the ground.

If the deeper structures of the ear are affected, the delicate structures involved with balance can become involved. The signs could then include:
- Head tilted to one side.
- Loss of balance — the cat may stagger, especially when turning, and may even fall. The cat's 'righting reflex' is extremely sensitive, but this could be lost if the inner ear is affected. Normally, even if held upside down only a few centimetres from the floor, then released, the cat will turn and twist in a fraction of a second to land square on its feet. When this reflex is interfered with, the cat will be unable to climb or jump with any certainty, and may be reluctant to move about.

- Circling in one direction. If only one ear is affected, the cat may have a tendency to walk in circles. If the right ear is affected, the cat will circle only to the right, and vice versa if the left ear is affected.

EAR MITES

The most common ear infection of cats is infestation by the tiny ear mite *otodectes cynotis*. This is especially common in kittens. These mites feed on the delicate lining of the ear canal, causing irritation and discomfort and the production of a dark brown wax discharge. This wax is readily seen if you shine a penlight into the ear canal. In some cases it oozes from the ear, where it dries and forms irritating crusts.

Mild infestations usually do not concern the cat. If the infestation is heavy the cat could become acutely uncomfortable. By scratching at the ears the cat may inflict further damage in its efforts to relieve the irritation.

Diagnosis
A diagnosis is achieved by seeing the mites in the ear. Your vet will use an auroscope or otoscope, which combines a magnifying glass with bright illumination. The mites can then be seen as tiny white dots moving across the dark field of wax. You may be able to see them yourself if you shine a torch down the ear, but the mites are very small and it takes a keen eye.

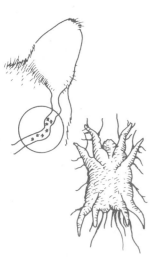

Ear mites can cause irritation and discomfort

Large amounts of very dark wax in the ears suggests ear mite infestation.

Treatment
Be gentle and careful whenever you handle your cat's ears. Read the section on cleaning ears and routine treatments.

A suitable insecticidal preparation can be purchased from your vet. These preparations generally have an ear wax solvent included in their formula, so separate wax solvents are not required.

132

The most common reason for lack of success in treating ear mite infestation is not continuing the treatment for long enough. You may have to continue treatment for three weeks. *Or,* treat twice daily for one week, cease treatment for the next week, then treat again the third week. This kills the mites that have hatched out subsequent to the first week's treatment.

Always treat both ears and all other cats and dogs in the household. Ear mites are easily transmitted between animals (although fortunately they will not infest humans).

Because some of the mites live on the cat's body as well, it is worthwhile to treat the cat simultaneously with an insecticidal powder or rinse.

OTHER PARASITES

Another mite which is sometimes found is *notodres cati.* Unlike the common ear mite which lives on the surface, this mite burrows into the skin. It produces intense irritation, raised lumps in the skin and dry, crusty flaky skin patches.

Notodres cati can affect cats and rabbits. It is not common, but when it occurs it is highly infectious.

Treatment
Rinse the affected areas with 0.5% malathion, (25 mls malathion diluted with 2 litres water) *or* 2½% lime sulphur.

Repeat the treatment once weekly for at least six weeks.

EAR INFECTIONS

The ear canal can become infected with a variety of organisms, including bacteria, fungi and yeasts. The name given to an infection of the ear canal is *otitis externa*, although many people refer to it as 'canker'.

The cause of ear infection (otitis externa)
Bacteria, fungi and yeasts are present in the normal ear canal. The cat's immune system is capable of resisting any build-up of these organisms under normal circumstances. Sometimes the environment within the ear canal changes, providing conditions suitable for these germs to multiply.

Such conditions can occur if wax builds up excessively in the ear, or if the ear is bitten or scratched by another cat or by the cat itself while scratching at an irritation within the ear, such as ear mites, or a grass seed.

Signs
A foul smelling discharge builds up in the ear canal and could spill out to matt down the hair at the base of the ear. Otitis externa can cause severe damage to the ear canal, and if neglected could penetrate the ear drum, leading to damage of the delicate middle and inner ear. This results in pain, loss of balance and even deafness.

Treatment
The treatment depends on what particular organisms are involved. It may be necessary to send samples to be cultured by a veterinary pathologist, not only to identify the agent involved, but to determine which drugs will be most effective in treating it.

Ear infections can be caused by foreign bodies, parasites, bacteria fungi or yeasts. The treatment depends on the cause

In bacterial infections, antibiotic ear ointments are usually prescribed.

For yeast and fungal infections a different range of drugs is required. The precise choice of treatment should be left to your vet.

In severe or painful cases, or where a foreign body such as a grass seed is present, your vet may suggest that the ears be thoroughly cleaned while the cat is under a general anaesthetic.

Chronic (long standing) ear infections are not common in cats. Failure to clear up an infection quickly is usually either because you have not applied the ointment correctly (deep into the ear canal), or you have stopped medicating too soon. Most cases require treatment for at least a week, some require treatment for two or three weeks.

In some cases, the prescribed drug may be ineffective against a particular organism. Resistance by bacteria especially is an increasing problem.

If an ear infection is not clearing up, contact your vet as a change in the treatment may be advisable.

In practice we quite often see cases where an owner thinks his cat has ear mites, and has been diligently treating the cat for weeks without result, when in fact the cat has a bacterial or fungal infection that requires a completely different medication.

> Do not persist with ineffective home treatments for ear infections. Permanent damage could result.

FOREIGN BODIES IN EARS

Foreign bodies such as grass seeds may be caught in a cat's ear. These gradually work their way into the ear canal. Sometimes children poke things such as sticks into cats' ears. If you can see a foreign body in the ear and can pull it out easily with tweezers, or similar, then do so. However, if the object has penetrated deeply or resists a gentle pull then leave it, and consult your vet. The ear is too delicate to risk forcing it.

> Do not persist in vain attempts to remove objects from cats' ears as this may result in severe ear damage.

Sunburn can lead to ear cancer

SUNBURNED EARS

Cats with white ears that live in sunny climates are liable to sunburn of the ears. This can lead, in time, to cancer of the ears.

White skin lacks the protective pigments that prevent damage by the sun's ultraviolet rays. Unfortunately many white cats love to bask in the sun as they do not get as hot as dark coloured cats. Damage can occur to any area of white skin but is most common on the ear tips, eyelids and around the nose.

Signs
Signs of severe skin damage can take years to appear. The ear may appear to heal during winter only to flare up again a little more severely each summer.

The first sign is a red, flaky area around the rim of the ear, followed by a slight curling of the ear tip. Gradually, small scales appear and the owner may mistakenly believe the cat has been scratched. These sores progress to become dark scabs with raw, swollen areas beneath, that bleed profusely when the scab is knocked off.

In time, the condition may progress to a cancer known as 'squamous cell carcinoma'. The ear tip ulcerates and the erosive, destructive cancerous process begins to destroy the ear. The ear becomes thickened, inflamed and angry looking.

Treatment
Once the first signs are recognised, the best treatment is to avoid any further exposure to strong sunlight. If possible, the cat should be kept indoors between 10 a.m. and 4 p.m. in the hot summer months. This may be impracticable. In these cases, coat the ear tips with an ultraviolet blockout cream, available from chemists. A children's preparation is preferable to adult preparations and the most effective types are those that are absorbed *into* the skin rather than just sitting on the surface, as the cat will remove the latter during routine grooming.

Some owners have had success using a black felt non-toxic marker pen once a week to provide artificial pigment on the ear margins.

If the condition has been neglected and cancer has started, surgery is usually required. The affected part of the ear is amputated. Other treatments include cryosurgery (deep cold treatment of the damaged tissue) or x-ray therapy. Therapy using drugs is only of limited use at present.

BLOOD BLISTER OF THE EAR (*aural haematoma*)

Aural haematoma

A large swelling under the skin of the ear is probably an 'aural haematoma'. This is formed when a blood vessel bursts and bleeds into the area between the ear cartilage and the outer skin. This may be as the result of a fight or constant rubbing and scratching, or head shaking due to ear mites or other infections.

A blood blister is usually not particularly painful, but if it is not drained the ear will become distorted and scarred during healing, resulting in a 'cauliflower ear'.

Treatment
Your vet will drain the fluid from the ear, usually while the cat is under a general anaesthetic. The ear is then splinted so that it heals in its orginal shape with the minimum of distortion by scar tissue.

INFECTIONS BEYOND THE EAR DRUM (*otitis media and otitis interna*)

Infections that involve the middle and inner ear are potentially very serious. The delicate hearing apparatus can be permanently damaged, resulting in deafness. In addition, the organs of balance are situated in the inner ear (the semi-circular canals). These are fluid-filled tubes lined with sensitive nerve endings which allow the cat to perform dextrous feats of balance even in total darkness. If infection or inflammation is present, the fluid within the semi-circular canals can become frothy and the nerve endings give only confused readings so that the cat no longer knows where the upright position is and hence loses its sense of balance.

Signs
In mild cases the cat may only have a head tilt, holding the affected side down. As the condition progresses the cat may develop a tendency to circle in one direction and balance is progressively lost: at first the cat may stagger or stumble, but this progresses to a total inability to stand upright, so the cat remains crouched down and is reluctant to move.

Treatment
The treatment depends on the cause. If a bacterial infection is responsible then antibiotics, perhaps in combination with surgery to drain the pus, may be successful. Inner ear damage due to toxic drugs may clear spontaneously if the dose has been moderate, but in some cases the damage to the nerves is permanent.

In general, early treatment often gives a good chance of recovery. However, if the damage is severe or treatment is delayed the cat may be left with permanent hearing impairment or with a head tilt. This head tilt often becomes less obvious with time as the cat adapts to compensate for the permanently damaged nerves.

DEAFNESS

Deafness can be present from birth (termed 'congenital' deafness). This is the case with most blue-eyed white cats. This deafness is due to a genetic defect and there is no treatment. White cats with one blue eye and one eye of another colour are usually deaf only in the ear next to the blue eye.

Other causes of deafness
- Ear infections that are untreated or fail to respond to treatment can result in deafness.
- Drug reactions: some drugs, for example the antibiotic dihydrostreptomycin, may cause deafness.
- Old age: many cats become progressively deaf with advancing age. The reason for this is not known, nor is there any effective treatment.

THE EYE

Cats that are fed dog food without fresh meat or fish suffer from retinal degeneration due to lack of an amino-acid taurine. Exclusive feeding of vegetable protein similarly causes vision loss

The cat possesses an open eye socket or orbit. That is to say, there is no bony floor to the eye socket as there is in man. Instead of bone, the back of the eye socket is occupied by muscles. These strong muscles permit a widely opening, powerful jaw. This is needed for grasping and holding prey.

There is limited white of the eye visible when we look at the eye of the cat. Most of what we see is the eye window (or cornea). This is in contrast to man. The cat's large cornea allows a wide field of vision and also allows maximum light to enter the eye for night vision.

A cat does not see close objects in focus as we do. This is because the cat cannot change the shape of its lens, and therefore cannot focus the image sharply. To sharpen the image the cat narrows the pupils into slit-like openings.

The third eyelid of the cat is the pink or whitish 'skin' that is visible on the eyeball at the corner of the eye near the nose. It is especially noticed when it has no pigment on its edge. The third eyelid has a cleaning and lubricating function. It sweeps across the surface of the eye like a windshield wiper, spreading the tears and removing dust and foreign particles. It helps to compensate for the fact that a cat seldom blinks, and also helps to protect the surface of the eye from injury.

If the cat is unwell or debilitated the third eyelids may be partly drawn across the eyes (see 'Haws' page 146).

What gives colour to the eye?
Cats' eyes come in a variety of colours. This colour is due to pigment in the iris. Occasionally a cat is born with eyes of different colours. The most common eye colours are yellow and green, others include orange, blue and pink eyes. Pigment in the iris is needed to protect the retina from too much light. Lack of pigment (blue eye) can mean less protection against bright light. Blue eyes in Siamese can be associated with a thin, under-developed iris. A thin blue iris is not as good for the cat's comfort as a darker eye.

137

Light passes through the pupil of the cat's eye and is focussed onto the retina by the lens – from there the optic nerve transmits the information received to the cat's brain. At the back of the cat's eye there is a reflective layer of cells known as the tapetum which collects light to help the cat see better at night. It is the light reflected by the tapetum which makes cats' eyes glow in the dark.

The pupil and iris of a cat are comparatively larger than in the human eye, allowing a wide field of view and much better night vision. In darkness, the cat will enlarge its pupil to let as much light as possible pass through the retina. Conversely, in bright light the cat will narrow its pupils into slit-like openings to stop too much light passing through the retina. Cats can also narrow their pupils to sharpen the focus of nearby images.

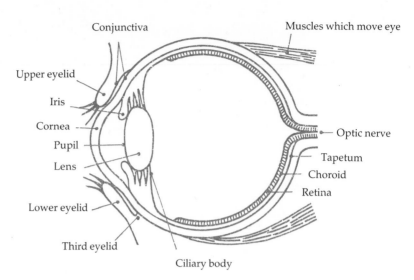

What does a cat see?

The shape of the cat's eye (see diagram) is such that the cat can better detect moving, rather than stationary prey. A cat detecting movement out of the corner of its eye will turn its head rapidly to bring the object into better view. A cat may fail to see a mouse sitting still against a grey background but if the mouse runs it stimulates the retina. The cat can accurately pounce on the moving target. It is doubtful whether cats have much ability to recognise objects at a distance. Rather than hunt like a dog or fox, cats prefer to lie in wait, springing at their prey when it is within striking distance.

Does a cat see at night?

While the cat's night vision is very much better than that of man, night vision is comparatively short range. No eyes can penetrate total darkness.

The cat's night vision is aided by a special reflecting shield at the back of the eye behind the retina (the tapetum). The tapetum is responsible for eye shine in the dark and reflects light so that the eye can be stimulated by low intensities of light.

While the cat cannot focus well, the extreme mobility of the pupil offers the cat good vision in greatly differing lights. It is remarkable that cats are so readily adapted to night vision, yet can enjoy good day vision as well. Most creatures of the dark, such as owls and moles, have very poor vision in bright light.

Colour vision in the cat

The cat's eyes have adapted to suit its specific needs as a hunter. There is little need for a cat to be able to distinguish colour, so it is not surprising to find that its colour vision is limited. It was once thought that cats had no colour vision at all, but experiments have shown that they can distinguish some colours from each other. Blue is probably their best colour and they appear to be able to distinguish various hues or shades of blue from each other. They are probably red blind, and have only a limited ability to distinguish green from blue.

The pupil

The pupil is the opening at the centre of the eye. It is surrounded by the iris. The iris changes the size and shape of the pupil. The ability of the cat's pupil to open wide or to constrict to a tiny slit allows hunting by day or night. If the pupils do not constrict to slits in bright daylight there is something wrong — see your vet.

138

How to examine the eye at home

You will need help to hold the cat as it will instinctively struggle and may scratch. Use a magnifying glass to examine the eyes carefully.

● Place the cat on a table near a window in good light. Pull the lower lid down for a general examination of the eye.

● Now close the curtains to darken the room and shine a penlight into the pupil. Watch for the pupil to get smaller.

EYE DISEASE

Signs

Consult your vet if any the following signs appear. Note the signs shown as '*' These are often overlooked as a sign of trouble.

VET TREATMENT
URGENT

*● Abnormal eye movement.
 ● Watery or red eye.
 ● Eye discharging pus.
 ● Swollen eyelids.
 ● Irritated eyelids.
 ● Blue, cloudy eye.
 ● Caked, crusty discharge on the eyelid.
*● Winking/squinting eye held closed.
 ● Rubbing at the eye.
 ● Bulging, protruding eye.
 ● Sunken eye.
 ● 'Skin' over the eye (prominent third eyelid). *Note* that a prolapsed third eyelid does *not* always mean eye disease.
*● Cat will not jump, bumps into things.
*● The young kitten does not run around freely.
*● Large pupil, eyes shine green during the day.
 ● White pupil. A cloudy lens (cataract) shows inside the eye as a white pupil.
*● Eye changes colour.

Some eye diseases cause the patient to be depressed, lethargic, 'not himself'.

If the eye looks smaller than normal, it could be:
 ● A sunken eye due to old age, malnutrition or dehydration.
 ● A small eye as a result of inflammation or injury.
 ● A congenitally small eye.

If the eye looks larger than normal, it could be:
 ● Dislocated eyeball (protruding forward due to injury).
 ● Infection/inflammation of the eye socket.
 ● Chronic glaucoma.

A widely dilated pupil may mimic a 'big' eye. The eyeball, however, may be normal in size. Compare carefully with the other eye.

If the eye is watery, it could be:
 ● Irritation from the eyelids e.g. entropion.
 ● Inflamed third eyelid e.g. from sunburn.
 ● Faulty tear drainage e.g. from adhesions and scarring following 'flu in the kitten, or poorly developed tear drainage in a short-nosed cat.
 ● Conjunctivitis.
 ● Injury, foreign body in the eye.
 ● Inflamed cornea e.g. corneal ulcer.
 ● Inflammation inside the eyeball.
 ● Glaucoma.
 ● Cat 'flu.

If the eye is red or inflamed, it could be:
- Conjunctivitis.
- Inflamed cornea.
- Inflammation inside the eyeball.
- Glaucoma/lens dislocation.
- Injury to the eye or eye socket.
- Haemorrhage.
- Cancer (feline leukemia, lymphosarcoma).

If the eye is blue/steamy-looking (cloudy instead of clear), it could be:
- Inflamed cornea.
- Inflammation inside the eyeball.
- Glaucoma/lens dislocation.

If the eyelids are swollen, it could be:
- Inflammation or infection of the eyelid skin.
- Injury.
- Severe conjunctivitis e.g. cat 'flu.
- Cancer.
- Inflammation or infection of the eye socket or eyeball.

If there is a change in the colour of an eye (iris changes colour), it could be:
- Inflammation inside the eyeball.
- Cancer.
- Haemorrhage (bleeding).

Note a cloudy lens (cataract) shows inside the eye as a white pupil.

BLINDNESS

A blind cat may cope so well in its own home that it is difficult to believe that it is nearly or totally blind. The cat may, however, bump into furniture in a dark room or move slowly about, nose down, feeling his way with his whiskers. A blind cat may misjudge when jumping up, although some (remarkably) can still jump the back fence.

If you suspect your cat is blind, examine the pupils very carefully for other signs of blindness. Two very large pupils, with little or no eye colour showing, suggests total loss of sight in both eyes. *Note* that light registering in one eye controls the size of both pupils so a blind eye may have a small pupil due to light entering the good eye. Shine a torch into the eyes. The pupils should contract to shut out excessive light. If they do not, disease is present. Try to test one eye at a time. The cat may be blind in only one eye.

Blind cats can manage well in their own environment. Long whiskers help. Some blind cats will even jump the back fence

140

How do I test a young kitten in the litter for decreased vision?
Move your hand in front of the litter. The sighted kitten will follow your hand, the kitten with poor vision will not.

How does a blind cat cope?
Usually very well, especially if the onset of blindness has been slow and the sense of smell and hearing are intact.

Helping a blind cat to cope
A blind cat is helped by:
- Familiar environment (do not move the furniture).
- A keen sense of smell and hearing (have the ears checked).
- Less need of vision than man.
- Another cat or dog in the household acting as a 'guide dog'.

If you suspect blindess keep the cat indoors until the eyes are checked or it may be run over or become lost.

Some common questions on cats' eyes

Why does my cat's eye shine green at night?
Reflection from a light such as headlights or a torch is due to the presence of a fluorescent reflective layer (the tapetum) at the back of the eyeball. In some cases, the reflection is red instead of green. This is sometimes called 'ruby eye' and it means that these cats lack this reflecting layer. The Siamese cat may possess a chocolate-coloured tapetum rather than a greenish one, or the tapetum may be absent altogether. This may mean that these cats don't see as well at dusk and after dark as normal cats which do have the reflecting layer.

Eyeshine is due to reflection through a large pupil from a layer at the back of the eye, which man does not possess. This layer helps the cat to see so well at night

Can bright sunlight cause eye damage?
The main danger of sunlight is to white cats or other cats with pink, unpigmented skin around the eyelids. Strong sunlight can cause sunburn and inflamed lids (and can lead to cancer). In cats already suffering from an eye disease, sunlight can make eye inflammation worse, so:

If your cat has a sick or sore eye keep him out of the sun.

What are the signs of eye pain? Is pain evident if a cat has a sore eye?
Winking, squinting of the eye, holding the eye half closed and avoiding light may all indicate eye pain. In severe cases of eye disease the cat may not eat, becomes lethargic or irritable. A sore eye often causes no obvious pain. The cat suffers and we don't realise it. After the eye is cured owners will often remark on how the cat is back to its old self.

Why is management of eye diseases different from other parts of the body?
The eyeball, even with expert care, never fully recovers from serious disease. The sooner eye disease is detected the better the chance of limiting damage. It is not possible to reverse damage done to the deep structures of the eye.

What 'sleep' and eye discharge is normal, and what is not?
Tiny glands at the front of the eye constantly produce a film of tears to keep the eye moist and lubricated. Residues of these tears or 'sleep' may accumulate in the corner of the eyes and then dry out. This is usually a light grey colour. Green,

141

yellow or watery or pink/brown discharge is not normal. Copious amounts of discharge are not normal.

EYELID INJURIES

VET TREATMENT
URGENT

Most eyelid injuries are serious. Very swollen eyelids can hide a badly damaged eyeball. Keep the eyeball moist (see page 149) and hurry to the vet. Extensive lid injury may require plastic surgery.

Why do extensive eyelid injuries harm the eyeball?
When the eyelids cannot cover the eyeball and sweep tears over the cornea, the eye becomes dry. Damage to the eye follows rapidly.

> If the eyelids cannot cover the eyeball keep the eye constantly wet while hurrying to the vet.

Stye
A stye is a small boil or abscess at the eyelid edge. It may need to be lanced and drained by your vet. Antibiotics are often needed.

Inflammation of the eyelids
Skin diseases can affect eyelid skin. Sunlight makes inflammation much worse so keep the patient inside. *Beware:* inflamed eyelids due to injury, infection or ringworm may cause an inflamed eye.
  Be careful that skin ointments prescribed to treat the area around the eye do not get into the eye. Have a 20 ml syringe of tepid, boiled tap water handy just in case. If medication accidentally gets into the eye, wash it out at once. Hold the syringe 2 cm from the eye and wash the eye out by squirting with the syringe.
  Note this precaution applies to *skin* ointments not *eye* ointments.

EYELID DISEASES OF NEWBORN KITTENS

The eyelids of the newborn kitten remain closed until about the tenth day. Opening of the eyes much before this can lead to blindess later. If the eyes open prematurely you should:
  ● Keep the eyes moist. Artificial tears are ideal but clean tap water will do.
  ● Seek veterinary help immediately. Your vet may have to suture the eyelids together.

Bulging eyelids
Bulging, closed eyelids in a newborn kitten mean an eye infection and can lead to loss of the eye. *Beware:* the infection may not be obvious, showing only as a swollen eyelid or a little pus at the corner of the eye.

> Swollen eyelids in a newborn kitten is an emergency. The eyelids must be surgically opened at once.

TAKE GREAT CARE!

  If you cannot see the vet immediately, gently ease open the closed lids with a toothpick to allow pus to drain out.
  After opening, apply antibiotic ointment continually to control the infection and keep the eyes lubricated. The eyelids must not be allowed to stick together until the infection has cleared.

142

Diseases seen at birth (congenital) are *not* necessarily inherited although some certainly are. Other inherited diseases are *not* evident at birth and only develop some time later.

Squint (turned eye/'cross-eyed')

This is most commonly seen in Siamese and is probably inherited. The cause of squint is due to maldevelopment of the visual pathways — that is the nerve pathways from eye to brain. Slight squint is not obvious. Use the slit-like pupils in broad daylight to help you examine for slight turning of the eyeball. Compare the pupils to see if the eyes are slightly turned towards the nose. Vision is present, appears adequate but is impaired. Let us breed for perfect sight, we can do better than breeding for 'good enough' vision in cross-eyed cats.

Cross eyes (squint) occur when the nerve pathways from the eyeball are abnormal. We should not accept this as 'normal' and should only breed from cats free of this disorder

Small eye

Some kittens are born with a very small eye or eyes. This is due to prematurely arrested development of the eyeball and causes imperfect vision.

Oscillating eyeball/jerky eye movements (nystagmus)

Generally speaking, oscillating eyeballs in kittens indicate blindness at birth. That is, the eye has not learned to hold still to see. Look for this especially in the Siamese kitten. The eye may be seen to be oscillating very quickly from side to side. In Siamese families this indicates some deformity in the eyeball itself or may be associated with abnormal pathways from the eye to the brain.

If nystagmus starts later in life, this may indicate a disease of the balancing system or inner ear.

Eyelids fail to open

If the newborn kitten's lids remain closed after twelve days of age, this is a danger sign. Failure of the eyes to open normally is usually associated with infection (neonatal conjunctivitis) which can cause blindness.

Absence of the upper eyelid

The absence of the outer part of the upper eyelid in the kitten causes exposure of the eyeball. Although this condition is congenital it is seldom noticed until the kitten is several weeks of age. Look for absence of the eyelid margin by comparing with another kitten. Surgery is needed as soon as possible to stop the eye becoming cloudy. While waiting for the kitten to become old enough for surgery, place artificial tears constantly on the eyeball. Alternatively, to protect the cornea, coat the eyeball with a bland eye ointment (and hope the mother will not lick it straight off).

Entropion (rolled-in eyelid) in the kitten (especially Persians)
In the normal eye, a hairless eyelid margin sits against the eyeball. If the lower lid rolls in, this must be surgically corrected because hair severely irritates the eye.
Sometimes the upper eyelid is rolled in as well.

ACQUIRED EYE DISEASES

VET TREATMENT
URGENT

Bulging/prominent/'big' eyes
Prominent eyes may be caused by injury, infection, glaucoma or more rarely, cancer. Infections that spread to the eyeball from the sinus also might cause the eye to bulge. Protrusion of the eyeball prevents eyelid closure. Lightly tap the corners of the eyelids with your finger to check whether blinking can cause the lids to meet over a big eyeball. Seek veterinary attention at once if the eyelids cannot cover the eyeball. While you are rushing to the vet, keep the prolapsed eyeball wet by squirting saline from a syringe onto the eye (see page 148).
A growth behind the eyeball is another cause of eye protrusion. The majority are malignant and respond poorly to treatment. You will notice a gradual bulging of the eye which gets worse over a matter of weeks.
Untreated chronic glaucoma can lead to increased size of the eye and protrusion. Chronic increase in pressure (glaucoma) enlarges the eyeball. This is seen mostly in old cats. The lens inside the eyeball becomes dislocated and damages delicate internal structures of the eye. Do not confuse a big eye with a big pupil — ask your vet to show you the difference.

Eye out of its socket
A hard blow to the head can dislocate the eyeball from its socket. Swelling behind the eye makes it extremely difficult to manipulate the eye back to its normal position. CAUTION: Do *not* make repeated attempts to manipulate a dislocated eye, as this may cause greater injury. Keep the eye *constantly* wet and rush to your vet!

My kitten's eye has been half closed ever since birth, what can be done?
This can be due to adhesions of the eyelids to the eyeball. Surgery may be helpful.

Sunken eye (enophthalmos)
The eyeball may recede when there is loss of substance in the fat 'cushion' behind the eye for example, in dehydration or rapid weight loss. Moreover, behind the eyeball there is a muscle which, when it goes into spasm, can pull the eye back into its socket. This might occur with a painful injury. Damage to a nerve in the head, neck or chest can result in a sunken eyeball and a small pupil (Horner's syndrome).
As the eye sinks back, the third eyelid becomes more obvious and there is an accumulation of mucus in the corner of the eye.

Eyelids held closed/squinting (blepharospasm)
Spasm of the eye-closing muscles is induced by pain such as from foreign materials in the eye. Irritation causes tightening of the muscles of the eyelids, closing the

144

eye and rolling the eyelids in against the cornea. Hair on the lids rolls in and rubs against the eyeball, causing further pain.

Inflamed/irritated eyelids (blepharitis)
Inflammation of the eyelids is common because the eyelids are frequently injured during cat fights. Scratches can easily become infected. This leads to itching and crust formation and the accumulation of pus and debris on the eyelids.

Inflammation of the eyelids often accompanies conjunctivitis. This can be due to many causes ranging from bacterial infection to mange mites and ringworm. The condition is made worse by self-mutilation. Hair is lost and the lid becomes thickened and ulcerated. *Note:*

- Skin ointments prescribed to treat the area around the eye must not be placed in the eye.
- Self-mutilation can be a problem.
- Keep the patient out of the sun.

TB (tuberculosis) of the eyelids
In some countries the eyelids of the cat can be affected by bovine TB. Lumps (tubercles) are seen on the eyelids and usually the cat has a generalised tuberculosis. With primary infection in the throat region, the lids become affected because the cat cleans its face with its paws. The affected cat is a health risk to man.

Eye rolled inward (entropion)
This condition occurs as an hereditary defect in some Persian cats, but can occur in any cat as a result of scarring of the lower lid, for example, following a bout of severe infection or laceration of the eyelid. The lower eyelid of old cats rolls in when the eyeball sinks too far in its socket. This may be due to loss of a fat pad at the back of the eye. Some cats have entropion because the eyelids are too big.

To diagnose entropion, look for absence of a lower lid margin. The rolled-in lid irritates the eye and causes a watery discharge. The defect can be corrected by surgery.

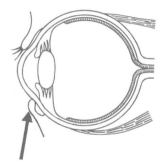

Rolled-in eyelid allows hair to irritate the eye. Look for absence of the normal eyelid margin on the eyeball. In some cats the eyelid opening is so large that the lid edge falls in

Tumours
Growths of the eyelid margin should be removed even if they only threaten to irritate the eyeball.

Cancer eye (squamous cell carcinoma)
Squamous cell carcinoma (SCC) is more common in older white cats. SCC typically begins on the lid margin but may occur on the third eyelid, or on the eyeball. When it first appears it looks like inflammation and not like a dangerous lump. Sunlight is more likely to damage unpigmented skin. Once the SCC has started, further exposure to sunlight is likely to make the condition worse.

Beware, a sore on the eye of a lightly coloured cat may be a cancer.

See your vet at once if a roughened sore appears on the eye.

Early removal offers the best chance of success. A neglected SCC can spread and is much more difficult to treat.

THE THIRD EYELID

The third eyelid, or nictitating (winking) membrane, is a protective 'extra' eyelid at the inner corner of each eye, next to the nose. When needed, the third eyelid can sweep across the eyeball like a windscreen wiper to help remove debris.

There are several conditions which can affect the third eyelid:

Prominent third eyelids (haws) can mean disease elsewhere in the body or disease of the eye

'Haws' (prominent third eyelid)

The third eyelid is held in position by very small muscles and when their nerve supply is disturbed, the third eyelid protrudes. The third eyelid can become more prominent due to many causes — some involving the eye but some due to conditions affecting the whole body. A prominent third eyelid can be due to many causes such as inflammation, adhesions of the third eyelid, intestinal disease, injury to the eye or neck or cancer.

The third eyelid looks like a 'skin' covering the inner part of the eye, usually about a quarter to a half of the eye being covered. Owners often mistakenly report that their cat has a film covering the eye. Some cases of 'haws' resolve on their own after about eight weeks.

Treatment

A prominent third eyelid is usually only one sign that there is eye disease or body disease. A veterinary examination determines the cause.

If the third eyelid is persistently prominent, should it be surgically removed?

No. The third eyelid is vital for eye health and should *never* be removed. If the third eyelid is removed, tear production is reduced and later the eye can become dry and very sick.

Pink third eyelid

A pink third eyelid is one that lacks pigment. Lack of pigment makes it appear prominent as it contrasts with the eyeball behind it. Pink third eyelids can become sunburned. Keep cats with unpigmented eyelids out of summer sun.

Cherry eye

There is a gland at the base of the third eyelid. Normally, this gland is small and tucked well out of sight. The gland may fall out of position and bulge out at the corner of the eye and become inflamed. This swelling is termed 'cherry eye'.

In mild cases of cherry eye the gland of the third eyelid can be returned to its correct position by the owner with the fingers. However, surgery is usually needed. The gland is stitched back into position. This gland should *not* be removed as it is vital for tear production.

> TAKE
> GREAT
> CARE!

CONJUNCTIVITIS (the commonest eye disease)

The conjuctiva is a thin membrane that covers and protects the white of the eye and lines the eyelids. It is usually transparent but becomes more obvious when it is inflamed.

Conjunctivitis appears as red, watery inflamed eyes. Common causes of conjunctivitis include:

- Allergies (to grass, pollen, house dust).
- Injury to the eye (cat scratch, after car accident, pricked by a bush).
- Foreign matter in the eye (grass seed, sand, etc).
- Sun irritation (especially in white cat lacking a dark protective pigment around the eyes or any cat with pink or pale eyelids.
- Chemical irritation (due to soap or shampoo or insecticide getting into the eye).

146

- Bacterial infection.
- Cat 'flu.

Other conditions of the eyelid, such as inturned eyelids, or inflammation of the skin around the eye (leading to the cat rubbing at the eye) can also result in conjunctivitis.

As a general rule, one watery eye suggests injury or a foreign body in the eye whereas two watery eyes suggests allergy or infection. Note that cat 'flu can start with one watery eye.

Rare causes of conjunctivitis are:
- Cancer.
- Parasite in the eye.
- Fungal infection.
- TB.

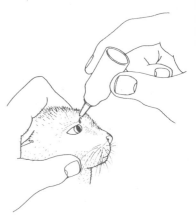

My cat has chronic conjunctivitis. Does he need to see the vet?
When conjunctivitis persists, it is worth visiting your vet because careful examination with magnification is required. The cause must be determined and the possibility of deeper eye disease investigated.

Treatment
Keep a cat that has inflamed eyes out of the sun. Very mild conjunctivitis, responds to decongestant drops. (Examples of these include Brolene and Otrivin.) But *beware* — if redness persists see your vet. Be especially suspicious if only one eye is red. This could mean there is a foreign body in the eye, or perhaps the inflammation is deeper than just the conjunctiva and the delicate inner structures of the eyeball are involved. Do *not* use antibiotic or cortisone as a routine first approach. We over use antibiotics and use cortisone wrongly. Your routine approach should be contact with your vet.

Lift the nose up with one hand and rest the hand holding the eye ointment or drops against the cat's head. Hold the nozzle well away from the eye so that the eye is not touched even when the cat moves his head. Place one drop onto the eyeball and hold the lids apart with the nose up for a minute or two. A match-head size of warm ointment is placed on the eyeball. For stiff ointments in cold weather, warm the naked end of the nozzle in warm water to make it flow more easily out of the tube

---

Do not treat a bloodshot eye casually. Always seek veterinary advice. A watery eye can be the start of cat 'flu or be an indication of deeper problems within the eye. Do *not* use antibiotic eye ointment without veterinary advice.

Can conjunctivitis be cured?
Yes, but the eyes may become inflamed again whenever they are irritated enough. Avoid the sun or other predisposing factors such as spraying insecticide to lessen the chance of relapse.

What happens with no treatment?
Conjunctivitis is an uncomfortable disease which tends to recur and cause more pain. Conjunctivitis typically does not cause visual loss but, if neglected, can lead to serious discomfort.

Warming eye ointment in an egg cup

Sudden swelling (chemosis)
Sudden swelling of the eyelids may be due to allergic reactions such as insect bites, hives, allergens in medications (e.g. neomycin); or it may be of unknown cause. Decongestant eye drops can decrease swelling. A markedly swollen eye needs urgent veterinary attention.

FOREIGN BODIES IN THE EYE

Foreign material such as dust, dirt, grass seeds and vegetable matter can become

147

trapped behind the eyelids. Signs include watering of the eye, blinking or squinting. The third eyelid may protrude.

Bacterial infection
Yellow or green pus discharging from the eye indicates bacterial infection. A scant, light grey discharge may be normal.

'Flu viruses
Most infectious conjunctivitis is due to viral upper respiratory tract infection — sometimes called URTI. Anti-viral drugs are needed for the eyes. If pus comes from the eyes, antibiotic ointment is needed as well.

Viral infection of the kitten's eyes can cause severe damage to the conjunctiva and cornea, causing the eyelids to stick to the eyeball.

My cat has a very swollen eye. What should I do?
The eye can become so swollen from allergy or injury that the eyeball cannot be seen. Cold packs may be used to reduce swelling. *Beware:* the eyeball may be seriously diseased. See your vet as soon as possible.

My cat is sneezing and his eyes are watery, what do I do?
Do not treat this lightly. There may be an early respiratory tract infection. See your vet if the eye discharge becomes thick or if the cat becomes ill (see page 107 on feline respiratory disease).

My kitten seems well but has had a runny eye ever since we got him. What do I do?
Cat 'flu is a common cause of scarring of the tear ducts and faulty tear drainage. If it worries the cat, surgery may be indicated. An artificial tear duct can be inserted in the eye. This is delicate surgery and should preferably be done by a specialist with an operating microscope. If the cat is not worried by it we usually leave it alone.

VET TREATMENT
URGENT

Treatment
First examine the eye as described. If the foreign body can be seen, you can gently remove it with blunt-nosed tweezers. When there is dirt in the eye, irrigate the eye with a salt-water solution (one teaspoon of salt to 500 mls water). Alternatively, soak a wad of cotton wool and squeeze it into the eye. Thorns which cling to the surface of the eyelids can be removed with tweezers. Those lying deeply should be removed by a vet. If the foreign body is caught behind the third eyelid, obtain professional assistance.

The cat may persist in rubbing his eye after treatment. In this case some foreign matter may still be in the eye or corneal damage may have occurred.

TAKE
GREAT
CARE!

FACIAL STAINING

My cat's face is stained a brown or rusty colour at the corners of the eyes. What is the cause?
Breeds with a white face can have a red-brown stain on the facial hair below the eye. This is due to tears overflowing from the eyelids and running down the face. This chronic wetness plus pigments in the tears turn the hair a rusty colour.

But why do the tears overflow?
Every normal eye is constantly covered with a thin film of tears that keeps the eyeball lubricated, sweeps debris and bacteria from the eye and prevents the cor-

148

Flat nosed cats may also have faulty drainage of tears. Let us breed cats with normal sized noses to avoid tears spilling on the face

nea from drying out. In most cases, these tears are drained away by the tear ducts Sometimes these tear ducts become blocked or are too narrow. Instead of being drained away into the nose, the tears spill over onto the face. In other cases, the tear flow may be excessive, overwhelm the capacity of the tear ducts and spill over. Such excessive tear flow can result from chronic irritation to the eyes, for example, from misdirected eyelashes, or entropion (see page 145).

Tear stains in Persians

Staining is seen most often in Persians, but other cats also can be affected. The breed standard for Persians calls for large prominent eyes and a flat face. In consequence, the pooling space at the inner corner of the eye might be too small — or the tear duct might not be in the best location for effective drainage. Narrowing of the tear duct is another possibility.

> Avoid breeding for a flat face. It can cause an overflow of tears with unsightly staining of the hair below the eyes.

Treatment

You can improve your cat's appearance by clipping the hair close to his face. Under veterinary supervision an antibiotic, tetracycline, is given by mouth for three weeks. The tetracycline replaces that part of the tears which cause tears to stain fur. If the stain returns after treatment, then long-term administration might be considered. Unnecessary use of any antibiotic is, of course, highly undesirable.

DRY EYE

An eye without its covering of tears is called a dry eye (also called *keratoconjunctivitis sicca* or KCS). Note that dry eye is due to disease of the tear glands which produce the tears (not the tear duct, which drains the tears to the nose). No tears means no protection or lubrication to keep the eyeball healthy. A dry eye can easily be overlooked. It is a very irritating and potentially blinding disease.

A dry eye looks similar to other inflamed eyes except that pus sits on the surface of the eyeball rather than accumulating in the corners of the eye. If the tear flow is adequate, pus does not stick to the eyeball.

Home care of dry eye

The dry eye needs to be kept constantly wet and clean. This can usually be

achieved by applying artificial tears or a special formula supplied by your vet that stimulates tear production as well as lubricating the eyeball.

Is permanent relief of dry eye possible?
Yes. If the condition is severe or non-responsive to treatment, your vet may advise surgery. In this operation, a salivary duct is transplanted from its original opening inside the mouth to the eye, so that the eyeball is kept wet and lubricated with saliva. (This operation is termed a parotid duct transposition.) Although saliva is not quite as satisfactory as normal tear secretions, it is an adequate substitute.

THE BLUE OR STEAMY EYE

Inflamed/ulcerated cornea (blue eye)
The clear 'window' in the front of the eye through which light enters is called the cornea. If it is injured or irritated it may become inflamed and swell with fluid, changing from its normal clear transparency to a bluish colour. When inflamed the cornea appears cloudy or steamy.

Injury, allergy, infection, glaucoma and cancer can cause corneal damage. (*Note:* A cloudy eye is not a cataract, which involves a deeper structure — the lens, see page 153.)

> A blue eye (cloudy cornea) indicates serious eye inflammation or increased pressure in the eyeball. Seek advice immediately.

EYE ULCERS

Causes of eye ulcers
- Injury.
- Inflammation.
- Infection.
- Foreign body.
- Lack of tear film (dry eye).
- Faulty lid function.
- A prominent eyeball.
- Extra lashes.

Signs
A red, sore, watery eye which may be slightly blue. Half-closed eyelids may hide the ulcer and the cat may wink one eye.

> A half-closed eye suggests a serious disease such as a corneal ulcer or a foreign body.

Treatment
Ointments may be sufficient in very mild cases. Otherwise your vet may elect to stitch the third eyelid right across the eye. This 'bandages' the eye and is extremely useful in protecting the eye and accelerating healing. The vet may use a button to stop the stitches cutting into the skin of the upper lid. This looks peculiar but works very well.

BLACK PLAQUE ON THE CORNEA

The cat can contract a unique disease of the eye which, if not treated, can give rise to long term irritation. The first sign may be that the cat's eye begins to water. When the lids are held open for inspection, a brown area or black plaque can be seen on the eyeball (on the cornea). The condition is not curable, but surgery can prevent the eye ulcerating extensively and so make the cat comfortable.

GLAUCOMA

Glaucoma describes the result of many eye diseases in which there is an increase in pressure within the eyeball. The eyeball contains fluid (aqueous), the amount of which is kept remarkably constant by a delicate, sensitive balance between production and drainage of fluid. Reduced drainage causes increased pressure, or glaucoma. Glaucoma can be very slow and insidious in its onset. Early cases are difficult to detect. Special instruments (tonometers) are necessary to detect early glaucoma, so diagnosis can be very difficult even for a vet. A specialist veterinary ophthalmologist's examination may be required.

Glaucoma is treatable rather than curable. Once it has been detected, constant treatment and vigilance is required to keep it under control.

Increased pressure in the eye (glaucoma) is one of the causes of red eye, undetected headache, blue eye and is usually seen in older cats.

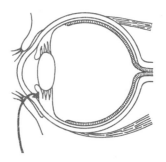

Reduced drainage at the indicated angle inside the eye leads to the eye becoming cloudy and causes considerable pain. The cat will typically not complain and becomes much brighter and happier following effective treatment

Can cancer cause glaucoma?
Yes. Cancer due, for example, to feline leukemia or malignant melanoma, can cause glaucoma.

How do you detect glaucoma?
The eye suffering from glaucoma is usually red and cloudy. The pupil is larger in size than the other eye and does not respond to a light shone on it. (The opening of the normal pupil should quickly contract when a bright penlight is shone through the pupil. Check one eye's reaction to light compared to the other eye.)

Treatment
Veterinary (often specialist) treatment can be very successful in controlling glaucoma, but glaucoma is usually not curable. Treatment may include medication directly onto the eye or given by mouth, and surgery. If glaucoma is detected too late, blindness results and the eye becomes very large. Glaucoma is painful. The vet might recommend removal of the eye. We are not always as aware of the pain of glaucoma as we should be. It is common for owners to say after surgery, 'I didn't realise the eye was worrying him so much — he is back to his old bright self now the eye has been removed.' In some cases, however, the cat is not worried by the blinded eye.

Should the eye be removed?
If the eye is painful, removal is the quickest way to relieve pain. Do not fear the look of an empty socket. When the hair regrows around the operation site, it will look most acceptable. Very few problems of after-care ever occur. If you want an artificial eye for your cat, discuss this before removal. Cats which have an eye removed usually manage extremely well, although they should not be allowed to roam as they are liable to be run over.

If I leave a large eyeball as it is will it cause problems?
If the vet tells you the pressure in the eye is low (pressure is best measured by a tonometer), the eye can be left as it is. Plastic surgery to make the eyelid smaller will protect the eyeball and prevent disease from exposure and drying. If the pressure within the eye is high, it is usually better to remove the eye. Alternatively an artificial implant can be placed in the eyeball to make the eye comfortable and pleasing in appearance.

DISEASES INSIDE THE EYEBALL

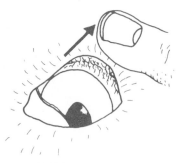

Pull the upper eyelid back to see if the white of the eye is red. This is a most important part of the eye examination. A red eye needs a vet.

Red eye
Most red eyes are due to conjunctivitis. Occasionally, however, red eyes are due to a much more serious disease: inflammation inside the eyeball *(uveitis)*. The distinction is significant. Conjunctivitis is merely uncomfortable rather than blinding. Uveitis causes more pain and can lead to blindness.

My cat's eye is red — how long do I wait to see the vet?
A bloodshot eye may need veterinary treatment at once — there could be a very serious inflammation inside the eyeball. Damage within the eye cannot be reversed. The best we can do is to minimise further damage.

Inflammation in the eyeball
Inflammation inside the eye quietly destroys vision. The earlier this inflammation is detected, the better chance there is of reducing the damage. Immune reactions rather than infection in the eyeball are a common cause of serious red eye and loss of vision. Untreated inflammation becomes very painful.
   Some possible causes of inflammation within the eyeball include:
   ● A blow to the eye or head e.g. following a road injury.
   ● A foreign body (e.g. grass seed, gunshot) within the eyeball.
   ● A result of other conditions, such as ulcerated cornea.
   ● As part of general body diseases, for example: toxoplasmosis, feline infectious peritonitis, cryptococcosis and histoplasmosis.
   ● Immune reactions.
   ● Cancer of the body (e.g. feline leukaemia) or of the eye.
   ● Many cases are of unknown cause. Allergies to virus or bacteria are suspected in some cases.

Does aspirin help to heal inflammation in the eye?
Yes. Low doses (10 mg/kg bodyweight) of aspirin each forty-eight hours or so is safe and effective to treat eye inflammation. Make sure the cat is *not* dosed daily. Too much aspirin is poisonous. The right dose relieves inflammation and pain. Consult your vet.

Can cancer cause inflammation in the eye?
Yes. Leukaemia/lymphosarcoma is the most common cancer affecting the eye. Even when the whole body is affected, inflammation of the eyes may be the first obvious sign. Other cancers such as malignant melanoma also cause a red eye and cataract. Cancer in the eye is very serious.

152

Blood in the eye
Blood within the eyeball itself suggests very serious eye disease. It may occur after car accidents or similar trauma, or it may be apparently spontaneous. Feline leukaemia can show as blood in a red inflamed eye. Try to prevent bleeding by:

- Keeping the patient as immobile as possible (in a cage, if necessary) in a quiet dark room.
- No exercise at all.
- Seeking veterinary advice as soon as possible.

CATARACTS (white pupil)

A cataract is a cloudy lens. It is seen as a hazy eye or white pupil. Light cannot get through the affected lens to reach the back of the eye. A cataract is seen as an opacity within the eyeball. This is easily confused with corneal disease, which is on the surface of the eye.

What causes cataracts?
Any disturbance to the eye which upsets the delicate lens chemistry can cause the lens to become cloudy. The usual cause is inflammation inside the eyeball sometimes following injury to the eye. A disease in the body (e.g. diabetes), inflammation or disease in the eye, a blow to the head, old age can all lead to cataracts. If the cat contracts a disease during pregnancy, cataracts can even form in kittens while they are in her womb.

My litter of kitten has cataracts. Are they inherited?
No. Cats do not suffer from inherited cataracts.

Can cataracts be cured medically?
No. In some cases eye drops that enlarge the pupil can allow some vision past a cloudy lens, but the change within the lens remains. Occasionally spontaneous partial disappearance or resorption of cataracts occurs in cats under three years of age.

My old cat has a blue lens. Is this a cataract?
Usually not. The blue lens you see in most old cats is not from disease, but due to the hardening of the lens with age.

My cat is getting cataracts — what should I do?
An immediate examination by an eye specialist before the lens becomes too cloudy will determine whether the back of the eye (beyond the cloudy lens) is healthy. It is vital to learn if the retina is healthy should surgical removal of the lens be considered later on. There is no point in removing a diseased lens if the back of the eye is also diseased.

What is cataract surgery?
Surgery involves removing the affected lens to allow light to get to the sight receptors which are at the back of the eye. Surgery may be considered if there is no disease beyond the cataract or elsewhere in the eye. Results of surgery in the cat are generally good.

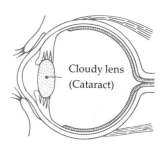

Cloudy lens (Cataract)

When the lens becomes cloudy vision is decreased. See your vet as soon as any cloudy part is seen. Cataracts can be removed surgically and (unlike in man) no artificial lens needs to be placed in the eye after surgery

Do cataracts always mean an operation?
Certainly not. In most cataracts, surgical extraction is not indicated. Moreover, medical treatment may be needed for other disease in the eye. Many cats manage very well in spite of dense cataracts.

My old cat is blind from cataracts. Do I need to have the eyes checked?
Yes. While surgery in old cats is generally not indicated, beware — cataracts can dislocate inside the eyeball and cause glaucoma, which is painful.

My cat has diabetes. Will he get cataracts?
Eventually, yes. However, careful drug control of diabetes can slow down the formation of cataracts in the cat. See your vet regularly. Careful specialist examination helps to identify early signs of cataract from diabetes.

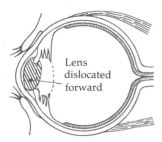

In older cats the lens in the eye can work loose, fall forward against the cornea and make the eye blue. To avoid pain, the lens is removed or relocated towards the retina

Lens dislocated forward

My old cat's eye suddenly looks more blue and cloudy. Should I see the vet?
Yes. Sudden changes often reflect painful conditions. For example, his lens may have suddenly fallen forward against the cornea. This not only affects vision but can be painful. In addition, we need to check that the lens of the other eye is not loose and about to dislocate. You may be referred to a specialist for this examination.

DISEASES OF THE BACK OF THE EYE

Generally speaking, diseases at the back of the eye are not readily evident to the owner. By the time disease is advanced enough to cause blindness, changes at the back of the eye cannot be reversed and the disease is incurable.

> Diseases at the back of the eye are a hidden cause of vision loss. Most are due to unknown causes.

Causes of vision loss at the back of the eye include:
- Immune mediated disease.
- General infection.
- Anaemia.
- Injury.
- Faulty diet.
- Cancers.
- Inheritance or (rarely) high blood pressure.
An end result of disease is retinal atrophy (wasting).

What is retinal atrophy?
The normal retina is composed of ten layers. In retinal atrophy the retina becomes thin. The ten retinal layers thin down to a few layers.

Do cats get detached and/or inflamed retinae?
Yes. Most commonly as a complication of a generalised disease such as feline infectious peritonitis, feline leukaemia, toxoplasmosis, cryptococcosis or histoplasmosis.

Can a faulty diet cause blindness?
Yes. The cat is peculiar to other animals in that food low in an amino acid called taurine will cause wasting (atrophy) of the retina. A faulty diet fed for a long time

154

can slowly cause loss of vision. Feeding cats exclusively on dog food, or exclusively on, for example, a fish diet can cause disease at the back of the eye.

What is FCRD?
This stands for feline central retinal degeneration — the retina becomes thin. It may be due to feeding insufficient taurine. Early signs of FCRD are not obvious. Areas of 'thin' retina are seen with an ophthalmoscope.

Why is commercial dog food bad for the cat's vision?
There is not enough taurine in dog food for the cat.

Is inheritance important in retinal atrophy?
Retinal atrophy may be inherited in Siamese, Persian and Abyssinian cats. Inherited retinal atrophy is, however, rare compared with other causes.

INHERITED EYE DISEASES

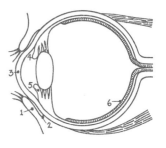

It is fortunate that inherited eye disease in cats is so rare compared with the dog. With care we can avoid the inbreeding/line-breeding practices that have done so much to cause pain and suffering in our canine friends. Two breeding fashions in the cat, however, must be commented upon:

The first is the practice of breeding short-nosed cats. A faulty tear duct can result, and this leads to an increase in problems of tear drainage in these cats.

The other is the breeding for lack of pigment or for albino or part-albino cats. Pigment is necessary to protect cats from the harmful effects of sunlight. Cats with unpigmented eyelids get far more conjunctivitis and eyelid cancer than do those with pigmented eyes.

Sites of inherited diseases –
1. Eyelid rolled in
2. Third eyelid out of position
3. Cornea cloudy
4. Glaucoma
5. Iris thin
6. Retina thin

> Beware: indiscriminate line-breeding has caused a great number of inherited diseases in the dog. Don't let this happen to the cat.

Siamese cats are called 'sub-albino'. They certainly have a pretty coat colour, but with a lack of pigment in the eyes, they may also have thinner irises. This means some Siamese cats cannot readily close the pupils and are less able to exclude bright light from the back of the eye and so are less comfortable in bright sunlight.

Not only does lack of pigment in the eyeball make the cat uncomfortable in bright daylight, but lack of pigment can also mean lack of vision. Before we breed animals with less colour than the pigment given to them by nature, let us have regard to the problems people with pale blue eyes or albino people experience. Albino people suffer great discomfort in bright light and cannot see very well either. They tell us it is unpleasant to have pink eyes, therefore avoid breeding for lighter colours in the eye, however attractive they may appear. Breed for dark eyes.

The following is a list of inherited eye diseases or abnormalities which affect different breeds. Note that factors other than inherited causes *may* produce these signs (symptoms) or diseases.

Breed	Signs/diseases to which breed predisposed
Abyssinian	Retinal atrophy.
Siamese	Black plaque on the cornea.
	Cloudy cornea (Storage disease MPS VI).
	Enzyme deficiency in the retina and brain (gangliosidosis).

155

Breed	Signs/diseases
Siamese	Strabismus (squint).
	Oscillating eyeball (nystagmus).
	Thin under-developed iris (iris hypoplasia).
	Retinal atrophy.
Persian	Black plaque on the cornea.
	Entropion (rolled-in lower eyelid).
	Oversized eyelid opening.
	Lack of upper eyelid development (agenesis/coloboma).
	Retinal atrophy.
	Watery eye (abnormal tear drainage).
Rex	Thin, under-developed iris (iris hypoplasia).
Stump-tailed Manx	Blue, cloudy cornea (corneal dystrophy).
Burmese	Everted third eyelid.
	Cherry eye.
	Watery eye (abnormal tear drainage).
	Dermoid (hairy growth on eye).

Skin And Coat

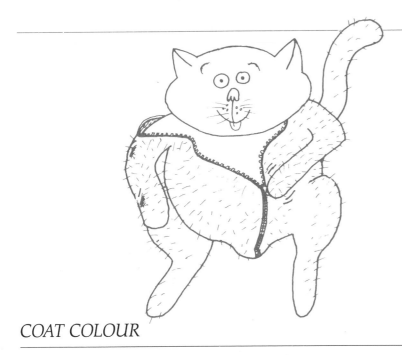

COAT COLOUR

Although dogs come in all shapes and sizes, cats don't. Even though there is some subtle variation in body size and facial features there are not the dramatic contrasts seen between breeds and cross breeds of dogs. For this reason it is the cat's coat — its colour, length and texture — that is used to identify individual cats.

SOLID COLOURED CATS

Solid coloured cats have no patterning, shading or flecking on their coats. Solid coloured kittens may have some slight tabby markings but these disappear with maturity. Black is the best known solid colour. Brown first arose accidentally from a genetic change to the black colour. Selective breeding has firmly established this colour change.

In Great Britain, brown is referred to as chocolate and in North America it is called chestnut or caramel.

Another accidental genetic modification changed the colour intensity of both the black and brown colours. These paler or 'diluted' shades have produced a

Chinchilla (silver tipped); silver tabby; tortoiseshell; white spotting; seal point Siamese; lynx point Siamese

variety of lighter coloured cats, including the grey (or blue) and fawn (or cinnamon, lavender or lilac) cats.

Orange coloured cats are usually not considered to have solid coats. This is because, by definition, solid coloured cats must be free of tabby markings and this is not genetically possible in an orange cat as tabby markings and orange colour are inherited together. The orange (or red) colour is also susceptible to the same colour changes or dilution that the black and brown colours are, producing a pale orange or cream coloured cat. The cream coloured cats are also tabbies although it is often very difficult to distinguish the markings. Many breeders have tried to dissipate the tabby pattern on orange cats through selective breeding programmes. Even though they have had some success, tabby markings usually persist around the face, legs and tail. In longhaired, orange cats, tabby patterning is less obvious because the long hair helps disguise it. Interestingly, red or cream colouration is also genetically linked with a factor that helps determine the sex of the cat. Because of this link, most red or cream cats are male.

TABBY CATS

Tabbies are found worldwide. Tabby is the natural pattern of the domestic cat. The tabby pattern arises from the combined action of two particular inherited factors, called the 'agouti' factor and the 'marking' factor. The agouti factor has a role in controlling the distribution of colour along each individual hair shaft. Visually it produces horizontal yellow banding across black hairs. This colour distribution is the universal camouflage pattern, found in many mammalian species — not only the cat (such as the rabbit). Hairs naturally slope backwards along the cat's body giving a speckled, greyish colour between the solid tabby stripes or blotches. This disrupted pattern gives effective camouflage as it obscures the continuity of the body outline and blends subtly with natural backgrounds. In the large wild cats, disruptive patterns are extensive — for example the tiger's stripes, leopard's spots and jaguar's rosettes.

There are three different marking factors found in the domestic cat. These include the 'mackerel' pattern, the 'blotched' pattern and the 'Abyssinian' pattern. Of these three patterns, it is the mackerel or 'tiger-striped' tabby that is the original type. Unfortunately the fine curving stripes of the mackerel tabby are not commonly seen in domestic cats today. The blotched or classic tabby is now the most popular marking. Although this pattern is very variable, breeders aim for a 'butterfly' pattern on the shoulders and an 'oyster' or blotch encircled by one or more unbroken rings on each flank.

The Abyssinian is a marking pattern that is also recognised as a specific breed of cat. Breeders have selected a particular body type to wear the Abyssinian markings and in doing so have established the breed standards. All Abyssinians have tabby markings on the face and sometimes also faintly on the legs and tail. The rest of the body has generalised 'ticking' or agouti flecking. This type of coat is sometimes called a 'bunny coat'.

As in solid coloured cats, tabbies also come in different shades. The best known are the brown and red tabbies. A brown tabby is correctly termed a chocolate or cinnamon tabby. When black tabby markings are present on a white background (no flecking) it is known as a silver tabby. Other colours include red, cream, lilac and cameo.

The basic Abyssinian is a red-brown flecked colour called cinnamon or sorrel. When this colour is genetically lightened it is known as fawn or beige. There are many other coloured Abyssinians including blue and lilac.

158

WHITE AND ALBINO CATS

Not all white cats are albinos. An albino lacks any pigment at all, not just in the hair or skin. The eyes lack pigment and are a pink colour. The pink is due to the colour of the blood vessels which are normally concealed by pigment in the retina and iris. In white cats the eyes are blue or orange.

TORTOISESHELL CATS

Tortoiseshell colouration produces a mosaic pattern of patches using orange (or cream) contrasted with black (or grey) or brown (or fawn). Tortoiseshell cats are usually female. This is because female cats have two similar sex factors, one from the mother and one from the father, both of which can carry a code for a different colour. Tortoiseshell cats need these two colour codes, one for orange (or cream) and one for a contrasting colour such as black or brown. The final distribution of colour varies with the individuals because the two colours compete randomly from the tip of the tail to the point of the nose. All this is determined before birth.

Male cats, in contrast to female cats, have only one sex factor that is capable of carrying a colour code. Hence there is no competition and therefore no mosaic results. This does not mean that all male cats are either a solid colour or tabby as there is yet another factor (not sex linked) that can produce white patches with any of the solid colours or tabby markings.

SPOTTED CATS

Cats with a coat of two colours are known as piebald. There is great diversity in the proportion of white hair that combines with the contrasting colour. It may vary from a mere splash of white down the chin and chest, or a flash of white down the nose or a solitary white sock, to an intricate pattern all over the body. The genetic factor producing the spotted pattern may be combined with any other coat colour or type. Generally, white appears with black, brown or ginger. Combinations of white and colours such as grey or fawn or white with tabby markings or tortoiseshell are also possible.

The longhaired Birman is a breed of cat in which Siamese markings have been united with the white spotting factor. The breed standards for the Birman restrict the white spotting to the feet only, producing four white socks.

BURMESE

Originally the term 'Burmese' referred to a unique shorthaired sleek coat type, not to a breed. Over many years breeders selected a distinct body type to wear this illustrious coat and in doing so have set the standards for the Burmese as a breed.

Adult Burmese are solid coloured cats. Kittens may sometimes appear shaded. Their coat has an unusual soft texture, much softer than their domestic shorthair contemporaries.

Burmese exhibit many different coat colours, similar to those seen in domestic shorthairs although the tones are much lighter. So the Burmese gene softens not only the texture of the coat but also the colour. The original Burmese colour (still considered by some to be the only true Burmese colour) is a deep seal or sable brown. A genetic mutation in the seal brown colour factor has produced a lighter (or more 'dilute') variation, blue. Through selective breeding this new colour has become firmly established. The Burmese blue is a distinct silver-grey with an eye-catching sheen to it.

Other recently developed colour variations include chocolate (also called champagne) which is a pale honey colour with slightly darker head and ears, and lilac (also called platinum) which is a very pale grey with a slight pinkish tinge and darker head and ears.

Both the chocolate and the lilac Burmese are almost white when born. They gradually darken with age.

The red, cream and tortoiseshell Burmese are recent additions to the breed. The tortie (tortoiseshell) Burmese has smaller, more finely intermingled patches of colour than the domestic shorthair, producing a delicately mottled coat.

A few of these more recently developed colours are not recognised for exhibiting in some countries.

SIAMESE

Pigment or colour production in Siamese occurs where the temperature of the skin drops below a certain critical temperature. The temperature at the ears, mask, legs and tail (the 'points') is usually measurably lower than the body core temperature. As a result a variation in the pigment or colour production occurs at the points. Visually the points of a Siamese cat are usually much darker than the rest of the body. A Siamese cat that spends a lot of time outside will develop darker body hair. This is due to a generalised drop in body skin temperature and a consequent increased production of pigment all over the body. If a patch of body hair is clipped from a Siamese, when the hair regrows it is usually darker than the surrounding hair. This is because shaving removes the insulating barrier between the skin and the environment and so the skin temperature falls thus increasing the pigment production in the new hair. Interestingly, Siamese cats also develop darker body hair with age. The reason for this is unclear but perhaps it is due to a decreased sensitivity of their temperature monitoring mechanisms with old age.

A Siamese that spends a large percentage of its time in front of a heat source will have not only pale body hair, but also lightening of the hair colour on the points. This is because when the skin temperature is continuously elevated all over the body, pigment production is decreased.

Similarly a Siamese that has a limb bandaged or in cast for an extended period will have lighter hair on that leg than on the others, when the old hair grows out. There is no effect on the colour of the existing hair. This is due to the bandage or plaster keeping the leg warmer and therefore decreasing pigment production.

The coat colour lightens if the cat habitually sits in front of a fire

Siamese kittens are born white. The temperature receptors in the skin are not fully functional until they are a few weeks old so pigment production does not occur until then.

Colours
Colours at the points vary in shades. The seal point (black point) is the original Siamese colour. There are three other basic colours: blue point, chocolate point and lilac point. These are all solid colours and there should be no tabby striping on the points. With selective breeding, a genetic variation was produced, incorporating the agouti factor (see 'Tabby Cats' page 158).

As a result of this, the tabby or lynx point Siamese emerged. These cats occur in the same colours as the solid point Siamese but they have tabby striping at the points. These are known as seal-point tabby, blue-point tabby etc. In some countries they are not recognised as true Siamese and are known as colour point shorthairs.

Red and cream Siamese have also been developed. As orange colour and tabby markings are inherited together, red point and cream point Siamese always have tabby striping at the points. The striping is less obvious in the cream point as it is in a pale contrast colour. As with the tabby points, the red and cream are not accepted as true Siamese in all countries.

Tortoiseshell colouration on the points is also possible. These cats are referred to as tortie-point Siamese. A tabby, tortie-point has also been bred and it is known as a torbie-point.

Other Siamese-type breeds

Himalayans
These are longhaired cats with Siamese markings. They are also known as colour points.

Birman
The Birman is a variation of the colour point. It is a longhaired cat with Siamese markings combined with four white feet. White markings can also appear on other parts of the body but this is not acceptable in a show cat.

The Tonkinese
The Tonkinese is a cross between a Siamese and a Burmese. It is produced by mating a Siamese with a Burmese. The Tonkinese has dark points (like the Siamese) but these blend subtly into the body colour (which is darker than the Siamese but lighter than the Burmese).

COAT TYPES

Short hair is the cat's natural or 'wild' type of hair coat. The texture varies greatly from breed to breed. Among the shorthaired coats are ultra short, curly haired breeds such as the Rex. The degree of curl in these cats may vary from a gentle wave to as tight as a coiled spring.

Normally a cat's coat consists of three types of hairs, the guard, awn and down hairs. In Cornish Rex the guard hairs have been bred out to achieve an ultra soft, short wavy coat. The texture of this type of coat is produced by the natural wave of the awn and down hairs. The Devon Rex has all three types of

Coat types: Longhair coat (for example, the Angora); Shorthair (for example, British Shorthair); Rex: short, tightly curled coat

Long hair type

Short hair

Rex (short, curled coat)

hairs present but the guard hairs are very short. The whiskers of these cats may also be reduced to curly stubs or may be missing completely.

The longhaired cats such as the Angora and Persian have different coat modifications. The Angora has extra long guard hairs that produce a long silky body cover. The Persian, in addition to these long guard hairs, has developed long down hairs as well. In some Persians these down hairs are as long as the guard hairs. This effectively doubles the thickness of the coat. Persians may have hair up to 12.5 cm in length.

Hairlessness

Due to a genetic mistake, a kitten can be born without hair. Some cats have been bred selectively for this trait. This breed is known as the sphynx or Canadian hairless. These cats are naked (other than for some fine downy hairs). They have poor cold tolerance and must be provided with fitted coats during cool weather.

GROOMING YOUR CAT

Daily grooming of longhaired cats is essential to prevent knotting and matting. In shorthaired cats a brush and comb twice weekly is adequate. Old cats or sick cats may lose interest in grooming themselves. Regular grooming by you under these circumstances is usually appreciated by your cat and will help maintain a healthy coat.

Coat care should be started when the kitten is about three months old. The cat then becomes accustomed to the activity. Most cats enjoy brushing provided you are gentle but firm. A cat that hasn't been brushed before will probably be a little wary at first. Introduce the brush gradually. A little brushing at a time. The cat will soon see there is nothing to be frightened of. It may help if the cat associates grooming with a reward, such as a fishy treat.

Grooming equipment

A natural bristle brush is best. Synthetic bristles can cause hair damage, especially in longhaired cats. To remove dead hairs effectively, comb against the lie of the hair with a metal comb.

Bathing

A bath may become necessary if the cat gets very muddy or soiled by diarrhoea, oil or other tenacious material. A badly soiled cat may be reluctant to lick itself clean because of the offensive taste. Ingestion of some materials such as sump oil is potentially dangerous. These toxic materials must be removed by bathing.

When bathing the cat, use a shampoo specifically formulated for cats. If this is not available, then a mild baby shampoo or a mild pure soap will do. These are less likely to irritate the eyes or skin than perfumed soaps or strong shampoos. Detergents manufactured for dish or clothes washing are unsuitable — do *not* use them on your cat. Always thoroughly rinse any soap or shampoo from the coat afterwards.

How do I bath my cat?

First: *be prepared.* Some of the things you will need include:

- A baby bath, trough or sink.
- A shower attachment or a bucket and jug for rinsing.
- Towels, a suitable soap or shampoo.
- Hair-dryer or fan heater.
- Someone to help you.

Stand your cat in the bottom of an empty sink or bath. Get a firm grip of the scruff then gradually wet the cat all over with lukewarm water. Spare the head unless it is also dirty. In this case wet the head with a sponge. Talk to your cat in reassuring tones while you are doing this. Pour on the shampoo then lather and rinse. Repeat if necessary. Make sure the final rinse is thorough. Gently squeeze out as much water as possible from the cat's coat (especially in longhaired cats) then wrap him in a towel. Allow the towel a few minutes to soak up water from the coat before removing it. Rub the cat briskly with a dry towel. It is best to finish the drying process with a hair dryer or fan heater because cats that remain damp could become chilled. If the cat will co-operate, brush the hair as it dries. If not, put the cat in a basket or cage near a heat source to dry, but not too close.

Bathing removes some of the natural oils from the coat. It may take a week for the customary sheen to return to the hair.

Dry shampoos

Although these products are sometimes used on show cats for the final fastidious clean-up, they are not a very efficient way of removing dirt and debris from heavily soiled coats. The powder is dusted into the coat and then brushed out, taking some of the dirt with it.

Matting

Matting can be a serious problem in longhaired cats. Try to *prevent* it happening.

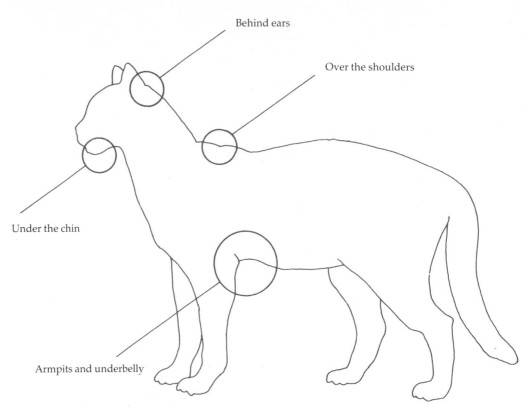

Behind ears

Over the shoulders

Under the chin

Armpits and underbelly

Areas most likely to become matted

Daily grooming will ensure that tangles don't turn into immovable wads of hair. Matting starts in areas that are difficult for the cat to groom. The most commonly affected areas are between the shoulders, behind the ears, under the chin, under the arms and legs and beneath the tail. Matts under the arms and on the chest can become a problem as some cats resent having these areas brushed. By dividing a large matt into smaller matts and combing these clumps you may be able to tease apart some of the tangled hair. In other cases it will be necessary to cut the clumps of hair out. Use blunt ended scissors and take special care not to nick the skin. Whatever you do, do *not* wet the coat when trying to remove a matt — it will make it worse.

Matts should always be removed *before* bathing.

In longhaired cats that either won't tolerate brushing or that have been neglected, electric clippers may be needed to shear off the matted hair. In extreme cases a general anaesthetic may even be necessary.

Fur balls/hairballs
Hair is continually shed from the cat's coat. The tongue of the cat acts as a comb and helps remove these loose hairs. The barbs on the cat's tongue trap the hair and they are swallowed. During periods of heavy moulting (spring and summer) particularly in longhaired breeds, hair may accumulate in solid masses in the stomach. These are called hairballs and are eliminated either by vomiting (this is a normal and quite natural occurrence and not a cause for concern), or they may pass into the intestines to be expelled in the droppings. If a hairball is very large, constipation may occur. Regular dosing with liquid paraffin (dose: ½ teaspoon twice weekly) during the moulting period helps to clear hair from the bowel. Mix the paraffin with food or syringe it straight into the mouth.

164

Cats irritated by hair trapped at the back of their throats may cough.

Hairs may become entwined around the teeth and irritate the gums. As a result, the cat may paw at the mouth and drool and there may be a foul mouth odour. You should be able to remove these fairly easily. A general anaesthetic is sometimes needed in an obstinate cat.

> If you remove the dead hairs by daily grooming most of these problems can be avoided.

Removal of paint from the cat's coat
Allow the paint to harden, then cut off the paint and hair. *Never* use thinners or solvents on or near the cat's skin as they can cause severe chemical burning of the skin.

Removal of crude (e.g. sump) oil from the cat's coat
Wash the cat in vegetable oil or margarine several times. Both of these products combine chemically with sump oil and allow it to be removed more efficiently. When most of the oil is removed, wash the cat with warm, soapy water (use a mild toilet soap). Rinse thoroughly. Repeat until all traces of oil are eliminated.

CLAWS (nails)

Should I clip my cat's nails?
Nails grow continuously so cats must keep their nails trimmed and sharpened. They do this by actively clawing at objects such as the base of trees and posts. You may provide a scratching post if you like. Natural wearing down also occurs during daily activities such as climbing. Cats that don't exercise because they are housebound, elderly or sick can grow excessively long nails. These cats need regular nail trimming, particularly on the front paws. Trimming a cat's nails is a simple, painless procedure if the cat co-operates.

Before the nails are clipped, identify the pink part of the nail (the 'quick'). Avoid cutting into the quick as it contains nerves and blood vessels.

If a nail does start to bleed exert pressure over it with a cottonball for five minutes if you can, although most cats resent this attention. Otherwise, don't worry as the bleeding will soon stop spontaneously. The cat will not lose much blood.

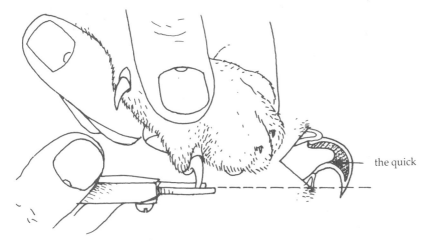

the quick

Nail bed infection
Infections can occur in the nailfold. These infections are difficult to treat successfully and may become chronic.

Treatment
Mild cases may respond to antiseptic soaks or painting with gentian violet or acriflavine. In severe cases, or in cases that are not responding to treatment, the nail may need to be removed. This allows the infected area to drain.

Infection may involve bacteria, yeast or fungi. The choice of drug treatment will vary accordingly. Your vet will advise you on the most appropriate treatment for your cat. In most cases the nail will grow back normally after the infection has been cured.

PARASITIC SKIN DISEASES

Infection of the nail bed

Fleas
Almost every cat is going to get fleas sooner or later, so all cat owners should read this section.

> Fleas are the most common cause of skin disease in cats.

Most of the flea's life cycle is spent *off* the host. A single cat can support as many as 15,000 fleas. Each female flea lays about 200 eggs in her lifetime, so high numbers of fleas can build up quickly.

Signs
Fleas spend most of their life off the cat, so just because you don't see any this does not necessarily mean they are not present. Look instead for indications that they have been around. Fleas leave evidence of their presence as flea dirt. Flea dirt is actually flea excreta and consists mainly of digested blood. These droppings appear as small black specks within the coat. They are most readily seen by pushing the hair back against its natural lie. Flea dirt is present in the highest concentrations around the tail base and neck. If you are not convinced that the matter you find there is flea dirt, then brush some of the specks on to a piece of white paper. Add a few drops of water to the specks and within a few seconds the water turns reddish brown due to the blood pigments in the excreta. This is evidence that what you are seeing is digested blood and not just dirt.

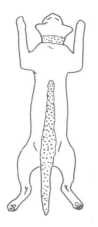

The dotted areas are liable to become inflamed in flea allergy dermatitis and in miliary dermatitis

What do flea eggs look like?
Flea eggs are pinpoint sized, white and oval in shape. They are very hard to see with the naked eye. They are resistant to many insecticides.

What damage do fleas do?
Fleas can cause four problems:

1. Transmit disease and parasites (especially tapeworm).
2. Cause skin irritation and itching, leading to vigorous scratching and licking which in turn damages the skin. This may preoccupy some cats to such an extent that their appetite wanes and they lose weight.
3. Fleas suck blood. This can cause anaemia if they are present in large numbers.
4. After prolonged exposure to biting fleas some cats develop a sensitivity (allergy) to flea saliva. This can result in a severe skin condition termed 'flea al-

lergy dermatitis'. Once sensitised, even a single flea bite may trigger an acute itch (*see* 'flea allergy dermatitis' page 168).

How to control fleas and repel future infestations
Your aim is not only to kill fleas on the cat but also to repel other fleas. Always follow the manufacturers' instructions carefully when using any insecticidal preparations.

● Flea powders: (active ingredients could include: carbamates, dichlorvos, propoxur, rotenone (don't use on your kittens), iodofenphos. There is a wide range available — most are effective but some need to be applied frequently, usually *twice* weekly to maintain protection. Apply flea powder by dusting it down the cat's back and then brushing it well into the coat and all over the body. Then take a damp cloth and wipe it lightly over the cat's body to remove any residual powder. This reduces the amount of powder the cat ingests while grooming and is especially important in the kittens as they are more susceptible to the insecticides.

● Insecticidal sprays: (active ingredients could include, carbamates, dichlorvos). These can be effective but many cats resent being sprayed. *Beware:* don't spray around the cat's eyes, nose or mouth.

● Insecticidal rinses: e.g. malathion. These are generally quite effective and give longer lasting protection than either sprays or powders. *Warning:* rinses can be very dangerous if not used properly. Read the instructions carefully and follow dilution rates precisely. Beware of using rinses where open wounds or raw areas of skin are present. Only use rinses that are specifically labelled as being safe to use on cats, or that have been dispensed to you by your vet for your cat. Many products that are suitable for dogs are poisonous to cats.

● Applying a flea rinse: proceed as for *'washing the cat'* (page 163) but do not rinse the insecticide out.

● Insecticidal shampoos: (some active ingredients may include, carbamates, pyrethrum, piperonyl butoxide). These preparations kill fleas on the cat at the time of bathing but they don't have much residual insecticidal action. For this reason they should be used in combination with other flea control methods such as powders or collars.

● Flea collars: (containing drugs such as dichlorvos, carbamates and propoxur). Two main types are available. One type produces an insecticidal vapour. These should be used with caution as the skin and eyes of some cats are sensitive to the vapour. Do *not* use them on sick cats, or cats with an eye problem. The other type of collars have microfined particles of insecticide that gradually work their way through the coat. These have fewer side effects than vapour collars. Watch for any signs of irritation on the skin of the neck and remove the collar immediately if any redness develops. If the inflammation is severe or persists, consult your veterinarian.

Remove flea collars before bathing the cat.

Vapour type collars should be removed if they become wet — e.g. when it rains.

Treatment of the surroundings
In heated homes fleas can multiply all year round. The cat's bedding should be powdered or sprayed. Vacuum cracks and crevices as fleas love to breed in these dusty areas. Burn the contents of the vacuum cleaner when finished. Insecticidal surface sprays may be used around furniture and skirting boards. All other animals in the house should also be treated for fleas.

Treatment of young kittens
Kittens suckling from a queen that has fleas often have fleas too. If the flea bur-

FLEAS !!!

den is high, severe blood loss and even death could occur in these kittens. In this situation it is essential to eliminate fleas on the queen. Either a flea powder or rinse can be used. Take special care to wash the nipples clean after using any insecticidal preparation as young kittens are very susceptible to these poisons. Kittens themselves may be dipped in lukewarm water for two to three minutes to drown any fleas on them. Keep the head out of the water but make sure the fur on the head is saturated by dabbing it with a wet sponge. Dry them thoroughly using a towel and then a hair dryer or fan heater. *Beware* of overheating the kitten. Fresh clean bedding should be provided and the old bedding burnt.

Flea allergy dermatitis (or miliary dermatitis)

Some cats develop an allergy to flea saliva. These cats become extremely sensitive to *any* flea bite. A single bite can result in severe skin irritation. By scratching and licking themselves the skin is further damaged. The sensory nerves of the skin become inflamed and exposed, creating an even more intense desire to scratch. This leads to a vicious cycle: itch, scratch, itch, scratch.

Sores develop. These are felt in the skin as numerous small crusty lesions. They have a characteristic distribution.

Treatment

If the condition is severe, it may be necessary for a vet to relieve the irritation with a dose of cortisone or a similar drug to allow the damaged skin time to heal. During this period start a vigorous campaign to eliminate fleas on the cat and in the immediate environment.

Stick fast flea (echidnophagia gallinacea)

The stick fast, or poultry flea, prefers birds but can infest cats. They usually feed around the head and ears of the cat and may resemble mud stuck to the skin and hair. These fleas do not move about when disturbed but hang tenaciously to the skin. These fleas are controlled using the same methods outlined for general flea management.

LICE

Lice rarely occur in healthy, well cared for cats. They are usually seen only on

168

neglected, run down or sick cats. Cats suffering from disease may become listless and cease grooming.

Lice can then take advantage of the cat's disinterest and parasitise it. Cat lice don't like other animals, so an infested cat is not a risk to humans or other pets. There are two types of lice. Some are biting lice. These cause skin irritation. Other types suck blood and cause anaemia.

Signs
Lice may be found anywhere on the body. The skin becomes itchy and the hair matts or falls out. There may be self inflicted sores where the cat has licked the itchy skin. The tiny white lice can be found by looking under the matts. Lice eggs ('nits') are attached to the hair shafts and give the appearance of scattered flour on the cat's coat.

Treatment
Matts of hair should be removed by clipping. The cat should have an insecticidal rinse once weekly for one month. *Or* wash the cat in an insecticidal shampoo and then apply an insecticidal preparation. This should be repeated weekly for one month.

If the skin is extensively damaged, veterinary advice should be sought before the cat is treated with any insecticidal preparation.

The problem that caused the initial self neglect should also be remedied.

MANGE

A mange mite

For centuries the word 'mange' has been incorrectly used to describe a multitude of skin conditions. A 'mangy' cat was understood to be poorly kept or rundown. In fact mange is a specific skin condition caused by mites that infest the skin. In cats the most significant cause of mange is a particular mite called *notoedres cati.*

Are some cats more susceptible to mange than others?
Mange is no longer a common condition. Insecticides now available are very effective. When mange does occur it is usually seen in cats that are not robust, such as the very old cat or in a litter of young kittens that are poorly nourished.

Mange is highly contagious between cats.

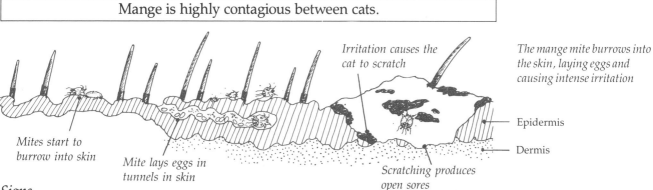

Irritation causes the cat to scratch

The mange mite burrows into the skin, laying eggs and causing intense irritation

Mites start to burrow into skin

Mite lays eggs in tunnels in skin

Scratching produces open sores

Epidermis

Dermis

Signs
The mites burrow deeply into the skin, causing intense itching and irritation. The cat continuously rubs, scratches or licks the affected areas. Mange usually starts on the edge of the ears and then progresses to cover the face, eyelids and neck.

The feet may be affected if mites are transferred from the head to the feet during grooming. In the same way mites may be transferred to the tail base and hind legs. The whole body may eventually become affected.

Other signs include self-inflicted sores, hair loss, areas of thickening and wrinkling of the skin. Bacteria may invade the broken skin and cause serious infections.

Treatment
When the condition is extensive, veterinary attention is necessary. Treatment may include antibiotics, insecticides and perhaps drugs to relieve the itch.

In mild cases a 0.5% malathion rinse repeated once (in ten days) will kill the mites and allow the skin to heal. All cats in contact with the infected cat should also be treated with malathion. The mite can survive only a short time off the cat so bedding and grooming equipment are not a source of re-infection.

Prevention
Regular treatment with insecticidal preparations such as are used for flea control will effectively control mites.

Are people affected by cat mites?
The cat mite can survive for only a short time on people. During this time minor skin irritation may occur. It is only on the skin of cats, rabbits or foxes that it can take up permanent residency and cause extensive skin damage.

RABBIT FUR MITE (cheyletiella parasitivorax)

The rabbit fur mite occasionally causes skin problems in cats. Irritation to the skin, caused by the mite, creates profuse dandruff along the cat's back and flanks.

Treatment
Use *one* of the following:
* Selenium sulphide shampoo effectively kills the mite and removes the scurf. This should be repeated weekly for three treatments.
* Malathion rinses (or similar insecticidal rinse).

This mite can also infect humans, causing itchy dry skin on the hands, forearms or chest. Occasionally the affected skin may blister into sores.

FLY STRIKE

Fly strike occurs when blow-flies lay eggs in matted hair, especially around the tail or open wounds. After the eggs hatch the maggots burrow into the skin, producing extensive skin damage. They also carry bacterial infection into wounds.

Treatment
The matted hair and hairs surrounding damaged skin should be trimmed away. Use a mild antiseptic such as dilute hydrogen peroxide to flush the wound. Remove as many maggots as possible and then apply an insecticidal, antiseptic powder or cream to kill any remaining maggots and to prevent reinfestation.

In some cases veterinary attention may be necessary, especially if the area involved is extensive and the cat resents attention to it.

Prevention
Don't let matts of hair build up. Aged or debilitated cats may be unable to groom themselves properly and it is your responsibility to keep them free of matts. Don't let loose droppings accumulate in hair around the hind legs. Longhaired cats with

170

diarrhoea will inevitably form some matts soiled with faeces. These must be trimmed away. The area around the tail base should be examined routinely for matts.

TICKS

Ticks can infest cats as opportunist parasites. They do not actually multiply on the cat and are usually picked up when a cat is stalking through vegetation where ticks have been rubbed off livestock. As the ticks suck blood, they increase in size and change colour to a grey-purple. They cause a skin reaction at their point of attachment and should be removed.

Treatment
Place an inverted bottle of alcohol or methylated spirits over the tick. It will soon release and drop off, or paint the tick with nail polish remover (acetone). Do not squeeze the tick or just break off the body.

BOT FLIES *(habronema spp. draschia spp)*

Found in some parts of the USA and Europe, these produce a different form of fly strike. The maggots migrate through the skin and are seen as swellings along the neck, back, sides, belly, eyelids, nostrils or jaw. The grub breathes through an opening at the top of this swelling. These lumps may become infected and full of pus, especially if the grub dies.

Treatment
First, remove the grub by squeezing the lump or gently pulling it out using tweezers. Then flush the lump with antiseptic solution. In cases where there are multiple swellings, veterinary treatment may be needed.

RINGWORM

Ringworm is an unfortunate name as this skin condition is not caused by a worm at all. It is caused by a fungus. Originally it was believed that the characteristic round ringworm sores were caused by a worm burrowing around in circles under the skin. In fact, the reason ringworm sores are round is because, like the ripples produced when a pebble is thrown into a pond, the fungus starts in one spot and spreads in all directions simultaneously.

The incidence of ringworm is highest in hot, humid climates such as Southern America, Northern Australia, Spain and North Africa but is seen in most parts of the world.

Signs
Symptoms appear two to four weeks after infection and vary greatly in appearance. A mild infection may have produced only a few broken hairs on the face or ears. There may be small round or oval patches of hair loss on the head, ears,

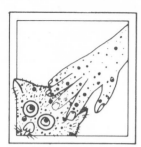

forepaws or back. In some cases the lesion may be mistaken for food stuck on the end of the cat's nose or face. In severe cases there are large areas of hair loss with crusty scaly scabs. Occasionally ringworm fungus may cause infection around the toenails.

Unlike ringworm in man, the sores are not particularly itchy. There may be mild irritation, but generally the cat pays little attention to them and general health is unaffected.

Young cats are more susceptible to ringworm than older cats. Following infection a strong immunity to reinfection develops.

Diagnosis

If you suspect your cat has ringworm you should consult your vet. He or she may shine an ultraviolet light (called a 'Wood's lamp') on the suspicious area as this causes some ringworm to fluoresce. A sample of the affected hair and skin may be sent to a laboratory for examination. Sometimes the vet may be confident enough of the characteristic appearance of the ringworm lesion and will treat accordingly without obtaining laboratory confirmation.

Treatment

Many mild cases are self-limiting and will clear up without treatment. Because ringworm is transmissible to humans (children are particularly susceptible) treatment may be advisable. If there are only one or two ringworm sores the area can be painted with tincture of iodine or washed with antiseptic soap to kill the fungal spores. The hairs around the area should be clipped but you must disinfect the scissors afterwards and burn the clipped hairs. If there are many sores it may be more effective to shampoo with a fungicidal product e.g. hexetidine.

Rinsing in 1:200 dilution of 45% captan is also effective. Either treatment should be repeated twice weekly until the sores resolve.

In severe or persistent cases, an anti-fungal drug called griseofulvin may be given orally for three to six weeks. It is highly effective, but is available only by prescription and should be used under veterinary supervision.

It is advisable either to burn or disinfect bedding and to disinfect grooming equipment. Fungal spores can remain infective for six months if not destroyed.

Disinfectants such as iodophos, formalin and alcohol are effective against fungal spores but are too toxic to be used on the cat itself.

Is ringworm contagious between cats?

Yes, but older cats often have a good immunity to ringworm and usually don't develop lesions. If your cat has been in contact with a cat with ringworm, griseofulvin can be given to prevent ringworm developing. You should discuss this with your vet as griseofulvin can only be given under veterinary supervision. Some cats can carry the fungal spores around in their coat without showing signs of having ringworm. These cats can act as sources of infection for other animals (and people). Because of these 'carriers' once ringworm gets into a cattery it is very difficult to eliminate.

Can people catch ringworm from cats?

Yes, but ringworm can also be picked up from many other sources including other people, dogs, or even directly from the soil. Children are especially susceptible but adults can be infected too. Ringworm is not a particularly severe condition in humans and usually responds quickly to ointments and lotions. In some cases it becomes deep seated or spreads rapidly. Don't take chances, see your physician for advice.

172

Feline endocrine alopecia

Hair loss (alopecia) is sometimes seen in neutered cats. It is much more common in castrated males than in spayed females.

Signs

There is no itchiness or change in the appearance of the skin. The only sign is a thinning of the hair coat in a symmetrical pattern. There is never a total loss of all body hair. A few fine hairs may remain on affected areas. The cat shows no other signs of illness.

Treatment

This condition is sometimes difficult to treat succesfully. Some cats respond to hormone treatment. Finding the actual cure for the condition is often a matter of trial and error. Treatment is continued until the hair regrows. In some cases the condition does not recur, in others a low dose of hormone may be needed intermittently for life. This is a matter for you and your vet to discuss.

Feline acne

Cats may sometimes develop blackheads (comedomes) or pimples (*pustules)* on the face, mainly around the lip margins or under the chin. These may be quite severe producing small abscesses that are difficult to cure.

Cats that don't wash and groom themselves properly under their chins and around their faces are prone to this condition. Dirt accumulates and blocks the pores. Oily secretions then accumulate and blackheads form. These may become infected, producing pimples and small abscesses.

Treatment

First thoroughly clean the neglected areas with mild antiseptic soap or antiseptic skin solutions then swab the area with methylated spirits. In some cases antibiotics will be necessary to clear up the infection.

Prevention of recurrences

In cats prone to acne, it may be necessary to clean the chin routinely for them. Alternate between an antiseptic agent such as hexachlorophene, and a defatting agent such as alcohol or methylated spirits. It is usually only necessary to treat these cats twice a week to prevent a flare up.

Stud tail

This is a common condition in uncastrated males. The male cat, under the influence of the male sex hormone testosterone, produces an oily secretion from glands at the base of the tail. This can result in an unsightly, greasy patch of hair in the gland area. This is particularly noticeable in light coloured cats. This usually does not concern the cat unless the area becomes irritated or infected.

Treatment

Wash the area with a cat shampoo, a baby shampoo or mild toilet soap to degrease the area and eliminate the stain. This may need to be repeated daily especially in the breeding season (spring). If infection occurs your vet may advise the use of antibiotics. Castration is the only effective way of eliminating the problem permanently.

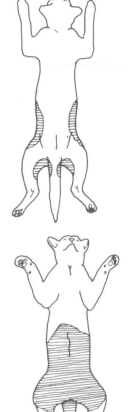

The pattern of hair loss in feline endocrine alopecia

Feline acne

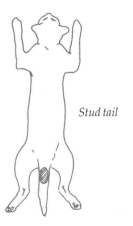

Stud tail

173

Hypothyroidism
Hypothyroidism means a deficiency of thyroid hormone. This condition occurs only rarely in cats.

Signs (variable)
- Symmetrical thinning of the hair coat, mainly on the neck and body. The hair remaining is dull, brittle and easily pulled out.
- Darkening of the skin, due to the increased pigment production.
- Thickened skin.
- Other signs are variable but may include lethargy, dullness, cold intolerance, tiredness, depressed sexual activity and obesity.

Diagnosis
Your vet may take blood to investigate thyroid hormone levels. But in many cases this test is not conclusive.

Treatment
Thyroid hormone tablets.
  Response to thyroid hormone replacement is slow and hair regrowth will not be seen for at least three to four weeks. The cat should be brighter in one to two weeks.

FELINE MILIARY DERMATITIS

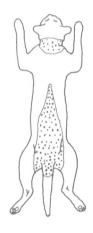

Some cases of feline miliary dermatitis (FMD) are caused by flea bite allergy (*see* 'Fleas' page 166). Other causes include food allergy, excessive fish diets, vitamin B deficiency or hormone disorder.

Signs
- Multiple, small, scabby sores across the rump, lower back and neck areas. These scabs are not always visible but they can be felt by stroking the cat.
- Thinning of the hair coat in the affected areas (also makes sores more obvious).
- Thickening of the skin.
- Scratching, licking and biting at the sores causing more skin damage and hair loss.

Veterinary treatment
May include the use of steroids, vitamin supplements, dietary changes or hormone replacement. Treatment is usually very successful but in some cases may have to be maintained at a low level for life.

LICK SORES (acral lick dermatitis)

These areas are affected in cases of miliary dermatitis

If a cat persistently licks an area of skin, the rasp-like action of the tongue will eventually damage the skin and produce a sore.
  Licking is a normal part of grooming but some cats concentrate their attention on one particular area, and a problem begins. Boredom is the main cause of overgrooming although some lick sores start as a wound, graze or insect bite. Licking may start as a casual habit. Some cats achieve a tension release by grooming themselves in much the same way a child relieves anxiety by sucking its thumb. Constant licking, however, irritates the nerves in the skin and an itch develops.

174

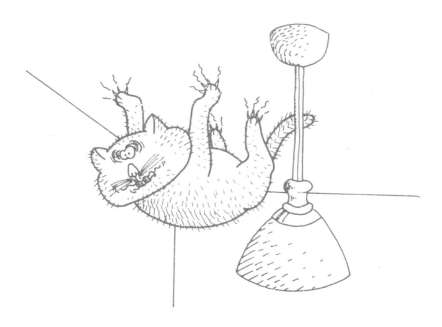

Nervous cats seem to be particularly prone to skin disease especially lick sores

The cat then licks more, partly to relieve the itch — and the skin becomes further damaged. Continuous licking prevents healing and eventually can create deep ulcers.

Signs
At first, hair loss is noticed where the cat is persistently licking. If licking persists the area becomes red and inflamed, the skin breaks and an ulcer forms.

Treatment
A lick sore can be difficult to clear up. Treatment should commence as early as possible. If the skin is hairless and red, providing the cat with distracting toys or a companion may relieve boredom and prevent the problem advancing further. If the skin is ulcerated or the cat cannot be distracted, veterinary treatment is required.

Veterinary treatment
Cortisone is often used to relieve the skin irritation as this reduces the cat's desire to lick, allowing the skin to heal. In neurotic cats, hormonal treatment may be successful. In refractory cases surgical removal of the sore may be considered.

Prevention
Where boredom is the cause, you could try some of the following:
- Provide more 'people' attention.
- Allow the cat a window to look out of.
- More feline company — a new cat. But *beware* — this can backfire and even make the problem worse.
- Avoid close confinement for long periods.
- Give toys to divert the cat's attention.
- Leave a radio playing when you leave the house.
- Try to minimise any suspected sources of anxiety.

Read the chapter on 'Behaviour', page 47.

Are some cats more susceptible than others?
Highly strung, nervous cats are the most likely to develop lick sores.

FOOD ALLERGY DERMATITIS

Although food allergies occur in cats, they are not common. Such allergies may occur at any time of the cat's life with or without a sudden dietary change.

Signs
A generalised itchiness with reddening of the skin, wheals ('hives') or small scabby sores.
   Sometimes vomiting and/or diarrhoea.

Treatment
An 'elimination' diet is the best approach to identify the offending food. The cat is placed on a bland diet containing few ingredients with no preservatives or additives. The idea is to feed a protein source that is not normally part of the cat's diet. Choose from fish, chicken, minced beef, lamb or mutton and feed it for ten to fourteen days. If food allergy is the problem, there should be a remission of the skin lesions within this time. If the change in diet seems to have succeeded, try feeding a small amount of the suspected food again (e.g. canned or dry food it normally eats). If signs of the allergy reappear within twelve to twenty-four hours the offending food is identified. If this food is not the cause (that is the signs do not reappear) continue adding back other components of the diet on alternate days until the one causing the allergy is eventually identified.

FELINE LEPROSY

Feline leprosy is not a common condition. It is not the same as human leprosy and is not transmissible to humans. The cause of the disease is the rat leprosy bacillus *mycobacterium lepraemurium*. It is transmitted to cats through a bite from an infected rat.

Signs
Painless, firm lump(s) under the skin of the head or limbs. The skin over the lump may ulcerate and infect. The cat usually has no other signs of illness.

Treatment
Surgical removal of the lump under a general anaesthetic may be necessary.

GUT

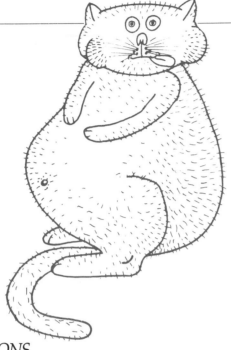

THE NORMAL FUNCTIONS

The cat's digestive system has been adapted to deal with its natural diet of small rodents and other small animals.

Mouth
The teeth are designed to catch, hold and kill the prey, then to shear off small pieces. The tongue forces these pieces of food back into the oesophagus. Saliva is mixed with the food to lubricate its passage and to start digestion.

Oesophagus
A muscular tube connecting the mouth and stomach. Food does not simply fall down the oesophagus. Powerful muscular contractions push the food through the neck and chest into the stomach. The cat can therefore swallow with its head lowered.

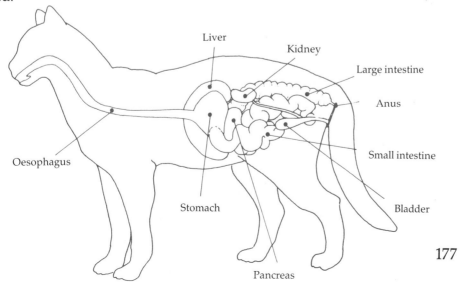

177

Stomach

It is a common misconception that most digestion occurs in the stomach. It only starts here. The stomach is a muscular sack in which the food is thoroughly mixed with the saliva plus secretions of acids and digestive juices from the stomach's wall.

When the food has become semi-liquified, a muscular ring valve (the pyloric sphincter) at one end of the stomach opens to allow some of the contents into the first part of the small intestine — the duodenum.

The small intestine

The three parts of the small intestine are, in sequence, the duodenum, the jejunum and the ileum. In the duodenum, more digestive enzymes are added to the food. The digestive secretions of the liver and the pancreas are piped in via the common bile duct.

The digestive process continues throughout the small intestine. When the food has been broken down into elementary units that are small and simple enough, these are absorbed through the gut wall. The digested foodstuffs are taken by blood and lymph to the liver. The basic components arrive in the liver as fats, carbohydrates, protein, vitamins and minerals.

The liver is a complex organ, responsible for final digestion, and production of the various body fuels required by the body's tissues. The liver also stores many essential vitamins, minerals and energy reserves. It is also the site of toxin breakdown, vitamin and digestive enzyme manufacture and bile production.

Meanwhile, whatever is left over in the gut moves from the small intestine to the calcum and large intestine.

The large intestine

The main function of the large intestine is to extract and resorb most of the remaining fluids and salts from the bowel contents. What is left is waste.

The terminal part of the large intestine is the colon. Wastes are stored here until they are dried out enough to be voided as faeces, or stools.

REGURGITATION AND VOMITING

Regurgitation

Regurgitation of food may at first seem to be the same as vomiting, but there are differences. Regurgitation is a relatively passive emptying of the stomach, and usually results from overeating. The food is brought up fairly sluggishly, in contrast to the more dramatic, forceful act of vomiting.

If your cat frequently regurgitates food, try feeding more often, but much smaller quantities. Regurgitation could be due to a blockage or obstruction, so consult your vet if your cat regurgitates food after eating if this is out of character.

Vomiting
Vomiting is a natural reflex, designed to clear the stomach of potentially irritant or toxic matter. Vomiting is also a part of many disease states. It does not necessarily indicate that the stomach itself is the seat of the problem.

Vomiting can be differentiated from regurgitation by the behaviour of the cat. Initially there is anxiety, increased salivation and swallowing. Stomach contractions gradually become more violent. Then, with rhythmic contractions of the diaphragm and abdomen, the food is forcibly expelled, usually to the accompaniment of a sharp cry or groan.

Vomiting can be a useful function that eliminates substances that could otherwise cause further problems. It may also be a sign of serious disease.

When to call the vet
If the cat is vomiting *and:*
- The cat is listless or physically depressed.
- There is profuse diarrhoea.
- There is blood in the vomit.
- Vomit is 'faecal' in nature, that is, more like bowel motion than stomach contents.
- Vomiting is persistent.

Some minor causes of vomiting that you can deal with

Grass eating
Sometimes cats will eat specific types of grass to induce vomiting. This is generally just to clear the stomach, perhaps because it is overfull or partly blocked by some indigestible matter such as a hairball or feathers from a bird.

Once the cat has vomited, the condition is usually resolved. If the grass eating is abnormally frequent, consult your vet.

Travel or motion sickness
For highly strung or emotional cats your vet may supply you with a mild sedative before a long trip. Do not use human travel sickness preparations unless on the advice of your vet. Most cats travel without vomiting, although they may yowl constantly.

Constipation
Toxins are absorbed from the bowel of the constipated cat, making it nauseous. Vomiting may result.

Worms
A heavy burden of roundworm may prevent the normal passage of food. Sometimes roundworm irritate the stomach itself, although they usually live in the small intestine. Treat as for worms (see page 193).

Gulping
Some cats rush their food, gulping it down and failing to chew it at all. These cats can ingest quite a large volume of air with the food. The stomach becomes over distended, triggering a reflex-clearing vomit.

Treatment

Cut the food finer, and feed smaller amounts more often. You may have to give four or five small meals a day.

Feeding a less appetising food, such as dry food, may also work.

Sensitivity to a particular food

You may note that your cat is vomiting whenever he eats a particular type or brand of food. This could be a reaction to the food itself, or to a preservative or additive in the food. Change the cat's diet to a bland food that is unlikely to cause problems, such as chicken or mutton. When the cat has returned to normal, offer a *little* of the suspect food. If vomiting is repeated, your suspicions will be confirmed.

If the cat is reacting to one of the preservatives or additives in commercially manufactured foods you may have to experiment a little before you discover a range of foods that your cat can cope with.

Stress

Some emotional or highly strung cats vomit when excited or upset. This may occur when the cat is fed alongside other cats. Nervous cats are usually better fed separately not just a few feet from the other cats, but in a separate room. Allow the cat a few days to adjust to this new routine. Other stresses can similarly result in vomiting. It can be difficult to discover what is upsetting the cat. Read the chapter on 'Behaviour' for some ideas.

Types of vomiting that do require investigation

Vomiting blood

The blood could come from the mouth, oesophagus or stomach. When a cat vomits blood after a car accident, it does not necessarily indicate serious internal damage. Quite often, the blood has come from a cut tongue or a knocked-out tooth.

Possible causes of bleeding in the oesophagus or stomach include laceration by foreign bodies such as bone splinters, fish hooks or needles, or bleeding from ulcers or tumours.

Projectile vomiting

In projectile vomiting, the stomach contents are ejected forcibly and without much warning to land up to a foot away from the cat. Projectile vomiting usually indicates a blockage at the start or early part of the duodenum. The most common site is the 'exit valve' from the stomach (the pyloric sphincter). This is a muscular ring that normally seals the stomach, opening only to let regulated amounts of food out of the stomach and into the small intestine.

Blockages could be caused by hairballs, growths or foreign bodies such as bits of plastic or rubber.

In some kittens, projectile vomiting starts when they are given solid foods. In such cases, the cause is often a constriction or 'stricture' of the pyloric sphincter. The kitten can open the sphincter enough to let liquids through, but solids cannot pass.

Treatment

Surgical. Usually it is successful and the kitten can develop without further complications.

GASTRITIS

Gastritis means 'inflamed stomach'. The primary sign of gastritis is vomiting.

Some of the causes of gastritis include:
- Eating spoiled foods.
- Eating food contaminated with insecticides or herbicides (neither are particularly common as the cat is very careful about what it eats).
- Ingesting irritant substances while grooming. The cat's fur could become contaminated with materials such as sump oil, or the owner may dust the coat with insecticide but neglect to remove the superficial powder. In these or similar situations, the cat's fastidious grooming habits may result in the ingestion of toxic amounts of these substances.
- Ulcers. Stomach ulcers are rare in cats. They sometimes occur as part of other conditions such as advanced kidney disease.

Home treatment for gastritis
Home treament should only be contemplated if the cat is still bright and alert, the vomit is free of blood, and there is not an accompanying diarrhoea. If the vomiting persists despite home treatment, consult your vet.
- 'Rest' the stomach. Give *no* food for at least twelve hours. In mature cats you can safely wait twenty-four to forty-eight hours.
- Give small amounts of water only. No milk. If the cat drinks too much at once this may trigger another vomit. Give only a few teaspoonfuls every thirty to sixty minutes. Or give an ice block to lick if the cat will cooperate.
- After twelve to twenty-four hours, offer a *small* amount of a readily digestible food that you know your cat likes. These foods should preferably be cooked and minced first as this aids digestion. Suitable foods include chicken, mutton and white fish.
- If the first one or two teaspoonfuls are accepted and kept down, wait at least an hour and then offer a little more.
- Do not rush things. Success is more likely if you return to the normal diet slowly. Feed little and often for the next two days, then gradually go back to normal routine over the next two to four days.
- Avoid rich or indigestible foods such as heart, liver, raw, fatty meat or rich canned foods for five to seven days.

Medications that may help
Some cats will accept medication without too much fuss. Do not persist in trying to force medication into a cat that has been vomiting if you meet vigorous resistance. You are likely to cause more vomiting.

Preparations such as Kaomagma or others containing kaolin, pectin and antacids may be obtained from a pharmacist. Ask for a children's preparation, and specify that there *must not be any morphine derivatives* in the preparation. (Cats react very badly to morphine.)

DIARRHOEA

The cat's bowel motions are normally a little softer and less well formed than, for example, those of a dog. Stools of the consistency of putty are considered quite normal. Diarrhoea is defined as very loose or fluid bowel motions.

Most cats experience mild bouts of diarrhoea from time to time. This need not alarm you. Treatment is not necessary unless the diarrhoea becomes persistent — but it usually clears up spontaneously.

Some causes of mild diarrhoea include:
- Overeating.
- Unfamiliar foods, which are consequently not digested properly.

- Rich foods, such as liver or too much milk.
- Stress. Diarrhoea is quite a common reaction to stresses such as a new cat in the neighbourhood, thunderstorms, overexcitement, or moving house.

Persistent or severe diarrhoea should not be neglected. Diarrhoea can be caused by such a wide range of factors that it may simplify the situation if you can first identify what sort of problem your cat has:
- Hypermotility (bowel is moving too fast).
- Malabsorption (food is not being broken down into basic components which could then be absorbed, or bowel wall is diseased and is unable to absorb foods).
- Infection (by bacteria, virus or parasite).

	HYPERMOTILITY	*MALABSORPTION*	*INFECTION*
Colour of stool	Green to yellow.	Pale grey to yellow.	Great variation, from light and frothy to black and tarry.
Consistency	Watery.	Greasy.	Very fluid, may be gas bubbles.
Smell	Not particularly abnormal, perhaps a little strong or sour.	Rancid.	Foul, very offensive.
Frequency	Two to four times normal.	Two to four times normal.	Very frequent — up to several times an hour.
Some likely causes	Irritant chemicals, heavy worm burdens, stagnant water, rotting carrion, some bacterial toxins, rich or very fatty foods.	Liver or pancreas conditions, inappropriate or indigestible foods, overeating, intolerance to a food or additive, internal parasites (e.g. hookworm).	Bacterial infection, viral infection, e.g. infectious feline enteritis, allergic reaction to drugs, poisons.

Notes on chart
- There are some agents, such as internal parasites, that could — directly or indirectly — cause *any* of the three types of bowel problems.
- The severity of the effect depends on the amount of toxin or poison involved. A small dose may produce little or no change. A lot could be fatal.
- The overall health of the cat must also be considered. In very young or old cats, or in debilitated cats, diarrhoea is always significant and potentially serious.

When to call the vet
- If diarrhoea is accompanied by vomiting.

- If cat is lethargic, listless.
- If there is blood in faeces or vomit.
- If there is severe abdominal pain.
- If diarrhoea persists or returns after home treatment.

Home treatment for mild diarrhoea

Aim
Rest the bowel. Give it time to recover. The bowel is capable of rapidly repairing any damage once the irritant has been eliminated.

Method
Withhold *all* food for twenty-four hours (eight to twelve hours for kittens). Exclude any milk or dairy products. Provide plenty of clean water instead. Glucose (*not* sugar) can be added to the water, ½ teaspoon per cup. After a period of fasting, offer a small amount of a bland, easily digested food such as cooked, minced chicken, or white fish, veal, minced hamburger steak (cooked, and fat drained) or cooked egg. If the cat will accept it, mix some boiled rice with this food. Select a food your cat is used to, and is known to like. Serve it at blood temperature. Give a *little*, every few hours. Total for the first day should be no more than half the normal ration. Do not rush to get the cat back to normal routine. Take three to five days to return gradually to a normal diet.

Medications that may be useful
- Aluminium hydroxide gel (e.g. Kaomagma or Kaopectate). Dose: Adult: ½ to 1 teaspoon per 5 kg three times daily.
- Activated charcoal: ½ to 2 tablets daily.

Chronic diarrhoea
If your cat suffers recurring bouts of diarrhoea or if the diarrhoea fails to clear up with simple treatment, you should consult your vet. Take a faecal sample with you. Better still, drop a sample in a few days prior to your visit to allow time for the sample to be examined for the presence of such things as parasite eggs, undigested foods and digestive enzymes.

ENTERITIS

Enteritis is more severe and serious than simple diarrhoea. The lining of the gut wall is damaged — perhaps due to bacterial infection (such as salmonella, clostridia and E. coli) or viral infection (such as feline infectious enteritis).

Signs
Include some or all of the following:
- Abdominal pain: the cat may assume a hunched posture, and be reluctant to allow you to feel its abdomen. The abdomen is tensed against the anticipated pain of your probing fingers.
- Loose, watery or ill formed faeces. The cat may strain frequently, passing only small quantities of foul smelling faeces.
- Faeces have a strong, penetrating and offensive smell.
- Bad breath.
- Increased thirst.
- Vomiting.
- Listlessness or extreme lethargy.

VET TREATMENT
URGENT

Treatment
Veterinary attention is essential.

CONSTIPATION

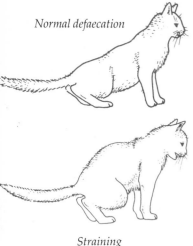

Normal defaecation

Straining

Constipation is the infrequent passage of faeces. As a result, the faeces become hard and dry and therefore difficult or painful to pass.

Signs
Because cats tend to be private in their toilet habits, owners may not detect this problem until it is well advanced.
Signs you may note:
● Difficulty passing motion.
● Frequent attempts to defaecate: squatting, straining then digging to bury an imaginary motion. (*Beware:* this is also a sign of cystitis, or blocked bladder, see page 204.)
● Dry, hard faeces. May be blood-flecked.
● Loss of appetite, lethargy and dullness.
● Vomiting.
You may be able to feel the contents of your cat's abdomen. Constipation is detected as a large sausage-shaped mass lying parallel to the cat's backbone.
Constipation is usually insidious in its onset. It is frequently detected only when the cat is severely distressed. Constipation is no joke. It is potentially very serious.

Some causes of constipation
Cats vary in their susceptibility to constipation. Most cats are never bothered. With others, it requires constant supervision to prevent it.

Diet
Dry foods may predispose to constipation, especially if the fluid intake is inadequate. Most dry foods contain adequate amounts of fibre. Some do not.
Bones are very constipating. If your cat likes bones, but tends to become constipated, eliminate them from the diet. 'All meat' diets or diets that are primarily meat, lack sufficient fibre and can cause constipation.

Age
As cats get older, the bowel muscle tone deteriorates. Some cats become unable to push out faeces.

Hair
The shedding of large amounts of hair in spring or when the cat is ill can lead to the formation of hard, coarse faeces wound up in masses of hair.

Exercise
Fat, lazy indoor cats are far more likely to become constipated than active, outdoor cats. If a cat that is normally allowed to roam outside is shut indoors for an extended period this could lead to constipation as these cats are often reluctant to use litter trays.

Injuries
Injuries to the pelvis are fairly common in car accidents. The pelvis may be narrowed as a result, and this could lead to constipation.
Other injuries that make passing faeces painful or difficult include injuries to the back or spine, or to the tail.

Home treatment for constipation
The aim of treatment is to lubricate the passage of faeces and/or soften the mass that has already formed. You could try *one* of the following. Do not use them all at once.

- Liquid paraffin (from a pharmacist, not a garage).

Dose: ½ to 1 teaspoon twice daily by mouth.

- Oil emulsions (e.g. Agarol).

Dose: ½ to 1 teaspoon twice daily by mouth.

- Olive oil or other vegetable oils.

Dose: 1 to 2 teaspoons twice daily. Not as effective as liquid paraffin or oil emulsions.

Note: do not use these oil preparations continuously as they could interfere with absorption of some foods from the bowel, notably some vitamins. Use for a maximum of three days.

- Faecal softeners: e.g. Coloxyl (dioctyl sodium sulphosuccinate).

Use a children's preparation. Dose rate is as for a six to twelve month child or use commercially available cat laxatives. Dose according to manufacturer's instructions.

- Enemas: if drugs fail, an enema may be necessary. An enema is the infusion of a solution into the rectum. It should be performed only by an experienced person. A general anaesthetic is usually given because most cats are unwilling to cooperate with this procedure.

When to call the vet
If home treatment is not successful within one day or if the cat is uncomfortable, vomiting or otherwise distressed.

Beware! What you may think is constipation *could* be a blocked bladder. This is potentially fatal, so see your vet if the cat is not responding.

VET TREATMENT
URGENT

Preventing constipation
If your cat is known to be prone to constipation, you may be able to prevent recurrences. First, ensure your cat is getting a properly balanced diet with plenty of fibre. You can increase the amount of fibre in the diet by adding natural, unprocessed bran. Try adding one teaspoon a day, then increase or decrease this amount according to the effect.

There are 'bulk producers' available commercially. These are substances that can be added to the cat's food to produce a bulkier moister stool that is soft, and therefore easy to pass. These products can be obtained from your vet or pharmacist. Examples include sterculia granules (normacol) and sorbitol.

If your cat is prone to constipation you should also ensure there is always plenty of water available. Encourage exercise — physically put the cat outside several times a day if necessary.

EXCESSIVE PASSING OF FLATUS *(wind, farting)*

The production of some gas in the bowel is normal. Passing large volumes of foul smelling gas from the anus is not. Most of the gases produced in the bowel are absorbed into the blood stream and eventually eliminated, mainly through the lungs. If too much gas is produced, some will leak out of the anus.

The control of this excessive gas is usually easy, but some cases frustrate all efforts of treatment.

The first step is usually to change the cat's diet. Some foods result in the formation of large volumes of gas, for example, uncooked carbohydrates, peas,

beans and other legumes, slightly tainted meat and some vegetables. Review your cat's diet and remove any suspect foods.

Feed less at each meal. Small meals are more likely to be properly digested, with a consequent reduction in the amount of gas produced. Feed three or four small meals a day.

Change your brand of cat food. Some cause a lot more gas production than others.

Some old cats have poor muscle tone in their bowel, and this makes it harder for them to restrain the passage of gas through the gut. This could result in the intermittent, uncontrolled passage of foul gases. These cases are harder to solve. A general effort to improve your cat's overall health is worthwhile — vitamin and mineral supplementation, worming, good diet and so on.

Sometimes medications help. Activated charcoal mixed with the food absorbs surprisingly large volumes of gas. Unfortunately, few cats will accept food medicated with charcoal. The addition of a small amount of natural, unflavoured yoghurt may help.

Your vet may supply you with preparations that slow bowel motility. Perhaps there is a chronic bowel infection that could be treated with antibiotics, or a chronic parasite problem that should be dealt with.

INDIGESTIBLE OBJECTS SWALLOWED (foreign bodies)

Cats are careful about what they eat. Adult cats rarely swallow potentially dangerous objects. They may however inadvertently swallow indigestible items such as hard shelled insects or small birds. Kittens, on the other hand, due to their natural curiosity are more liable to swallow indigestible objects such as string, wool, small balls, foam rubber and so on. Eating cotton can lead to serious consequences if there is a needle on the other end. Fortunately, these needles are usually swallowed blunt end first. It may pass right through the gut, or it may lodge in the throat or neck, or it may perforate the gut.

If you know or suspect that your cat has eaten a needle (or similar) seek veterinary attention.

186

These indigestible objects can lead to obstruction of the bowel. Never pull on a piece of string or cotton hanging out of the cat's anus. You could cause further damage such as pulling a needle through the bowel wall.

OBSTRUCTIONS OF THE BOWEL

Possible causes include:
- Indigestible foreign body such as insect shells.
- Pieces of rubber, or plastic and bits of polystyrene foam.
- Balled up string, cotton or foam.
- Twist in the bowel, or a telescoping of the gut into itself ('intussusception'). These twists or telescoping can be a sequel to acute gut infections or inflammation or to heavy worm burdens.

Signs
The signs depend on where the obstruction is and whether it completely blocks the bowel or not. It may only cause a *partial* blockage.

In the case of a total obstruction of the stomach or small intestine, the signs are dramatic and may include the following:
- Vomiting.
- Acute depression/listlessness.
- Tense, painful abdomen.
- Disinclination to move. Hunched appearance.
- Body temperature may fall due to shock.

If the obstruction is partial or is in the large bowel, the signs are less noticeable. They may include some or all of the following:
- Listlessness, depression, lethargy.
- Foul breath.
- Loss of appetite.
- No, or few, bowel motions.
- Occasional vomiting, perhaps faecal in character.
- Dehydration (dry, tacky skin).

Diagnosis
Your vet may be able to feel the obstruction, or may x-ray the cat or even perform an exploratory operation if the cat is in severe distress.

Treatment
Seek expert veterinary treatment.

VET TREATMENT
URGENT

PANCREATITIS

The pancreas is an unspectacular organ until something goes wrong with it. The pancreas lies alongside the stomach, nestling close to the duodenum. It has two functions:
- To produce insulin.
- To produce digestive enzymes. These are essential for the digestion of

187

food in the bowel. The pancreas and the liver are the key organs in digestion.

When things go wrong

Acute pancreatitis
If the pancreas becomes damaged or inflamed, its cells break apart, releasing the digestive enzymes they contain. Unfortunately, the pancreas itself is not immune to the action of these enzymes. The pancreas literally starts to digest itself. This is dangerous — if the damage is extensive and a large volume of enzymes are released, the entire pancreas can be affected. Acute pancreatitis is extremely painful and potentially fatal.

What causes acute pancreatitis?
In most cases, we don't know. Some are started by bacterial infection, some by penetration of a foreign body such as a needle, some by viral infection. In many cases there is no apparent trigger.

Clinical signs
- Acute, debilitating pain.
- Cat may adopt a 'praying' position in an effort to minimise pain.
- Vomiting, may pass loose, yellow faeces.
- Shock: pale gums, rapid weak pulse.
- Cat reluctant to move.

Treatment
Your vet will attempt to ease the inflammation in the pancreas and alleviate the pain. Most respond well, but treatment is not always successful.

After the crisis
If the damage to the pancreas has been extensive you will have to be careful what you feed your cat. The aim is to feed small amounts of readily digestible foods. Supplementary pancreatic enzymes are available and can be mixed with the food prior to serving it. Your vet will give you a suitable diet, telling you what you can and cannot give.

Avoid fatty foods and sudden changes in diet. Stick to a fairly bland diet. The wrong diet can precipitate relapses.

Chronic pancreatitis
Chronic pancreatitis is not a dramatic condition. The pancreas gradually becomes less productive for a variety of poorly understood reasons. It gradually produces less and less until there are not sufficient enzymes for efficient digestion.

Sometimes bouts of acute pancreatitis gradually reduce the amount of functional pancreas tissue. In most cases there has been no known history of bouts of acute pancreatitis, although many owners report that, in hindsight, the cat did have episodes of being off food for a few days. These episodes *could* have been mild bouts of pancreatitis, insufficient to cause overt signs of pain but enough to reduce gradually the pancreas' output.

The clinical signs are not of a painful abdominal crisis, but of maldigestion.

Signs
- Weight loss (or failure to gain weight).
- Ill formed bowel motions — greasy, yellowish but may become rancid and foul smelling.
- Undigested food in faeces (usually need to detect this microscopically).

Treatment
Pancreas enzymes are commercially available to supplement the cat's own pancreas production, and to increase pancreas enzymes to a level to allow normal digestion. Fortunately they have become relatively inexpensive. They are mixed with the cat's food. Response to treatment can be excellent.

DIABETES

There are two forms of diabetes. Both are rare in the cat. (Note: diabetes *mellitus* is the form better known in human cases.)

Diabetes insipitus
In this form, the cat's kidneys are unable to concentrate the body's waste products into a relatively small volume of urine. As a result, the cat produces vast quantities of weak urine.

Signs
- Increased thirst.
- Increased volume of urine passed.
- Increased frequency of urinating.

Diagnosis
Laboratory tests to determine the specific gravity of the urine.
   The cat is then given a restricted water intake for twelve to twenty-four hours to see if it *can* concentrate the urine.

Causes
The causes are complex. The anti diuretic hormone (ADH) is sometimes involved. Some cats do not produce enough ADH. Others have enough but the kidneys fail to respond to it.
   Treatment is often unrewarding.

Diabetes mellitus
The pancreas fails to produce enough insulin. Insulin is essential for the cells to be able to utilise their basic energy source, *glucose*. Insulin enables glucose to enter the cell.
   Without the presence of insulin the cells cannot get glucose from the bloodstream. Because they lack glucose within their cell walls, they signal for more. The body responds to this apparent glucose lack by releasing more. The level of glucose in the blood stream rises higher and higher. The cells are oblivious to the potential amount of glucose available. Without insulin, it is useless to them. The level of glucose in the blood eventually rises so high that the kidney cannot retain it all. Glucose starts to spill out into the urine. This urine is 'sweet' due to its high glucose content. The ancient Greeks noted the sweetness of a diabetic's urine — hence the name 'mellitus', Greek for 'sweet'.

Clinical signs (some or all of the following)
- Increased urine output.
- Frequency of urinating.
- Thirst.
- Hunger.

189

- Weight loss.

Blood and urine tests show abnormal levels of glucose.

Treatment

Supply insulin.

At present the only successful form of replacement is by daily injection of insulin. The amount of insulin required must be constantly monitored. If too much is given it can 'burn' excess glucose, leaving the blood glucose level too low and a 'diabetic coma' can result. The amount of glucose needed is usually determined by daily urine testing. This is extremely difficult to obtain in most cats. If you want to take on treatment for your diabetic cat you will need an excellent working relationship with your vet, a very cooperative cat and a lot of patience and determination. But it can be done.

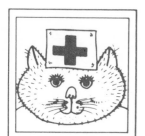

NURSING

LIVER DISEASE (hepatitis)

VET TREATMENT
URGENT

The liver is the powerhouse of the body. It manufactures and stores the basic food units required by the body, manufactures essential vitamins, stores minerals and vitamins, breaks down toxins and poisons and produces digestive enzymes and bile.

Signs

The liver has remarkable reserves of functional tissue, so signs of liver injury may not become apparent until extensive damage has been done. The liver has such a wide range of functions that the clinical signs of liver disease are quite varied. Laboratory tests are usually required to confirm a diagnosis.

Some signs that *could* be associated with liver disease include:
- Vomiting.
- Pain in abdomen, especially on right side under the rib cage.
- Swollen abdomen.
- Diarrhoea (especially a greasy, yellowish stool).
- Listlessness.
- Jaundice (yellowing of the visible mucous membranes, the gums, conjunctiva, lips of vulva).
- Dark coloured urine.

What is hepatitis?

Hepatitis means 'inflamed liver.' There are many causes of hepatitis from poisoning to bacterial or viral infection. In humans, the term 'hepatitis' is commonly understood to mean the infectious viral form. These particular viruses do not affect cats. Nor can humans contract the feline 'hepatitis'.

190

Causes of liver disease (hepatitis)
Include:
- Poisoning.
- Bacterial and viral infection.
- Cirrhosis (scarring of the liver).
- Cancer (often seeded, or 'secondary' tumours).
- Heart disease.
- Fatty infiltration of liver.
- Damage by toxins absorbed from other parts of body, for example the gut.

Diagnosis
Blood, faecal and other tests may be needed before treatment is proceeded with. X-rays may be helpful. Sometimes exploratory surgery is indicated, especially if a tumour or obstruction is suspected.

Treatment
Veterinary treatment is essential. Treatment can be complicated and prolonged. On recovery, it will be essential to provide your cat with a diet that puts the minimum of strain on the liver's resources.

The following diet is called a 'liver protection diet':
1½ cups cottage cheese
½ cup cooked, drained rice
1 large hardboiled egg
2 teaspoons Brewers yeast
3 teaspoons glucose
1 teaspoon maize/corn oil
1 teaspoon potassium chloride (KCL) also called 'No Salt'
2 teaspoons DCP powder
Feed a small amount (1 to 2 tablespoonsful) several times daily.

The major drawback of this diet is that many cats won't eat it. You may have to increase the protein or introduce meat.

If all else fails, feed the cat according to these rules:
- Give a little, often.
- Avoid fats.
- Give lean, white meats (chicken, rabbit, fish) in preference to rich, red meat (beef).
- Give a daily vitamin and mineral supplement.

ANAL SACS AND GLANDS

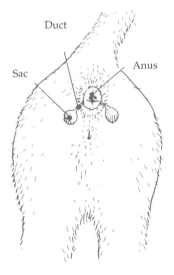

Position of the anal sacs

The cat has two small sacs located one on either side of its anus. These are sometimes called 'scent glands.' They contain an extremely foul smelling secretion. A little of this secretion is expressed onto each bowel motion. Their function is presumably to mark the droppings with the cat's own individual scent. This aids in boundary or territorial marking, or in identifying the presence of a new cat in the area.

Problems occasionally arise if these anal sacs become overfull. This occurs if the duct through which they empty becomes blocked. Secretions then build up within the sac and the subsequent swelling in the sensitive perineal region causes discomfort to the cat.

The secretions within the sacs may become dried up (impacted/inspissated) and therefore difficult or impossible to pass. This is sometimes associated with

191

chronic constipation as the sacs are not emptied regularly. The reverse can also occur if the sacs are swollen and painful, the cat may find it painful to pass faeces, and therefore becomes constipated.

Signs
- Cat licks anxiously under the tail.
- Rubbing bottom along the floor.
- Suddenly turning round to look at the tail (as if pricked by a needle).
- A swelling, redness or a discharge in the area around and beneath the anus.

Treatment
Unless an infection has developed, the sacs may be expressed by manually squeezing them. Your vet will show you how to do this. It is simple enough, but be gentle, and *beware!* The secretions from the anal sacs may be ejected unexpectedly and with considerable velocity. They are extremely foul smelling.

> TAKE
> GREAT
> CARE!

The anal sacs can also become infected, and fill with pus. An abscess may develop causing a painful swelling below and to one side of the anus. These abscesses usually burst, leaving a ragged opening that discharges a little pus or a blood-stained fluid.

If anal sac problems are severe or recurring, your vet may advise surgical removal of the glands. The cat suffers no apparent handicap from their loss.

INTERNAL PARASITES, OR 'WORMS'

There are several types of worms that live in the intestines of cats.

Roundworms, (toxocara cati, toxascaris leonina)
Roundworms are a *very* common parasite of kittens. Adult cats may also be affected.

All kittens should be treated for roundworms.

Roundworms are quite large. They can grow up to 18 cm in length, although they are usually less than half that.

How kittens can become infested with roundworm
- By eating roundworm eggs. These may be present in vast numbers around the nest at birth. There may be large numbers of eggs stuck to the mother's fur and skin, especially around the nipples. The kittens ingest these while suckling. Eggs may also be ingested through contaminated foods, or while the kitten is grooming.
- By ingesting roundworm larvae (the immature form) contained in the queen's first milk, or colostrum. These larvae have been dormant in the mammary glands until stimulated by the hormones of late pregnancy to continue their development and to be released when the kittens begin to suckle.

How adult cats can become infested with roundworm
Adults can be infested when they eat food contaminated with the sticky roundworm eggs, or when they eat prey such as mice, birds and some insects. These are called 'intermediate hosts'. These intermediate hosts have swallowed roundworm eggs, which then encyst within their body and so remain potent until the cat preys upon them.

192

Massive numbers of roundworm can build up in the intestine, especially in a young kitten. This can seriously damage their health

Each worm can grow up to 10 cm long. Each female could lay 200,000 eggs every day

The eggs are passed in the droppings.

The eggs develop into larvae which migrate via the liver and lungs to eventually arrive in the intestine. Final development into an egg-laying adult then occurs

The eggs develop to the infectious stage. They can remain infectious for many months.

The cat picks up eggs while grooming or by eating contaminated food. Kittens pick up eggs when suckling

The roundworm life cycle

What harm do roundworms do?

In small numbers they cause little harm. Larger numbers can cause irritation and thickening of the gut wall, which interferes with proper digestion and absorption of food. Intermittent diarrhoea may result. Kittens fail to thrive and may develop a distended pot belly.

The larvae of one of the roundworms (T. Cati) migrates through the liver and lungs as part of the life cycle. If sufficient numbers of larvae are involved, significant damage can be inflicted on the liver and lungs.

Diagnosis

Because roundworm is so common in kittens, many vets recommend the routine worming of all kittens without necessarily getting a positive diagnosis of infestation first.

If a diagnosis is required, a laboratory examination of the cat's faeces will detect microscopic roundworm eggs, *if* the kitten has egg-laying adults in its intestine. It takes about two months for an egg to develop into a mature egg-laying adult worm. Young kittens could therefore have a heavy burden of immature worms without having eggs in their droppings. So *beware!* A 'negative' faecal test does not necessarily mean that the kitten does not have worms.

Treatment

Kittens: Start as early as four to six weeks of age. Treat every two to four weeks until five months old and then every six to eight weeks until twelve months old.

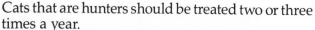

Adults: Cats that are hunters should be treated two or three times a year.

Pregnant queens should be treated at least once in the last three weeks of their pregnancy. For effective drugs, check the list at the end of the chapter. Ask your vet first for one he/she recommends, especially if you are using it for a pregnant queen or for young kittens.

A health warning: young pups are more dangerous as a source of roundworm than kittens. Nevertheless — be sure to worm your kitten regularly.

Children could pick up roundworm eggs, especially when stroking young kittens or a recently queened female. These eggs can also be picked up from sandpits or garden areas where cats defaecate. Finger-sucking toddlers are especially at risk. These roundworm eggs may develop into larvae that can migrate through the intestine and into organs such as the liver where they can cause serious damage. It is possible for them to reach and injure the eye and brain. The larvae never develop into adult worms, so — contrary to common belief — children do not develop worms from cats (or dogs).

TRANSMITTED TO HUMANS

Preventive measures
- Treat your cat for roundworm.
- Be certain children wash their hands after handling kittens or queen; *or* don't allow them to play with the kittens at all.
- Sandpits should be covered when not in use to prevent them from becoming toilet areas for cats.

Hookworms (ancylostoma spp, uncinaria spp)
These are only small worms — one or two centimetres long — but they can cause serious damage to the cat's delicate intestinal lining. Some are blood suckers. Others feed on the intestine's surface.

Ancylostoma species, found mainly in summer rainfall areas, are vigorous blood suckers.

Uncinaria species, found mainly in winter rainfall areas, are milder in their effects although heavy infestations are debilitating and cause intestinal upsets.

How does a cat become infested with hookworm?
There are several ways:
- In a moist, unhygienic environment, the hookworm larvae burrow into the skin, migrate to the blood vessels and are swept into the lungs. After moving into the bronchi they are coughed up, then swallowed. The larvae mature into adults and take up residence in the cat's small intestine.
- Eating food contaminated with larvae.
- Infection can occur even before the kitten is born, although this is very rare. The larvae migrate into the uterus to infect the unborn kitten.

Signs
- Diarrhoea. Mainly dark, loose, may be bloody.
- Weight loss.
- General ill health, including poor coat, listlessness.
- Dermatitis due to invasion of larvae through skin.

Many cats show no clinical signs at all. A routine faecal examination annually at vaccination time will enable treatment where necessary.

These signs vary in degree according to the age and condition of the cat and with the number of worms parasitising it.

194

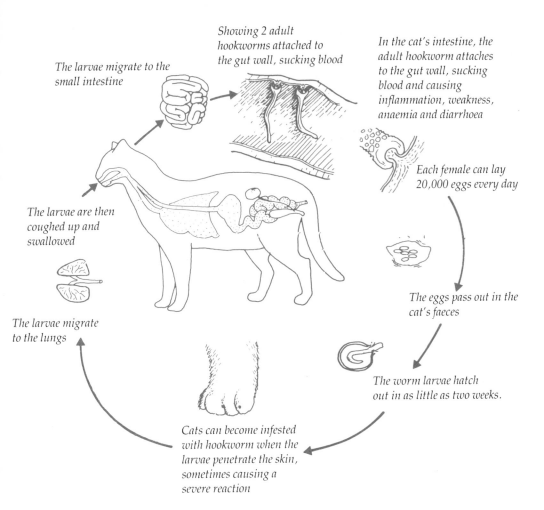

The larvae migrate to the small intestine

Showing 2 adult hookworms attached to the gut wall, sucking blood

In the cat's intestine, the adult hookworm attaches to the gut wall, sucking blood and causing inflammation, weakness, anaemia and diarrhoea

The larvae are then coughed up and swallowed

Each female can lay 20,000 eggs every day

The larvae migrate to the lungs

The eggs pass out in the cat's faeces

The worm larvae hatch out in as little as two weeks.

Cats can become infested with hookworm when the larvae penetrate the skin, sometimes causing a severe reaction

Hookworm life cycle

Diagnosis

Your vet will examine a sample of faeces for the presence of distinctive hookworm eggs.

Treatment

It is not sufficient merely to kill the worms in the cat's bowel. You must also prevent re-infestation. With all those hookworm eggs already in the ground, this requires a plan to counter the probability of a new build up of hookworm.

If the cat has already been affected severely, feed good quality food and include a reliable iron, vitamin and mineral supplement to help counter the anaemia caused by the hookworm.

Kittens:	Where hookworm is a problem, treatment can commence as early as four to six weeks of age. If the kittens have been diagnosed as having hookworm, initially treatment is required every three weeks for a minimum of three doses. In kittens over three months, treatment every three months is sufficient to keep the numbers down.
Adults:	Initially, treat three times at intervals of twenty-one days. Adult cats usually develop a good immunity to re-infestation with hookworm, so treatment once every summer is adequate as a routine.

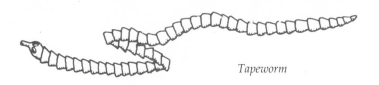

Tapeworm

Drugs to use
Check the chart at the end of this chapter. Always read the label carefully before use. Some preparations that are suitable for dogs are toxic for cats.

Tapeworms
There are many different types of tapeworm. All consist of a head, which attaches to the wall of the intestine, and a body composed of segments that look like many barrels stacked end to end. The hindmost segments contain many thousands of eggs and these are intermittently shed in the cat's faeces.

Some tapeworm reach sizes of over a metre in length but most are only a few centimetres long. Surprisingly, perhaps, tapeworm usually cause very little trouble except in old or debilitated cats. In an otherwise healthy cat, the tapeworm is tolerated well.

Occasionally tapeworm can cause a mild bowel upset, with diarrhoea or constipation. The tapeworm segments pass out of the anus where they may stick to the hairs around the anus resulting in an itchy bottom. In these cases, the cat may vigorously lick under its tail. Look for dried tapeworm segments. They resemble flattened dried up grains of rice.

How do cats become infected with tapeworm?
Tapeworm are not passed directly from cat to cat. To complete the life cycle, the egg must be eaten by an 'intermediate host' such as a flea, bird, mouse or rat. Further development takes place within this intermediate host. When a cat subsequently eats the intermediate host, the cycle is completed. The worm develops into an adult in the cat's intestine.

Diagnosis
Look for segments in the cat's faeces or attached to the hair around the anus.
As fleas are a source of re-infestation, flea control is important.

Are cat tapeworm dangerous to humans?
No. It is the dog hydatid tapeworm that is a human health hazard.

COCCIDIOSIS

Coccidia are microscopic parasites of the cat's bowel. Small numbers can be present without causing the cat any inconvenience. In the occasional case, significant numbers are present and a chronic diarrhoea may develop, resulting in weight loss and lack of condition. This is most likely to occur in kittens kept in crowded conditions on wet bedding — for example, in some pet shops.

Diagnosis
By laboratory examination of faecal samples.

196

Treatment
Response to treatment with sulphonamides is usually good. Your vet will pre-
scribe the correct dose.
The environment must be cleaned, disinfected and dried.
Disinfection can be achieved with sodium hydroxide, ammonia or other al-
kaline disinfectants.

DRUG		DOSE RATE	COMMENT
ROUNDWORM	Diethycarbamazine	50 mg/kg	Usually used at 5.5mg/kg for prevention of heartworm.
	Mebendazole	16-32 mg/kg	Should be given daily for three consecutive days.
	Nitroscanate	50 mg/kg	Fast for twelve hours, then give with food. Can cause vomiting.
	Piperazine	80-100 mg/kg	Many preparations available.
	Pyrantel	5 mg/kg	Available as chocolate-flavoured syrup or tablets.
HOOKWORM	Disophenol	10 mg/kg	Specific hookworm treatment.
	Mebendazole	16-32 mg/kg	Should be given daily for three consecutive days.
	Nitroscanate	50 mg/kg	Fast for twelve hours, then give with food. Can cause vomiting.
	Pyrantel	5 mg/kg	Available as chocolate-flavoured syrup or tablets.
	Thenium	10-35 mg/kg	
TAPEWORM	Praziquantel	2.5 mg/kg	Very safe and very effective.
	Bunamidine	50 mg/kg	Sugar coated tablets, don't crush tablets, take care not to get any in eye.

Kidney and Bladder

LE TOILET

THE KIDNEYS: *what they do*

The cat has two kidneys. Their function is to filter the blood and remove wastes. The by-products of normal body metabolism are potentially toxic, and must be constantly flushed from the body. If the kidneys fail, the resulting build-up of toxic wastes has a serious and ultimately fatal effect.

CHRONIC KIDNEY DISEASE

This is the most common condition to threaten the health of the ageing cat. Early recognition of warning signs can allow you to take measures that will prolong kidney function. This helps to keep your cat comfortable for months or even years longer than would be the case if the condition was not recognised and checked.

Signs
Signs do not start until about two-thirds of both kidneys are non-functional. Even though the kidneys have deteriorated only gradually over months or even years, the signs of disease often appear suddenly.
   Signs may include some of the following:
   - Increased thirst.
   - Increased urine production — the cat may start urinating during the night.
   - Appetite may increase or decrease — usually it decreases, because the cat is feeling ill.
   - Listlessness — physical and mental depression.
   - The coat becomes rough and unkempt.

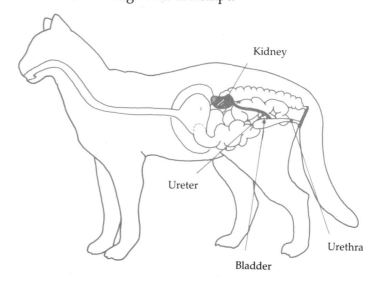

- Weight loss — this is usually insidious and often is not noticed until quite a lot of condition is lost.
  - Bad breath.
  - Mouth ulcers.
  - Vomiting and loose, often dark coloured faeces.
  - Joint and muscle pain and stiffness (not very common).

Why do these signs occur? What is happening?
As the kidney gradually deteriorates it becomes less efficient. It can no longer extract all the normal by-products and wastes of daily body metabolism from the bloodstream. In order to flush out these potential poisons, the cat must produce greater quantities of dilute urine. This means a loss of body fluids so the cat drinks more to compensate. For this reason one of the first signs of kidney disease is usually an increased thirst.

Drinking more helps only for a while, but gradually the toxic wastes build up. The body tries to expel them through other routes such as in the saliva or through the bowel wall. One of these waste products is urea, which is produced when protein is digested. When large amounts of urea are present in the saliva, the oral bacteria react with it to produce ammonia which can result in bad breath. Ammonia is an irritant and could also cause mouth ulcers.

Increased blood levels of urea and other wastes can cause loss of appetite, nausea, vomiting and listlessness. Anaemia may develop because of toxic depression of the bone marrow, meaning that fewer red blood cells are produced.

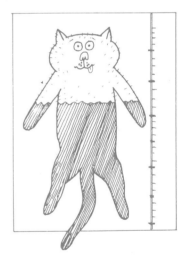

Toxic wastes gradually build up

Other changes take place in the bloodstream. There are disturbances in the levels of the vital body salts (sodium, potassium, calcium and others). When the kidney is healthy it maintains an exact and delicate balance of these salts. The damaged kidney cannot. As calcium is lost, replacement calcium is leached from the bones, gradually rendering them softer and weaker. If this process is prolonged, some cats develop lameness or could even fracture bones as they become increasingly fragile.

Diagnosis
The signs and history are suggestive, but your vet may want to do tests to confirm a tentative diagnosis. Urine tests are useful, but it is often hard to get a sample from a cat. Blood tests are usually taken. One useful test is to measure the level

of a waste product, such as urea, in the blood. There is normally *some* urea in the bloodstream, but if the kidney is failing this level rises and so gives your vet some idea of how much kidney function remains, and therefore what the prognosis for the cat is.

Treatment
Initial treatment by your vet may include:
- Antibiotics — to control any infection present.
- Vitamins — to overcome deficiencies and to help in tissue repair.
- Anabolic steroids — to help stop tissue breakdown.
- Fluids — at critical times these may be injected intravenously or under the skin.
- Peritoneal dialysis — this is a technique for removing wastes from the body. In humans, sophisticated machines are used to extract wastes from the bloodstream, but this is not feasible in the cat.

After the cat comes home you will have to follow up the treatment with good nursing and careful feeding.

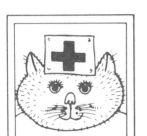
NURSING

Diet
The most important part of home treatment is a correct diet. The aim of this diet is to reduce the amount of protein fed as this reduces the amount of wastes formed. Unfortunately, many cats will refuse any dietary change.

In all cases of kidney failure you should feed *little* and *often* instead of giving one or two relatively large meals daily. This spreads the 'workload' of the kidney.

In some countries a commercially produced low protein diet is available for cats with kidney disease. If this is not available the following diet may be acceptable. This diet is high in energy to reduce the cat's need to break down protein.

Example of a restricted protein diet (14% protein):
>2 cups cooked rice
>1 cooked egg
>30 gm liver
>2 teaspoons maize oil
>½ teaspoon $CaCo_3$
>½ teaspoon iodised salt
>*Yield* 500 gm
>2 kg cat — 170 gm/daily
>5 kg cat — 350 gm/daily

This diet will be unpalatable to many cats. You may have to raise the protein content until it is acceptable — add some lean meat — preferably 'white' meat such as chicken or fish. Avoid rich red meats.

Vitamin and mineral supplements should be given daily — especially the B group vitamins and vitamins A and C. Multi-vitamin/mineral supplements help to overcome deficiencies and excess losses, and are also helpful in tissue maintenance and repair, and in stimulating appetite. Calcium, vitamin B complex and vitamin C supplements are particularly indicated. (Brewer's yeast is an excellent source of B vitamins.)

Other home care
Table salt should be added to the diet. This replaces the excessive amounts of sodium lost in the urine and it also encourages drinking. Sodium bicarbonate (bicarbonate of soda) can be used instead of salt. Add a total of about one quarter of a teaspoon daily in small amounts at a time.

Free access to clean water should always be allowed. Milk is not enough.

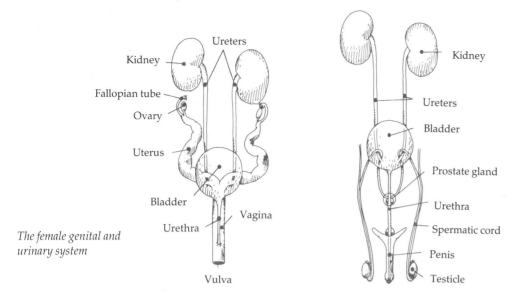

The female genital and urinary system

The male genital and urinary system

Warmth, avoiding stress (even just moving the furniture around can stress some cats) and tender loving care can make a big difference to the outcome of treatment. Try lots of it.

ACUTE KIDNEY DISEASE

Acute (sudden) kidney disease is not as common as the chronic form, and affects mainly younger cats (one to five years old).

Causes
Some possible causes include:
- Bacterial or viral infection.
- Toxic injury, including ethylene glycol (anti-freeze), carbon tetrachloride, lead, thallium, arsenic, tetrachloroethylene, drugs (some antibiotics), mercury.
- Shock: the blood supply to the kidney may be drastically affected in shock states, for example after a car accident. Kidney damage occurs due to oxygen lack.
- *Snakebite from a poisonous snake
- *Severe injury to other parts of the body or major surgery.
*In these states damaged blood cells and other debris and waste in the bloodstream can be trapped in the kidney and clog it up.
- Accidents (such as motor car accident) causing bruising or rupture of the kidney.

Signs
Some or all of the following:
- Loss of appetite.
- Abdominal pain, especially in the mid-back area.
- Increased or decreased thirst or apparent attraction to water. The cat may stand over the water bowl without actually drinking.
- Increased or decreased urine output (despite increased thirst).
- Vomiting.
- Dehydration.
- Urine changes — often has a strong smell, may contain blood or pus.

Treatment
If treatment is commenced early the damage can often be restricted. A return to

efficient function is possible in many cases. Treatment may include:
- Fluids — may be given intravenously, under the skin or orally.
- Antibiotics (if bacteria are involved).
- Vitamins, especially B group and C.
- Antiemetics — to stop vomiting and reduce fluid loss.

Diet
Your vet will prescribe a diet to follow while the kidneys heal, probably one similar to that given for chronic kidney disease.

SOME OTHER KIDNEY CONDITIONS

Glomerulonephritis
This term is mainly a technical distinction indicating that a particular part of the kidney — the glomerulus — is attacked first. The cause of many of these cases is linked to disturbances in the cat's immune system.

Ectopic ureter
A rare condition in the cat. It occurs only in females. The ureter (the tube that carries urine from the kidney to the bladder) does not empty into the bladder but instead by-passes it and empties into the vagina. As a result the cat constantly dribbles urine. The defect is present from birth. Treatment, if contemplated, is surgical. This surgery is difficult.

Cancer of the kidneys
The kidney is a relatively common site for 'secondary' tumours to grow. The parent or 'primary' tumour grows in another part of the body. Malignant cells bud off from the primary tumour and spread to other parts of the body, usually via the bloodstream, to grow in organs such as the lungs, liver or kidney.

Most of these tumours cause severe damage and the outlook for the cat is grave.

Cystitis
The bladder is a distendable muscular sack or reservoir used to store the urine formed by the kidneys until the cat is ready to eliminate it. Although the bladder is a relatively simple structure, things can go wrong. When they do, the result is often acutely uncomfortable.

Cystitis, meaning inflammation of the bladder wall, is a relatively common condition in the cat and one that can cause great irritation and distress.

Causes
Many cases of cystitis are associated with the formation of a coarse, sand-like deposit. This is explained in the next section (FUS).

Bacterial infection is probably the most common cause of cystitis. Some bacteria are normally present in urine but do not cause problems under normal circumstances. It is when these bacteria are able to multiply, or if particularly pathogenic bacteria gain entry, that cystitis flares up.

The factors that favour bacterial cystitis include:
- Urine stagnation: an important feature of the bladder's defense system is that it empties almost completely. Cats should urinate three or more times daily,

literally flushing out bacteria and wastes before they have time to do any damage. If the cat cannot (or will not) empty its bladder regularly then bacteria have a much better chance of multiplying to gain a foothold. Such a situation could occur if the cat does not get out to empty its bladder. For example the cat may be reluctant to go outside if it is raining or too cold. Or there may be a partial obstruction of the bladder or perhaps a disturbance of bladder function, for example due to spinal injury.

- Physical irritation of bladder wall from bladder stones.
- Irritation due to the bladder worm (these worms only rarely cause problems).

Signs

The first sign is usually that your cat begins to urinate more often, sometimes in unusual places such as in the bath or sink. Only small quantities of urine are passed at each attempt. As the condition develops, the cat spends more and more time squatting and straining, perhaps scratching at the ground, twitching its tail and looking around anxiously. The urine is sometimes bloodstained and may have a strong, offensive odour. The staining can easily be mistaken for a sign of constipation. Many owners waste valuable time treating these cats with oil or purgatives.

Most cats remain fairly bright and continue to eat. Most drink more.

Sometimes the cat does become listless and ill and may vomit and run a fever.

Treatment

Your vet will decide on the treatment according to the individual case. Treatment includes:

- Antibiotics if infection is present or suspected.
- Urine acidifiers to reduce new stone formation and suppress bacterial growth.
- Changes to the cat's routine. There are two aims:

VET TREATMENT
URGENT

1. Get your cat to urinate as often as possible; allow free access to toilet area. If it uses a litter tray, keep it clean. Some cats are so fastidious they will not use it once it is too soiled.

If the cat uses an outside toilet area make sure it goes out at least three times daily. In some cases you may have to pick it up physically and put it out.

Encourage exercise, as this in turn encourages bladder emptying.

2. Prevent the urine from becoming too concentrated. Encourage drinking, always allow free access to fresh water. Add salt to the food daily (an eighth to one quarter teaspoon daily). If your cat likes milk, then water it down before you give it. Feed sloppy foods as *part* of the diet. Avoid dry foods. These play a significant role in producing concentrated urine. Some dry foods are high in magnesium and should be avoided for this reason also (see FUS).

BLADDER STONES: THE FELINE UROLITHIASIS SYNDROME (FUS)

It is a source of amazement to many that 'stones' can actually grow in the bladder and kidney. These stones may only be small specks of crystal but in some cases can become very large — the size of a plum stone or even the plum itself.

There are many different types of bladder and kidney stones. Their cause, the type of damage produced and the correct treatment, varies with their different composition and positions. In man, kidney stones are the most common type. These cause intense pain if they are passed through the ureter (the narrow, sensitive tube joining the kidney to the bladder).

In the cat, by far the more common site is the bladder. Usually a sludge of a sand-like precipitate forms rather than a discrete 'stone'. This sand irritates the bladder wall, causing cystitis. In male cats it can cause a blockage of the bladder if it builds up to plug the urethra (see diagram below). Because the urethra of the female cat is relatively much wider it is less liable to become blocked.

Signs of FUS

First sign: (where there is cystitis and maybe a partial bladder block)
- Cat spends a lot of time in one spot, often the litter tray or a favourite toilet area.
- Straining (could be mistaken for constipation).
- Twitching tail.
- Licking penis or area under tail.

Later signs: (these develop if the bladder becomes completely blocked and the cat is unable to urinate)
- Penis may be protruded, swollen and red or congested with blood, turning it a blue or blackish colour.
- Tense, painful abdomen. Cat may have difficulty walking.
- Dark, blood-tinged urine may be passed in small amounts.
- Cat becomes listless, physically and mentally depressed.
- Loss of appetite.
- Vomiting.
- Howling in pain.

It is easy to misdiagnose your cat's condition as constipation, and many owners waste valuable time giving oil or laxatives. This delay reduces the chances of a favourable outcome.

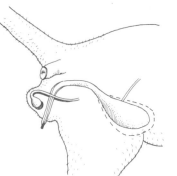

The penis can become blocked by a plug of precipitate (struvite)

A blocked bladder is an emergency. The cat will die without treatment.

Perineal urethrostomy: This operation results in the elimination of the narrowest part of the urethra, where blockages usually occur

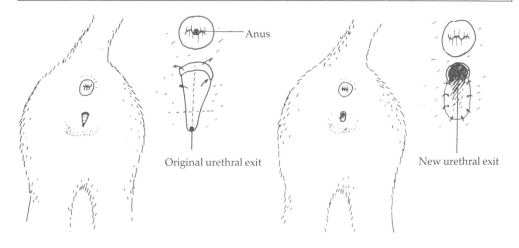

Anus

Original urethral exit

New urethral exit

(A) Before surgery. The penis is blocked. During surgery the tip is removed, the rest opened and folded back.

(B) After surgery. The penis has been partly amputated and partly opened up. The new exit for urine is higher up, much wider and less liable to blockage.

Treatment of a blocked bladder

The vet must relieve the obstruction and re-establish the free passage of urine. This usually requires the administration of a general anaesthetic and the passage of a fine tube (a catheter) into the bladder. This can be difficult. In severe or recurring cases your vet may advise a surgical procedure to eliminate the dangerous bottleneck in the penis where blockages usually occur. The most common procedure is called a perineal urethrostomy.

In our experience, the outlook after surgery is usually excellent.

Preventing FUS or the formation of stones

If any infection is present it will have to be eliminated, usually through antibiotics. Drugs that acidify the urine are useful in some cases. The main preventive measures concern the cat's diet.

The primary aim is to prevent the formation of concentrated urine and to prevent urine retention. Eliminating dry foods from the diet of cats suffering from FUS is a high priority.

In the majority of cases the substances precipitated in the bladder and urethra is a complex called struvite, an important element of which is magnesium. Research shows that diets high in magnesium are more likely to produce struvite formation. It follows that you should avoid giving cats that have a history of struvite formation diets high in magnesium.

Foods high in magnesium	Moderately high	Low
Beef	Rabbit	Milk
Heart	Potatoes	Tripe
Pork	Omelette	Bacon
Cod	Scrambled egg	Carrots
Herring	Roast chicken	Luncheon meat
Kippers		Cream cheese
Pilchards		Butter
Sardines		Dripping

Other measures to take

Encourage a high water intake

This is not always possible but try the following measures:
- Allow free access to clean water.
- If the cat drinks milk, water it down.
- Add liquids to the cat's food, either as straight water or in the form of gravies.
- Add some table salt daily to the cat's rations. About a quarter teaspoon daily is usually effective in increasing the cat's thirst.

Encourage the cat to pass urine frequently
- Allow free access to litter tray or an outside toilet area.
- Encourage exercise. This may mean physically putting the cat out at least three times daily or playing games that get the cat moving about.

Urine acidifiers may help

In some cases, using drugs (such as methionine) that increase the acidity of urine will slow the formation of new stones and may even dissolve those already formed. They are more effective if they are not given continually; a short course every few weeks is often more effective.

THE BLADDER WORM (cappilaria feliscati)

The bladder worm is quite common in some areas. It is a very fragile, thread-like worm measuring 1-6 cms long. It is difficult to see with the naked eye. Most infestations cause no problem, although in rare cases the worms may irritate the bladder wall enough to produce cystitis. Treatment is usually unnecessary.

URINARY INCONTINENCE (dribbling)

This is not a common problem in the cat.

Possible causes
- Inborn abnormality (see ectopic ureter, page 202).
- As a sequel to persistent bouts of FUS or chronic cystitis.
- Loss of nervous control, due to spinal damage or after trauma such as a car accident.
- An hormonal imbalance (in females).

Signs
The cat either constantly drips small amounts of urine or occasionally unconsciously passes urine, often during sleep or when lying resting.

Treatment
The treatment depends on the cause. Urine incontinence is always a case for your vet, not for home treatment. If urinary incontinence persists there is a high risk of bacterial infection spreading up into the bladder.

HEART AND LUNGS

THE HEART

The heart is a pump. It is composed of specialised muscle that expands and contracts unceasingly, tirelessly, throughout the cat's life. The heart must keep the blood constantly circulating throughout the body, supplying oxygen and nutrients and removing wastes, warming or cooling, keeping the body in harmony.

Heart disease in cats is not common especially in comparison with the incidence in humans.

The normal heart rate for cats is fast: 100 to 240 beats per minute. The cat's heartbeat can be felt by placing your fingers in the left side of the chest, just behind and above the elbow. With each heartbeat a pulse of blood can be felt in the major arteries. The most convenient artery to feel for in the cat is located centrally inside the back leg, in the groin area.

HEART FAILURE AND DISEASE

If the heart fails to perform effectively then the blood is not circulated efficiently and the entire body is affected. The clinical signs of heart failure are a result of this poor blood flow. When the heart is working ineffectively blood banks up in the cat's veins, waiting to be pumped through. Because the walls of veins are not completely waterproof, fluid (plasma) gradually leaks out into the surrounding area. The parts of the body that are most affected could be the lungs or the abdominal organs. It depends on which side of the heart is diseased. If it is mainly the left side, then the lungs become congested with fluid. If the right side of the heart is not functioning then fluid pools in the abdomen giving the cat a 'pot bellied' appearance.

When the lungs become congested some of the fluid pools in the air pas-

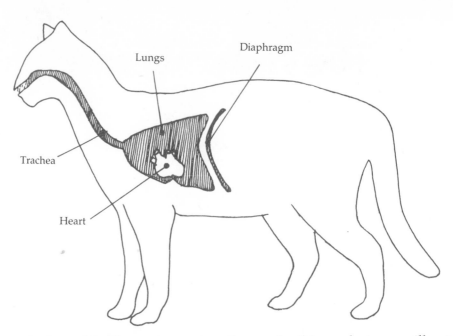

Lungs

Diaphragm

Trachea

Heart

sages (the bronchi). The cat intermittently coughs this up, but you will not see it as the cat immediately swallows it. This type of cough is typically a deep moist cough with a 'tinny' sound. It is termed a 'cardiac cough'.

Causes of heart disease

The exact cause for each individual patient is often not determined. Some of the possible causes include:

- Heart muscle deterioration, with fibrosis or scarring of the heart muscle ('cardiomyopathy'). This can occur even in young cats.
- Deterioration in the circulation in the heart muscle itself.
- Heart valve disease. (The major chambers of the heart are closed off by valves. If these valves become leaky, due perhaps to growths on their surfaces, the heart becomes inefficient.)
- Infections by bacteria or virus that damage the heart's muscular walls or the surrounding sac (pericardium).
- Congenital malformations of the heart or the large blood vessels.
- Trauma to chest.
- Tumours involving heart or structures near the heart.

Warning signs of heart failure

Coughing

Be suspicious of a deep, moist and resonant cough, particularly in an old cat. At first the 'heart cough' is especially notable in the early morning, or when the cat gets up from a rest and starts to move about. Later, the cough becomes more persistent. The cat will then cough intermittently throughout the day.

Exercise tolerance

The cat with heart disease tires easily and is reluctant to exercise, spending most of the day sleeping. If forced into activity, these cats will start to breathe very rapidly and may become breathless.

Restlessness at night

Some heart patients just can't seem to get comfortable at night. They are restless and seem to be 'on edge'. This is due to the discomfort of congested lungs or a tight, fluid-filled abdomen.

Exercise intolerance can be an early warning sign

208

Other signs may include
- Pale or bluish-coloured gums (lift the upper lip back to inspect the gums).
- Difficulty breathing or rapid breathing.
- As the cat's condition deteriorates the cat may have episodes of open mouthed gasping.
- Fainting spells.

What treatment is possible?
Heart conditions in cats often carry a poor prognosis.

It is usually not possible to cure the condition but it may be possible to control it.

Treatment is usually limited to drug therapy to improve the heart's performance plus good nursing to reduce the workload on the heart. This can be very effective in many cases. Techniques of heart surgery are advancing dramatically in sophistication and success rate.

In veterinary medicine the amount of heart surgery possible is limited by technical and financial constraints, but could be considered in selected cases.

Drug therapy for cats with heart disease
Excessive fluid build up may be relieved with drugs such as frusemide and other 'diuretics'. These must be used only under veterinary supervision.

The performance of the heart muscle can be improved by certain drugs for example, digoxin, propranolol and the theophyline-like drugs. The selection and dose rates of these drugs must be tailored individually to each case. You should establish a good working relationship with your vet. Ask for an explanation of the actions of any drug prescribed so that you will know when alterations in treatment might be indicated. Owners are usually very good at noting small changes in their cat's condition.

Good nursing
Rest is essential. The cat will usually look after this aspect of treatment quite satisfactorily. You can help by avoiding stress situations which could make the cat anxious or tense. These stresses include things *you* may not think of as stressful. For example, putting the cat outside at night may be stressful if there are other cats about (especially toms). They might threaten your cat. Other stress situations are more obvious. Don't let the dog or young children romp around or tease him. And this is certainly *not* the time to acquire a new pet in an attempt to 'cheer him up'. Such an invader of the cat's domain is likely to make his condition far worse, not better.

NURSING

Feeding the cat suffering from heart disease
The role of diet in the treatment of heart failure is not so critical as in man, but you should restrict salt as much as you can. (*Note:* if your cat also has kidney disease then talk to your vet about how much salt is advisable, as *some* is essential.) Most commercial foods are high in salt because it helps to make them palatable. In some countries, specially prepared low salt cat foods are available for cats with heart disease. Where this is not available you will have to cut down salt by giving more home cooked or fresh foods and less commercially prepared foods.

Foods which are low in salt include:
- Freshwater fish.
- Chicken (without skin), rabbit, beef, lamb, horsemeat.
- Egg yolk.
- Rice, macaroni, spaghetti.
- Unsalted butter.

Foods which are high in salt and which should be avoided include:
- Cheese and other dairy foods.
- Processed meats (including meat blocks, sausage, ham, bacon).
- Most tinned cat foods.
- Heart, kidney and liver.
- Shellfish.

HEARTWORM DISEASE

Heartworm are worms that live in the cat's heart and the great blood vessels near the heart. Heartworm is primarily a disease of dogs and is considered rare in cats. Infections may occur, especially under hot and humid conditions.

Lifecycle of heartworm
Heartworm is mainly a disease of hot or tropical areas but it is spreading. Ask your own vet for the current situation in your area.

Signs
The following signs may be present in heartworm disease. They also occur in other conditions, so they are only an indication of possible heartworm:
- A cough; usually chronic, persistent.
- Listlessness or lack of stamina.
- Weight loss (gradual).
- Fluid build-up in the abdomen.

Specific tests
Your vet can take blood samples to detect the presence of heartworm. X-rays could be useful as there are changes in the size and shape of the heart, especially in chronic cases.

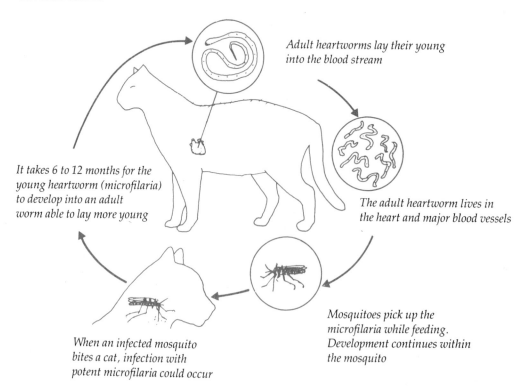

Adult heartworms lay their young into the blood stream

It takes 6 to 12 months for the young heartworm (microfilaria) to develop into an adult worm able to lay more young

The adult heartworm lives in the heart and major blood vessels

Mosquitoes pick up the microfilaria while feeding. Development continues within the mosquito

When an infected mosquito bites a cat, infection with potent microfilaria could occur

Heartworm life cycle

210

Treatment
Once the cat has adult heartworms living in the heart, treatment involves getting them out. This can be difficult. The worms can be killed readily enough by injecting the cat with a drug such as sodium caparsolate, but the problem is that the dead worms can then be swept into organs such as the lungs where extensive damage, even death, could result. Some vets favour surgery to remove the worms physically. Whatever the treatment, veterinary supervision is essential. *Do not* attempt home treatment. *Do not* give the preventive drug DEC (see later) if you suspect your cat already has heartworm.

Preventing heartworm infection
The cat is much less susceptible to heartworm infection than the dog. Routine preventive measures may not be necessary. Ask your vet for his opinion.

If you live in a 'heartworm area' and preventive treatment *is* decided on there are two approaches to consider:

1. Preventing infection by eliminating mosquito bites. If the cat can be protected from mosquitoes, preventive drugs may not be necessary. The cat should be kept inside, especially at dusk when mosquitoes are most active. You cannot rely on insecticide powders, rinses or collars to repel mosquitoes, although these can help.

Where it is not feasible or desirable to keep the cat inside, the second alternative is:

2. Drug therapy: a daily dosage of DEC (diethylcarbamazine citrate) at a dose of 6.25 mg per kg of the cat's body weight is a current preventive treatment. DEC is available as a syrup or palatable tablet. When DEC is given daily, the heartworm larvae, or *microfilaria*, that are injected into the cat by carrier mosquitoes cannot develop into the harmful adult stage.

THE LUNGS

The lungs occupy most of the chest. They are supported and protected by the ribs. The heart nestles between the lungs. Some of the descriptive terms used in dealing with lung conditions can be confusing, so you may find the diagrams helpful.

LUNG DISEASE

The cat has a remarkable capacity to compensate if part of the lungs are damaged. This can mean that there are very few signs of lung disease until the condition has reached an advanced stage where most of the cat's lung tissue is affected. By the time the cat shows obvious signs of distress, successful treatment could be very difficult.

Signs
A cat showing some of the following signs could have a lung or bronchial condition:
- Rapid breathing: over thirty breaths per minute is abnormal, unless the cat is very excited or hot.
- Difficult or painful breathing: this can be signalled by a hunched appearance. The cat typically crouches down with the elbows held out and away from the chest.
- Panting, or breathing with the mouth open: while dogs pant to lose heat,

cats don't. Open-mouthed breathing usually indicates that the cat is very distressed perhaps due to being very hot or terrified or because of serious lung disease.

● Pale or bluish-coloured gums: lift the cat's lips back to expose the gums. The gums should be a healthy pink colour. When the gums have a bluish tinge (termed cyanosis) it means the blood is not getting enough oxygen. When the gums are very pale it may mean anaemia or shock. When the gums are very dark, even blackish, this is usually due only to excessive pigment (skin colouring) and is not a cause for concern.

● Coughing: the character of the cough can be significant. A low pitched, moist, resonant cough is more likely to be from the chest, while a high pitched, dry, shallow cough is usually from the upper areas of the respiratory tract, for example the larynx or throat.

● Other abnormal breathing sounds: such as snuffling, snorting, bubbling, honking or wheezing.

● Other, less specific signs, could include: discharge from the nose, loss of appetite, a reluctance to get up and move about, fever, general malaise.

PNEUMONIA

Pneumonia means inflammation of the lungs. The most common cause is infection by bacteria or virus. These bacteria can be inhaled in droplet form from direct contact with another infected cat, or can come via the bloodstream or from a penetrating chest wound.

Parasitic invasion, such as by lungworm or roundworm larvae can also lead to pneumonia.

NURSING

Treatment
The treatment depends on the cause. If bacteria are involved, antibiotics are usually indicated. Viral infections have to run their course, although because they are frequently complicated by a 'secondary' bacterial infection, antibiotics may be used here also.

Rest is essential. This reduces the stress on the lungs. It may be necessary to confine the cat to a cage or to a small room, thereby forcing it to rest. This is termed 'cage rest' and is the equivalent of human 'bed rest'.

In acute cases, oxygen may be given, but this requires special facilities. Good nursing is essential. This includes good feeding, ensuring warmth and rest, proper medication plus lots of loving care. Pneumonia is a serious illness and effective nursing can make the difference between recovery and failure.

OTHER TYPES OF PNEUMONIA

Lungworm (caused by the parasite aelurostrongylus abstrusus)
Lungworm is a parasite which is widespread and found in most places including Europe, USA and Australia.

Infection occurs when the cat eats prey that is infested with lungworm larvae. Such prey may include snails, frogs, slugs, birds, reptiles or rodents.

The main sign of lungworm infection is a cough. This cough is especially severe in the early stages of infection because the young lungworms are relatively active and move around in the lungs thereby causing a great deal of irritation. The cough gradually becomes less frequent, but deeper and more resonant. If the infestation is severe, the cat's general weight and condition will deteriorate. Other signs can include a nasal discharge, sneezing and sometimes diarrhoea.

212

Diagnosis
Diagnosis is made by a laboratory examination of the cat's faeces to detect lung-worm eggs or larvae. Sometimes a procedure termed a 'tracheal wash' is performed. In this test, a small amount of fluid is injected directly into the cat's windpipe (the trachea), sucked out again, then examined for lungworm eggs or larvae.

Treatment
Drugs used include levamisole and fenbendazole. These should be used under veterinary supervision as they can be toxic, so correct dose rates are important.

Lung fluke (cause: paragonimus spp.)
Lung fluke is an infestation seen in some parts of the USA and South Africa.

Infection occurs when the cat eats raw crabs or crayfish. The severity depends on the number of fluke ingested. The main sign is a cough. The cat may bring up a rust-coloured (bloody) sputum. More serious damage occurs if the brain and spinal cord are invaded. The signs depend on what area of the brain is affected but could include a head tilt, or convulsions and fits.

Diagnosis
Microscopic examination of the cat sputum or faeces will reveal characteristic fluke eggs.

Prevention
Do not feed the cat raw crabs or shellfish.

PLEURISY

The lungs are coated with a thin membrane called the pleura. This also coats the chest wall. If the pleura becomes inflamed, due perhaps to infection by bacteria virus, fungi or parasites, or due to a tumour, the pleura produces a fluid that gradually builds up in the chest cavity, pushing the lungs away from the chest wall and therefore making breathing difficult and painful.

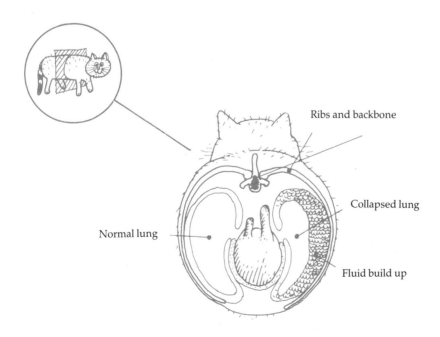

Ribs and backbone

Collapsed lung

Normal lung

Fluid build up

Pleurisy: Fluid builds up between the lung and the chest wall. In pneumonia, the congestion is within the lung itself

213

In many cases, the condition is far advanced before the cat shows obvious signs of distress. By this stage, treatment is difficult and often unsuccessful.

There are a variety of ways in which infection can gain entry. The most common is probably when lung tissue is ruptured, for example due to a kick or car accident. The air that is breathed into the lungs is usually contaminated by dust and other debris including fungal spores or bacteria. The lungs are adapted to cope with these contaminants, but the pleura is not. Agents that would be innocuous in the lungs can be responsible for severe infections in the pleural cavity.

Other possible routes of infection include penetrating chest wounds, such as by a broken rib, or bite wounds, or by extensions from lung infections. Some viruses have a specific affinity for the pleura and once present in the bloodstream will quickly establish themselves and start growing in the pleura.

BRONCHITIS

The bronchi are the airways of the lungs. Air comes down the trachea, which then branches out into smaller and smaller passageways taking the air deep into the lung tissue. When the bronchi become inflamed, due to infection by virus or bacteria, or inhalation of irritant gases, smoke or dust, allergic reactions, or invasion by parasites, this is termed bronchitis.

The primary sign of bronchitis is a harsh cough. This can vary in nature, and can be hard, dry, spasmodic and/or painful.

Treatment
The treatment varies with the cause and severity of the condition. The cause should be eliminated if possible — for example if the cat is being exposed to excessive fumes or dust.

NURSING

● Antibiotics are often indicated. Even if bacteria did not start the condition, they will commonly invade once the bronchi are damaged.

● Mucolytics: these are agents that break down the thick, tenacious mucous into a more fluid form that can be dislodged from the bronchi and eliminated from the lungs.

● Bronchodilators: the bronchi have a muscular component. This muscle can contract to narrow the passage through the bronchi. When the bronchi are inflamed there is usually some narrowing of the airways. Bronchodilators are drugs that can reverse this tendency, opening the airways and allowing easier breathing and more efficient expectoration of discharges.

● Humidifying the atmosphere or the use of inhalation agents can help (see the chapter on 'First Aid', page 17).

● Good nursing: improving the cat's general condition can stimulate the cat's own defences. Vitamin supplements do seem to help, especially vitamin A.

In troublesome cases your vet may use cough suppressants or corticosteroids to reduce the inflammation and the severity of the cough.

Treatment of long standing (chronic) cases of bronchitis can be unrewarding, especially if they have been present since kittenhood.

BRONCHIAL ASTHMA

Bronchial asthma is a condition where there is a spasm of the smooth muscle of the bronchi. This results in a substantial narrowing of the air passages through the lungs. The cat consequently has increased difficulty breathing. Affected cats make a distinctive wheezing noise.

Cats are not as liable to develop asthma as are humans. Siamese are more commonly affected than other breeds.

During severe bouts of asthma the cat may wheeze and cough, gasping for breath. It will be reluctant to move and may sit or lie in one spot with elbows out, breathing laboriously, perhaps even mouth breathing.

Treatment
Treatment includes the use of corticosteroids in injection, tablet or syrup form to control the bronchial spasm. Bronchodilators may also be prescribed.

Prevention
Bronchial asthma is not completely understood. The causes include an allergic reaction to agents (allergens) such as pollen or house dust. If the cat's attacks are seasonal only, then it is likely that some agent such as pollen is responsible. Short courses of corticosteroids during this season may be the best solution. Unfortunately, many cats are afflicted throughout the year. Corticosteroids cannot be used indiscriminately as they can have serious side effects if used for too long (these side effects include thinning of the skin, muscle wasting, increased bone fragility and decreased disease resistance). For this reason corticosteroid treatment must be carefully monitored. For long term control, a low dosage every second or third day can greatly reduce side effects. There may be other ways of handling the problem. If you can reduce the cat's exposure to the allergen this will help. Keep him inside when the pollen counts are high. You may try electronic air purifiers or ionisers — they have worked dramatically in some cases, but failed dismally in others. Naturopathic treatment is also worth consideration.

BONES AND JOINTS

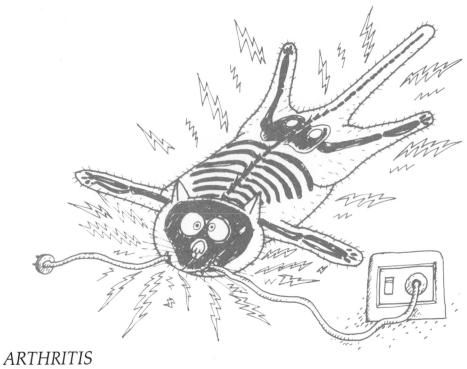

ARTHRITIS

A joint is a flexible connection between two bones. Its purpose is to allow movement. Some joints are relatively simple and permit only a limited range of movement. Others, such as the hip or the jaw, are quite complex and are designed to enable the two bones to move in several directions.

'Arthritis' means inflammation within a joint. This usually results in pain and a degree of lameness. For all its apparent familiarity to us, the condition 'arthritis' is often poorly understood by owners. One particularly common misconception is that arthritis and rheumatism are the same thing. (Rheumatism is a specific type of arthritis.) An understanding of what arthritis is, how it develops, and what you can do about it may help you to cope better with an arthritic cat.

Arthritis is not particularly common in cats, especially when compared with its incidence in humans.

What happens inside an arthritic joint?
A normal, simple joint consists of two bones sliding against each other. The ends of each bone are covered with smooth, hard cartilage. The joint is bathed, nurtured and lubricated by the thick, viscous joint fluid. The bone surfaces glide on an ultra smooth, virtually frictionless cartilage-bearing shell.

If the even surface of the joint is disturbed, inflammation and pain can result. Arthritic change often occurs first at the borders of the joint, so it is only on full extension or flexion of the joint that pain occurs. This inflammatory change can gradually extend to involve more and more of the joint. This is especially the case in degenerative arthritis. In infectious arthritis, the entire joint may be attacked simultaneously.

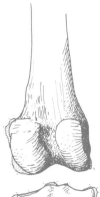
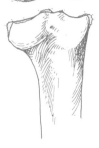

Arthritic changes within the knee joint. Some surfaces wear. Bony spurs and prominences can develop

216

There are several ways in which arthritis may develop:

Infectious arthritis (septic arthritis)
In infectious arthritis, the joint is invaded by bacteria or viruses which interfere with the smooth function of the joint by damaging the weight-bearing surfaces or the supporting joint ligaments and joint capsule. Infections can gain entry via the bloodstream, although the intrinsic defenses of the joint usually form an effective barrier to the invasion of most bacteria and viruses. It takes a very vigorous infection or some defect or flaw in the body's immune system to overcome this barrier. It is most likely to occur in a very young or old cat, or in a debilitated cat.

Infection can also gain entry to a joint directly through a bite wound or similar injury, or perhaps through an open wound from a car accident.

Degenerative arthritis
Degenerative arthritis occurs when the joint-bearing surfaces wear unevenly. This could be compared with the wearing out of a car's tyres. If the tyres are properly balanced and wearing evenly, you might get 70-80,000 kilometers' wear from them. If they are not, they could need replacement after only 20,000. Similarly, if a joint has become unstable (for example, due to damage to the ligaments or perhaps because of a fracture) the joint may wear much faster than normal. Because the joint surfaces are not gliding properly over one another the irregular wear leads to the development of arthritis.

The rate at which the joint degenerates depends on the instability of the joint. Cats with severe instabilities may develop degenerative arthritis within a few months of the joint being damaged. In other cases, the signs may not appear until late in life.

Auto immune arthritis (rheumatism)
This is a group of diseases in which the body starts to react against its own cells. Some factor affects the cells within the joint to make them appear 'foreign' to the body's immune system, which then attacks these *apparently* foreign cells. The resulting inflammation is termed 'auto immune' arthritis. Cats do *not* suffer from this form of arthritis. Because it is so common in humans, we have just mentioned it here.

Signs
Note that the severity of the signs varies with the amount of damage done to the joint and rate at which damage occurs. Signs could include:
- Hot, swollen joint.
- Pain: cat may limp or even refuse to bear weight on the joint.
- Stiffness, lameness. Cat may be slow or reluctant to stand up after rest.
- A general loss or reduction of normal free function.

Treatment
The treatment depends to some extent on the cause of the arthritis. The aim is to minimise further damage and to relieve the pain and inflammation.

When bacterial infection is the cause antibiotics are used, but it is difficult to get antibiotics into the joint and therefore to the site of infection. This is because everything that gets into the joint is filtered, purified and modified first. There is no blood within the joint. Instead, there is joint fluid which is responsible for lubrication and nutrition. Because the joint is 'protected' from antibiotics, infections within a joint may flourish. Although there are ways of overcoming this problem, it is nevertheless difficult to eliminate an infection once it has invaded a joint.

The treatment of degenerative arthritis involves controlling the inflammation thus reducing the pain, plus stabilising the joint if possible. This may involve repair of loose or broken ligaments. Reduction of any excess weight will help.

There is a range of drugs that can be used. Aspirin is quite effective but cats have difficulty in excreting it. If you use aspirin, you should not repeat the dose for at least two days. Better to leave the choice and dose rates of drugs to your vet.

BROKEN BONES *(fractures)*

A broken bone is the same as a fractured bone. The terms are synonymous. There are many different types of fractures, and they are classified according to their severity, the number of breaks, the degree of displacement and so on. The main types are as follows:

- Greenstick fracture: the bone is incompletely broken. There is no displacement. This usually occurs in young cats when the bones are still relatively flexible.
- Simple fracture: the bone is completely broken and there is some separation between the ends, but the skin is not broken.
- Compound fracture: some bone penetrates through the skin. Infection is potentially a problem.

Signs
Some or all of the following:
- Loss of function. The cat will not bear weight on a fractured limb. (A fracture of the pelvis might not result in total loss of function.)
- Pain, especially at fracture site.
- Swelling, due to bleeding and bruising. (This can be difficult to see, and the cat will resent your probing.)

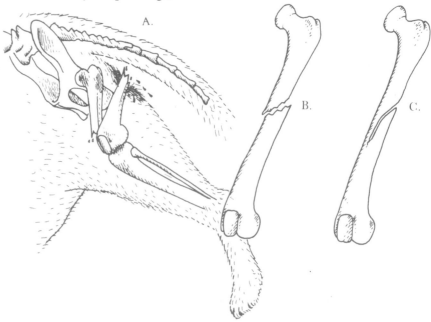

A. Compound fracture
(skin broken)

B. Simple fracture

C. Greenstick fracture

- Unnatural degree of movement. For example, the lower part of a limb may swing freely, or the end of the tail drag along. The limb may appear shorter or abnormally twisted.

If you are in doubt, it is useful to compare the damaged part with the same part on the other side of the body.

First aid
- Be careful. The cat may resent handling. (Read the chapter on 'First Aid', page 17.)
- Do not attempt to apply a splint.
- In transporting the cat, move slowly to minimise movement of the injured part. Let the damaged limb hang free.

Treatment
To mend, a bone must be set back in the correct position and then be held there rigidly for many weeks.

Plaster casts have never been particularly satisfactory in cats because they are heavy and the cat often resents the encumbrance. There are improved synthetic casting materials that are lighter, stronger and water repellant. These are much less uncomfortable for the cat.

'Internal fixation' involves the use of surgical pins, plates, screws and wire. Internal fixation is used commonly now. A major advantage of this method is that it allows some use of a limb while repair occurs. Healing is faster and there is usually not as much muscle wasting. The increasing sophistication of veterinary surgery now allows the successful treatment of most fractures with minimum discomfort and a rapid return to normal use.

SOME COMMON FRACTURES

Broken jaw
Cats falling from a height sometimes smack the lower jaw hard against the ground. The most common injury is to split the jawbone, although the shafts are sometimes also broken.

Broken tail
Because the nerves run through the tail, injuries can be serious. If there is much displacement of the broken ends there is likely to be nerve damage, resulting in a paralysed tail that may need to be amputated.

Fractured pelvis
Fractures of the pelvis are among the most common seen in veterinary practice. Most result from car accidents. The treatment depends on how much displacement has occurred. Many do not need any internal or external fixation. By simply putting the cat into a small cage and therefore forcing it to rest, the pelvis will usually heal quickly and with little apparent discomfort to the cat. The muscles of the pelvis go into 'spasm' and can effectively hold the fracture immobile while it heals — providing the cat does not jump or move too much. Most cats seem perfectly content to sit in a cage for the ten to fourteen days necessary.

If there is a lot of displacement, your vet may need to realign the bones and perhaps use internal fixation to keep them aligned.

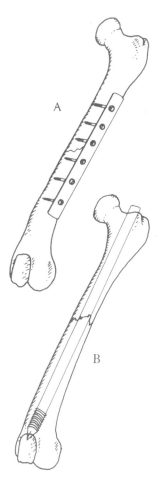

(A) Repair of fractured femur with a stainless steel bone plate and screws; (B) Repair using a steel bone pin

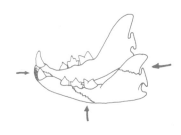

Common sites of jaw fractures

DISLOCATIONS

A dislocation occurs when a bone is displaced from its normal position within a joint. This usually requires considerable force. The joint capsule is simultaneously painfully stretched, and there is usually also some damage to joint ligaments and other supporting tissues.

The signs are similar to a fracture, and an X-ray may be needed to differentiate between them. The most commonly affected joint is the hip.

Dislocated bones are usually manipulated back into their correct position while the cat is deeply anaesthetised. The problem then is to prevent the damaged and unstable joint from re-dislocating. Sometimes the limb is bandaged in position, or perhaps surgery may be required to help stabilise the joint. 'Cage rest' is usually recommended for a few days.

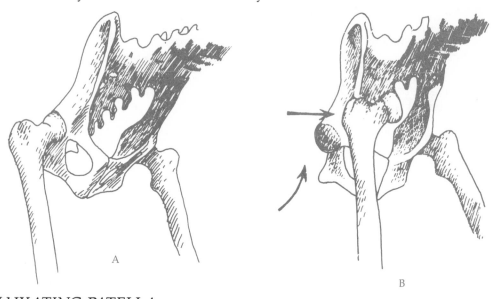

(A) Normal; (B) Dislocated hip (usually goes forwards and upwards)

LUXATING PATELLA

A congenital defect in the knee joint of some cats allows the kneecap to slip out of its correct position. (The kneecap should lie in a groove at the end of the femur.) This condition is common in some strains of the Devon Rex breed. Surgical repair is possible, but affected cats should *not* be used for breeding.

SPRAINS

Sprains are injuries to the joints, usually due to overstretching or rupture of the joint capsule or ligaments.

The main signs are pain, swelling and lameness. It may be difficult to distinguish between a sprain, a fracture, a dislocation or an acute infection of the joint (due for example to a bite) without a careful examination and perhaps an x-ray.

Treatment involves rest. Cats resent the application of ice packs which are used routinely in human sprains, and you must *not* rub on linaments or ointments designed for human use. These ointments can cause pain and skin damage, and the cat will try to lick them off causing salivation, distress and perhaps vomiting.

220

In most cases the cat will restrict activity itself, but try to avoid situations where the cat has to jump down from a height. If your cat is a climber it may be necessary to confine it in a cage for one to two weeks.

When to call the vet
If the cat has a simple sprain, then home treatment is usually satisfactory. However, because it is difficult to distinguish between a sprain and, say, a bite wound, or a dislocation, you should seek veterinary advice, especially if:
- Cat is listless, won't eat.
- Cat is in considerable pain.
- Injury deteriorates — especially if the swelling is increasing.
- Injury fails to respond to treatment.

VET TREATMENT
URGENT

RICKETS

Rickets is also called 'paper bone disease' and the 'all meat syndrome'. It is correctly called nutritional secondary hyperparathyroidism.

This condition is discussed in the chapter on 'Nutrition'. It is common in young malnourished cats. It is also seen in cats fed incorrectly on excessive amounts of meat, especially rich red meats such as heart, liver and beef.

Rickets leads to swollen joints, malformed bones, predisposition to fractures and even spinal deformity. If the cause is corrected by feeding a correctly balanced diet and perhaps also giving a calcium supplement, most cats will respond well, especially if they are still young. (See also chapter on 'Nutrition', page 60.)

Renal rickets
In old cats with chronic kidney (renal) disease, the bones can become weakened as calcium is reabsorbed from them. This occurs because the kidneys are not activating vitamin D which is needed to allow absorption of calcium from the gut. Because the body needs calcium, it starts to leach it from the bones instead. This weakens them and renders them more liable to fracture.

Treatment
Add vitamin D to the diet — but not too much. A few drops of cod liver oil three times weekly, or a teaspoon of liver three times weekly is sufficient.

BONE TUMOURS

A bone tumour is a serious condition, recognised by a sudden onset of lameness which progresses to a painful swelling, usually near a joint. The most common site is in the long bones of the legs. *Note*: it is hard to differentiate a bone tumour from a fracture.

The most common tumour is an osteosarcoma. This is a highly malignant tumour. Secondary tumours are liable to spread quickly, especially to the lungs — often before a diagnosis is even made.

At present, the only treatment that gives the cat any chance is amputation of the affected limb. This is only performed if x-rays of the lungs show that secondary tumours have not already established themselves there. Even so, the chances of the cat living for even a further six months are poor.

NERVES

Nerves form the communicating link between all parts of the body. They possess unique properties, but suffer from one significant disability: they are unable to heal once they have been badly damaged. If your cat suffers nerve damage your main aim is to minimise further damage.

SPINAL INJURY

VET TREATMENT
URGENT

A network of nerves radiates to and from the brain

Why is it so serious?
An unbroken, unimpaired link between the brain and the rest of the body is fundamental to good health. The network of nerves relays information from every part of the body. Vast amounts of data are transmitted to the brain. All conscious activity within the cat's body is initiated in the brain, but the nerves are essential for the execution of all voluntary, and many involuntary, body functions.

The spinal cord is composed of innumerable individual nerves running together through the spinal canal, protected and supported by the vertebrae. Any damage to the spinal cord has grave repercussions further afield in the body. If communication between the brain and a limb or an organ is lost, then all conscious and most unconscious control is also lost. If the nerves are badly damaged, this loss of control could be permanent.

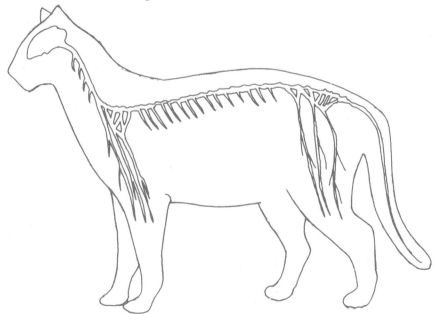

222

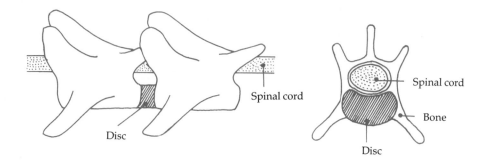

Side view of vertebra   End on view of vertebra

The spinal cord of nerves is surrounded by a pocket of air, enclosed by the protecting bone of the vertebral canal. Discs between each vertebra act as shock absorbers so a cat's spinal cord is very rarely damaged except by a serious accident.

If the spinal cord is cut or crushed in the neck, the cat will die. Control of the diaphragm is lost, and therefore the cat cannot breathe. In general, the closer to the cat's brain that spinal damage occurs, the worse is the outlook for the cat's future.

Causes
- Trauma is the most common cause. It requires violent physical force to overcome the protective defenses of the vertebrae, but serious damage could result from a motor car accident, a kick, fall from a height or gunshot wound or similar.
- Disc disease: degeneration or disease of the intervertebral discs (see diagram) can result in the protrusion of matter from the disc's nucleus into the spinal canal, causing pain, weakness or paralysis.
- Infectious disease: some infectious agents have a particular affinity with nerve tissue — notably the virus, rabies. Others occasionally involve nerves, for example:
  — Feline infectious peritonitis.
  — Toxoplasmosis.
  — Cryptococcosis.
- Tumours: the most common tumour involving the spinal cord is lymphosarcoma.
- Conditions that cause changes in the bones of the spine, or remodelling of them, can result in increased pressure on the spinal cord. These include:
  — Vitamin A overdose or poisoning.
  — Vitamin D overdose or poisoning.
  — All meat diet.
  — Rickets.

Signs
May include some of the following. The degree of damage inflicted and the location of the injury are critical factors in determining the severity of the signs.
- Pain, or altered sensitivity to pain: in severe injury, there is a loss of all sensation, including pain, beyond the injured area. In milder injuries, pain sensitivity could be increased.
- Paralysis: in mild injury there may be only weakness (paresis) rather than a total loss of function.

223

- Loss of sensation: this is often the first sign in degenerative nerve disease. Humans may complain to their physician of a tingling sensation or numbness, but in the cat you can only observe the effects of this loss of sensation. Because the cat lacks feeling or sensation in an area, it may inadvertently damage it. For example, a damaged tail may become fouled with urine. In cleaning the tail, the cat may damage the skin, causing inflammation and ulceration because it lacks the sensitivity to prevent the rough tongue from rasping the skin.

Other signs include
- Stiff forelegs.
- Dribbling urine, or involuntary retention of urine.
- Loss of normal bowel control: diarrhoea or constipation.
- Abnormal posture and movements.

Treatment

First aid
Your main task is to avoid further damage to the nerves. Once the vertebral column has been damaged it might no longer protect the spinal cord efficiently. Careless handling could result in further destruction of irreplaceable nerve cells.
- Find a board or a box with a firm bottom where the cat can lie flat without having to curl up. If the surface is smooth it is preferable to cover it with a blanket so that the injured cat does not slip around.
- Put the cat onto the board or into the box. This can be difficult. Take care. If possible, slide it onto the blanket, then — supporting it with the flat of both hands so that the spine does not sag — put the whole bundle onto the flat, firm supporting surface of the box or board.

If the cat struggles, or is uncooperative or is trying to bite or scratch, then first cover him with a large towel or blanket. Pack the material firmly around him, enveloping the entire body. Then move the whole lot — blanket, cat and all — into a box, doing your best to avoid bending the cat's spine.
- Get to a vet as soon as possible. Spinal injury is too serious for home treatment. When travelling, go slowly and smoothly. You won't help the injury by bouncing the patient around in a frantic dash to get to the vet.

Treatment should be commenced as soon as possible after the injury has occurred, and preferably within an hour. If treatment is commenced more than twenty-four hours after serious injury, then the chances of achieving a successful outcome are greatly reduced.

VET TREATMENT
URGENT

Veterinary treatment
Treatment of acute injuries may include treatment to reduce inflammation or swelling in and around the spinal cord and to control further bleeding. The damaged area may have to be immobilised. In some cases, surgical treatment is indicated to relieve pressure on the injured cord. Such surgery must be undertaken as soon after the injury as possible, and it should preferably be performed by a very experienced surgeon.

Treatment of chronic spinal conditions which have resulted in a gradual onset of signs is less urgent. The vet has time to assess the patient carefully before deciding on the most satisfactory course of treatment.

DISC DISEASE *(disease of the intervertebral disc)*

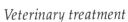

Disc disease is not particularly common in cats. This is in contrast to the situation in dogs and humans, where problems due to degeneration or rupture of the spinal discs are frequently encountered.

When feline disc disease occurs, it is usually the result of direct physical trauma, such as a motor car accident, although chronic deterioration with age does occur. Disc disease is most likely to occur in cats over fifteen years of age. The discs between the neck vertebrae are the ones most commonly affected. Sometimes the nucleus of the disc deteriorates, ruptures and presses on the spinal cord yet causes no apparent discomfort. This is possible only if the protrusion occurs very gradually. It is not uncommon to find, during routine autopsy, that an aged cat has protrusion of several spinal discs, although it had never shown clinical signs while alive.

If a disc protrudes as the result of trauma, sudden pressure may be applied to the spinal cord. This is usually aggravated by inflammation as the material in the disc's nucleus is very irritant. The cat will probably be in considerable pain and there may be weakness or paralysis.

POISONS THAT CAUSE NERVE DAMAGE

Cats are less likely to be poisoned than dogs, but could inadvertently ingest poisons with their food or during grooming.

The following is a list of some of the more common poisons that cause nervous signs. (For more details see the chapter on 'Poisoning', page 33.)
- Anti-freeze.
- Aspirin.
- Benzoic acid.
- Chlorinated hydrocarbons (insecticides).
- Lead.
- Mercury.
- Metaldehyde (snail bait).
- Organophosphates (snail bait and other pesticides).
- Streptomycin (an antibiotic).

FITS, SEIZURES, CONVULSIONS, EPILEPSY

Why fits or seizures occur
There is constant electrical activity in the brain, even during sleep and rest. The brain controls the entire body via messages transmitted as electrical impulses through the nerves. A seizure or fit is caused by a violent burst of electrical activity within the brain, similar to the surging discharge of energy seen as lightning during thunderstorms.

The fit, or electrical 'storm' occurs within the brain after there has been a gradual build up of electrical energy in a small area of the brain. This is usually due to some irritant focus such as a blood clot, an old scar, or to a more diffuse inflammation as might be caused by an infection or a poison. The electrical potential gradually builds up to a peak then suddenly, violently, discharges the energy. This is expressed as a fit, or seizure. The actual pattern of the seizure (its duration, the parts of the body affected and so on) depends on which part of the brain is involved, and on how large an area is affected. If the causative agent is gradually producing more pressure or irritation, as would occur if a tumour is growing within the brain, the fits will become more frequent and more severe. In other cases, the body may be able to get rid of the irritant, or contain it in some way, and the fits could cease altogether. This is usually the case in infections or poisonings that have been successfully treated — there is often no permanent damage, assuming treatment is commenced promptly.

Some possible causes of fits

Fits or seizures are generally precipitated by something causing localised pressure, inflammation or irritation in the brain. Some of the more common causes include:

- Head injury: bleeding may result from pressure on the brain, or scars may gradually form which eventually — weeks or even months later — produce a focus of pressure on the brain.
- Toxic chemicals, especially lead, also insecticides, anti-freeze and others.
- Infectious agents, especially toxoplasmosis, feline infectious peritonitis and cryptococcosis, but others may be involved.
- Tumours: lymphosarcoma following feline leukemia virus infection is the most common.
- Thiamine deficiency: due to a diet rich in raw fish.

Other conditions, when seizures or fits can be a major presenting sign, include:

- Liver disease.
- Kidney failure.
- Low blood sugar (hypoglycaemia).
- Milk fever/eclampsia.

Signs

- Sudden onset of violent, uncontrolled muscle spasms.
- Tremor.
- Collapse.
- Loss of consciousness (from transient to prolonged).
- Paddling movements of the legs.
- Stiffness or rigidity of the body.
- Involuntary salivation.
- 'Rage reaction', the cat growls and hisses, may not be aware of his surroundings, and does not react to normal stimulations, such as calling his name.

Most fits or seizures last only a few seconds, but may last several minutes. It always *seems* much longer at the time. Cats may have several convulsions in one day, then a period of apparent normal health, followed by another series.

Recovery from fits is usually spontaneous. Owners frequently erroneously believe that something they have done has produced the recovery — for example stroking the cat, or throwing cold water over it. In fact, there is virtually nothing you can do for the cat while it is in the grip of a convulsion. You should *not* interfere unless you have to as there is a real danger of being hurt. A fit that is continuous and does not spontaneously cease is termed *status epilepticus*. This requires urgent veterinary attention.

Upon recovery, the cat may be quiet and appear dazed or confused. Many will go away and hide in a dark, quiet place. Some temporarily become quite unpredictable, even vicious. Others crave affection, comfort and soothing.

Epilepsy

Epilepsy is characterised by a recurring pattern to the seizures one after the other, then an interval of days or weeks before the next series. In most other species, such as dogs, there is just a single fit, rather than a series. Epileptic attacks may start in the young cat around puberty, or they may start to occur some weeks or months after a blow to the head, such as could have been inflicted in a car accident. This latter is due to scar tissue which gradually contracts to produce a focal source of irritation to the brain.

Many epileptic attacks are classified as 'idiopathic' which means 'of unknown cause'.

Treatment
Treatment can be rewarding. Daily tablets will be necessary, plus a close liaison with your vet. It takes time to find the most suitable dose rates and the most effective drugs. Once the fits have been controlled successfully, the cat can usually live a normal life.

What should you do if faced with a convulsing cat?
● Most fits end spontaneously, so — stand back. Leave the cat where it is unless it is in danger (such as on a road or near an open fire). The cat is unlikely to die during a fit, unless it is very prolonged. *Note:* if you *must* move a convulsing cat, then first throw a large towel or blanket over it, completely enveloping it. Then move the whole bundle to a safer area.
● *Don't* put your finger into the cat's mouth. You will be bitten if you do. Cats virtually never swallow their tongue, so there is usually no necessity to try to open the mouth.
● Leave the cat until the convulsion has ended. *Do not* attempt to stroke, hold or cuddle the cat either during or immediately after an episode.
● Approach with caution. The cat may be unpredictable and could uncharacteristically bite or scratch through fear or confusion. Try to get it to a quiet, dark room. Once it has sufficiently recovered, transport it to the vet for examination.

DAMAGE TO INDIVIDUAL NERVES

Radial nerve paralysis
This is the most common 'single' nerve condition. We have probably all experienced mild episodes of radial nerve paralysis. If you fall asleep across your arm you may inadvertently put pressure on the radial nerve where it runs around your elbow. On awakening, you may have a temporary loss of feeling and strength in the arm. After a few minutes, and a period of 'pins and needles', the arm goes back to normal.

The radial nerve is more liable to damage than most because it runs close to the surface and lies on top of a bone, where it could be crushed. If hit hard enough, the damage can be serious — even permanent.

The most common cause of radial nerve paralysis is a car accident, but it could also be damaged in a fight, or if the foreleg is caught in a fence or a trap or something similar.

Radial nerve (foreleg) paralysis

227

Signs
- Affected foreleg cannot bear weight.
- Leg folds up when the cat attempts to stand on it or the foot may be dragged along the ground as the cat walks.
- There is a lack of sensation on the front of the foot over the top of the toes. Sores or ulcers may develop on the feet where they are dragged over the ground.

Treatment
The outlook depends on how badly the nerve has been damaged. If the nerve is only bruised, then treatment to reduce inflammation and swelling may prevent increased pressure on the nerve and therefore further damage. In many instances, recovery is spontaneous. Most cases improve or even recover completely within twenty-four hours. Others take up to several weeks.

If the nerve is severely damaged, it will not heal. In this case, treatment depends on how the cat copes with the affliction. Most handle the situation well, get around on three legs and avoid damaging the affected leg. If the cat is basically an outdoors cat it may not cope well as it will find climbing difficult and hunting virtually impossible. If the cat's normal activities are severely restricted and it is unhappy indoors then it may be kinder to opt for euthanasia or amputation at this stage.

Amputation of the affected limb could become necessary, especially if there has been other damage such as skin loss or multiple fractures. It could also be indicated if the cat is self traumatising the insensitive skin by licking or damaging it as the leg drags over the ground.

Other nerves that may be damaged
Two other fairly common nerve injuries that result in significant loss of function are:

1. Sciatic nerve damage in the hindleg (most likely as a complication of a fractured femur).

2. Damage to the brachial plexus which is a group of nerves lying between the foreleg and the body wall. The entire group of nerves is sometimes torn when the leg is forcibly pulled away from the body wall. Again — usually a car accident is responsible.

In the situation where much of the nervous control is lost, the cat cannot hold the leg up out of trouble so the limb impedes walking and will probably become ulcerated and infected. You unfortunately have only two options. Either have the limb amputated or have your cat humanely euthanised.

VITAMIN A POISONING

Vitamin A is an essential element in the cat's diet. However, it can be taken in excess and accumulate to toxic levels. This usually occurs in cats fed large amounts of liver, but could result from over-supplementation of cod liver oil and vitamin preparations.

Vitamin A excess can result in inflexibility of the spine

Signs
- Stiff neck. Usually first noticed because the cat cannot groom itself properly.
- Foreleg lameness. Usually intermittent at first.
- Pain in legs and body.
- Abnormal gait and posture.

228

These signs occur because vitamin A causes minerals to be laid down in the ligaments of the spine. The normally elastic ligaments become hard and inflexible. Excessive bone is also laid down in the neck vertebrae and back vertebrae. Initially this causes pain when the cat moves, and eventually produces rigidity of the spine so the cat cannot bend its neck or get much movement of the normally flexible spine.

If this condition is ̣iagnosed early, the excessive mineralisation of ligaments and abnormal bone formation may gradually resolve. The diet must be corrected and drugs such as corticosteroids may be needed to help relieve the pain and inflammation and to speed recovery. Advanced cases may be incurable.

THE ALL-MEAT DIET

Cats which are fed a predominantly or exclusively meat diet develop an imbalance of minerals, calcium and phosphorus. As meat is also deficient in other nutrients such as iodine, magnesium and several vitamins, the clinical picture may be clouded by other deficiency conditions, but basically this condition results in poor bone structure and is most common in young, growing kittens. Their bones have thin shafts, the joints swell and the cat is liable to joint pain. The long bones are easily fractured. In advanced cases the bone may even collapse in what is termed a 'folding fracture'.

Vitamin A poisoning can cause rigidity of the spine, lameness and pain. An early sign may be failure to groom properly

Signs
- Increasing irritability (due to pain).
- Lameness: often a 'shifting' lameness where first one leg then another is favoured. In fact all the legs are involved, but one is usually more sore than the others.
- Deformities of legs: usually bowing of the forelegs and swollen, mushrooming joints.
- Fractures.
- Constipation, as a result of deformity of spine or pelvis.

Treatment
Improve the cat's diet to a balanced one and give a calcium supplement for a few weeks. The best calcium sources are calcium carbonate (chalk), calcium gluconate or calcium lactate. Dose: 1 teaspoon or 1 tablet per 5 kg body weight per day. *Do not* use DCP (di-calcium phosphate).

An improvement is usually seen in kittens within a week or two.

Owners faced with a diagnosis of this condition quite often say 'But I give him milk. Isn't that a good source of calcium?' The answer is *yes*, it is, but although it can help prevent the condition from developing, it is unsuitable as a treatment because it lacks the required balance of calcium to phosphorus. A cat would have to drink 600 mls (1 pint) of milk daily to meet its calcium requirement!

THIAMINE DEFICIENCY (also called chasteks paralysis)

Thiamine is a vitamin — one of the B group. It is one of the few vitamins that the cat cannot produce itself. It must therefore be supplied in the diet. Fortunately, many of the cat's natural foods such as liver and kidney are rich in thiamine. Other sources include whole grain and green vegetables. Actual dietary deficiencies are not common. The usual cause of a thiamine deficiency is excessive destruction

of thiamine by a substance called thiaminase, which is found in some raw fish. Cats fed large amounts of this fish will develop chasteks paralysis.

Overcooking food, or the use of preservatives such as sulphur dioxide, can also destroy thiamine. Some commercial foods are marginally deficient in thiamine. Sometimes stress (such as illness, pregnancy or an emotional upset) can precipitate the condition.

Signs
- Loss of weight.
- Lack of appetite.
- Irritability.
- Progressive weakness.
- Vomiting.
- Eventually convulsions, loss of balance. Affected cats tend to walk with their head down and claws extended.

Treatment
Supplement the diet with thiamine and stop feeding raw fish. If nervous signs have started, an injection of thiamine will rapidly produce an improvement, usually within a day.

Even though commercial food manufacturers are aware of the problems, cases of thiamine deficiency still occur in some cats that have been fed one particular brand. Cats are unlikely to develop this problem if they are fed a variety of commercial products.

In severe cases there may be irreversible brain damage. These cats should be euthanised.

BENZOIC ACID POISONING

Benzoic acid is used as a preservative in some foods. It is toxic to cats and should never be used in their food. Poisoning may occur due to uneven mixing of the preservative during the manufacturing process.

Signs
- Incoordination.
- Muscle tremors.
- Blindness.
- Increased pain sensitivity.

Treatment
Remove the source of the benzoic acid.

Your vet may need to treat the cat to relieve any distressing symptoms.

STROKE

A 'stroke' is the common term for the syndrome that occurs following bleeding on the brain or due to a blood clot forming in the brain; resulting in a localised area of brain damage.

Strokes are not common in cats. They are most likely to occur in cats over ten years old.

230

Signs
The signs of a stroke are due to pressure on the brain or to the effects of oxygen starvation to a discreet area. The signs depend on which particular part of the brain is affected.

The sudden onset of one or more of the following signs could indicate a 'stroke':

- Loss of consciousness.
- Loss of function of one side of the body. This may involve only the face, or may be more extensive and involve one or both limbs on the same side of the body.
- Severe mental depression: a state of semi-stupor.
- Dilated pupil or pupils.
- Loss of balance, pacing and circling in one direction (consistently to the left or consistently to the right).
- Dramatic or sudden change in behaviour.

Treatment
Treatment depends on the severity and extent of brain damage. Most cats will spontaneously recover from a slight stroke with time, good nursing and perhaps some drug treatment from your vet. There may be residual problems, such as partial blindness, behavioural changes or recurring fits (epilepsy).

NURSING

CANCER

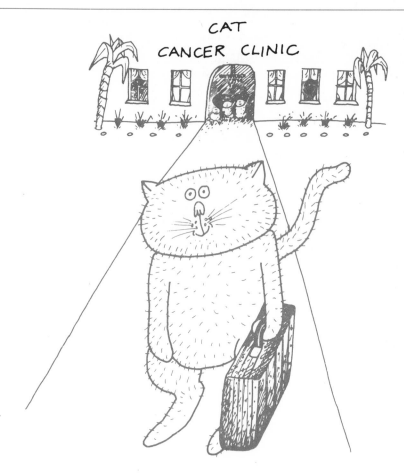

Few words evoke such sinister connotations as cancer. While a diagnosis of cancer may cause some dismay, the situation is by no means hopeless. Many cancers are treatable, especially if recognised and treated early.

A cancer is a growth which is beyond the body's control. Most of the body's cells are capable of multiplying but when they multiply it is to replace or repair damaged or worn out cells, or as a normal part of growth. It is when the body loses the ability to limit or constrain the multiplication of cells that a tumour develops.

Types of growths: benign vs malignant
A tumour is defined as any swelling or lump. A tumour can be any group of cells that are growing beyond the control of the host's body.

Tumours may be benign or malignant. Many tumours do not fit neatly into one category or the other. Others can gradually change their nature from benign to malignant. A definite diagnosis of tumour-type is not always possible.

A benign tumour is not a great threat to your cat's life. These tumours do not eat into surrounding tissue. They expand and grow from within, somewhat like a balloon being slowly blown up.

A malignant tumour is also called a cancer. This tumour grows out from its borders, invading and destroying surrounding tissues. Sometimes cancerous cells break away from the parent tumour and take root some distance away, growing as a 'secondary' tumour. Common sites for secondary tumour growth include the lungs, liver and abdominal cavity.

This brief summary of the basic characteristics of benign tumours compared to malignant tumours may help to make the distinction clearer.

CHARACTERISTIC	BENIGN	MALIGNANT
Rate of growth.	Slow.	Usually rapid.
Shape.	Usually regular — round or oval, with readily defined borders.	Irregular. Often difficult to tell exactly where the limits of the growth are.
Pain.	Usually does not concern the cat. Depends on the position of the tumour.	Often inflamed. May be swelling, pain and discharge. Cat is usually concerned.
Do they invade surrounding tissue?	No.	Yes.
Do they spread locally or to other organs?	No.	Sometimes.

How common are tumours in cats?
According to the results of one survey, every year an average of two in every one thousand cats develop a tumour.

What percentage of these are malignant?
In the cat, an unusually high percentage of all tumours are malignant — around 80%. This is much higher than for dogs or humans.

Why does cancer occur?
We do not know the full answer to this question, although part of the story is known.

Occasionally 'mistakes' or 'genetic errors' occur when new tissues are regenerating to replace worn or damaged tissue. Because of these errors, the tissue cells grow too rapidly. The body cannot restrain their growth and the cells multiply to produce a confused, disorganised mass of cells rather than an ordered structure. Usually, the body's immune system is able to regain control before these errors get out of hand, but some slip through. As the cat ages, the probability of these genetic errors occurring becomes greater. So the potential to develop some types of tumours increases with age. Other factors are known to increase the rate of genetic errors and consequently to increase the chance of a tumour developing. These factors are called carcinogens.

Cigarette smoke contains carcinogens. Radiation is a carcinogen. There are many other known carcinogens and these include some viruses (especially feline leukemia virus), ultraviolet rays and some drugs and chemicals.

Constant physical trauma or irritation can sometimes lead to cancer — for example the pipe-smoker has a far higher chance of developing cancer of the lip than the non-pipe smoker.

A summary of some of the terms used in this chapter may be useful for reference at this stage.

Tumour:	Any swelling or lump. Usually applied to a new growth of tissue that is *not* under the body's control.
Benign tumour:	A tumour that expands to occupy space, but does not invade the surrounding healthy tissue. Benign tumours are usually surrounded by a capsule.
Malignant tumour:	These tumours are composed of cells that aggressively take over areas previously occupied by normal cells. They invade and destroy. Groups of malignant cells might break off to be carried in the cat's circulation (blood and lymph) to start new tumours.
Primary tumour:	The initial or parent tumour.
Secondary tumour:	Tumours that have been started elsewhere by cells breaking off from the primary tumour.
Cancer:	A malignant tumour.
Neoplasm (or Neoplasia):	A new growth of tissue that is beyond the body's normal control. Adjective: neoplastic. (It would in fact be more accurate to talk in this chapter of 'neoplasms' rather than 'tumours', but because we feel the word 'tumour' is more familiar, we have stuck to it.)
Biopsy:	A sample taken from a live tissue, usually for microscopic examination, for example to determine whether a tumour is malignant.

My cat has a tumour. Should it be removed?

Your vet will judge each case on its merits and advise accordingly. It is not always possible to know whether a tumour is malignant or benign until a pathologist has examined a portion of it microscopically. If your cat has to be anaesthetised to obtain a biopsy, many vets will opt to remove the entire growth (if possible) rather than just take out a piece of it.

The position of the tumour must also be considered. A tumour that is growing, for example, on an eyelid or the lip may cause irritation or pain. If so, it should be removed even if it is thought to be benign.

Treatment of cancer (malignant tumour)

The main weapons against cancer are surgical removal and treatment of the mass with drugs, radiation or other therapies.

Surgical

Because of the invasive nature of their growth, it is often difficult to determine the precise borders of a cancer. The surgeon will usually try to take out not only the tumour, but also an area of apparently healthy tissue surrounding the tumour. The aim is also to remove any unseen cancer cells that might be infiltrating locally and which may otherwise grow to replace the primary tumour. It is not always possible to remove all of the potentially involved tissue. For example, the tumour may be on the skin of the face, or on an eyelid. Too much loss of tissue from these areas could be disfiguring, or perhaps the surgeon would be unable to close over the resultant wound.

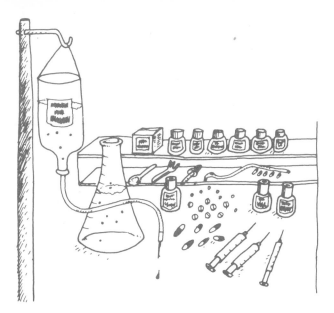

Drugs (chemotherapy)
There are many drugs and chemicals available that are known to be able to kill cancer cells. The problem in most cases is that their side-effects are very undesirable. Cancer cells are still the cat's own body cells and one major question that researchers are yet to answer is how the prescribed drug differentiates normal cells from cancer cells, and then selectively destroys the abnormal cells?

Chemotherapy is still in its infancy, but effective and safe drugs that kill cancer cells only and spare normal cells may soon be developed.

Radiation
The use of x-rays to destroy malignant cells can be very effective. Cancerous cells are more sensitive to x-rays than normal cells. Sophisticated machines are required that can focus the x-rays precisely into the tumour. Some tumours, especially skin tumours, can be effectively treated this way, but the apparatus is not widely available due to its expense.

Radioactive implants can be used. These are small 'needles' of radioactive material that are inserted into the tumour mass. They emit intense radiation over a very short distance and are capable of destroying some tumours without affecting surrounding healthy tissues.

Electromagnetic pulse therapy and laser beam therapy are two other forms of treatment which show promise, but are yet to be fully developed.

After a malignant tumour has been removed (or otherwise treated) why is the outlook for the cat's future still guarded?
The most common complication to arise in the treatment of malignant tumours is when the tumour cells have already spread to other parts of the cat's body. There is little point in removing the primary tumour if there are multiple secondary tumours growing elsewhere. If a malignant tumour is removed *before* it has had time to spread, the cat should recover to normal health.

SOME SPECIFIC TUMOURS

SKIN TUMOURS

The two most common skin tumours of cats are the squamous cell carcinoma and the basal cell carcinoma. Both are malignant. Fortunately, owners often detect them early enough for treatment to be successful.

Squamous cell carcinoma is more common in white or unpigmented skin on ear tips, nose and eyelids

What sort of growth justifies concern?

Any new lump or growth that appears in your cat's skin should be carefully examined. If it exhibits any of the following characteristics it should be checked by your vet:

- Rapid growth.
- Dark pigmentation.
- Irregular shape (rather than being round or oval).
- Open, ulcerated or raw surface.
- Is causing discomfort.

If a malignant tumour is detected and removed *before* it has spread to other organs the cat's life may be saved.

Squamous cell carcinoma

Usual sites:	Ear tips, nose and eyelid. Also lips and mouth.
Typical appearance:	Usually a single growth. Irregular in size and shape. Surface is usually ulcerated (open and raw). Eventually appears to be eroding away the skin. *Note:* early in its course, a squamous cell carcinoma can easily be mistaken for a bite or scratch wound.
Comments:	Excessive exposure to sunlight is strongly incriminated in the cause, although other factors are also involved. The ultraviolet radiation of sunlight is particularly dangerous to unpigmented skin, especially in areas such as the ears, nose and eyelids where there is no hair cover either. For this reason, white cats living in warm climates are at risk if they are allowed to lie in the sun.

Basal cell carcinoma

Usual sites:	Most common on back of head, neck and withers, but can be found anywhere.
Typical appearance:	Usually single, rounded and hairless lump with a rubbery consistency. Most eventually ulcerate.
Comments:	These tumours usually only invade locally, and do not commonly spread to other organs such as the lungs. Treatment by wide surgical excision can be curative.

MAMMARY TUMOURS

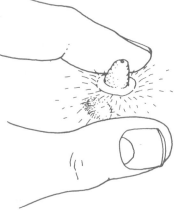

Early detection of mammary tumours gives a better chance of successful treatment

Tumours involving the mammary glands (breasts) comprise about 25% of all tumours occurring in female cats. They are rare in males, or in females spayed when young. Unfortunately, most feline mammary tumours are malignant.

The majority of the cats affected are old. Their average age is eleven years.

The tumours can be palpated as lumps in the mammary glands. The entire gland may become firm. The skin surface sometimes ulcerates, oozing a blood-stained fluid. They may attach firmly to the body wall, but are usually moveable.

Mammary tumours can be confused with mammary cysts. These cysts are fairly common in older queens and are due to a blockage of the milk ducts. They are firm and seem fluid-filled when touched. They are usually not painful.

Treatment

If detected early, your vet may recommend removal of the affected mammary glands, and perhaps of the entire chain of glands. An x-ray of the cat's chest may be taken first. If the tumour has already spread to the lungs, or other organs, or if the case is far advanced, successful treatment may not be possible.

LYMPHOSARCOMA

One-third of all tumours seen in cats are lymphosarcoma, a malignant tumour that is associated with infection by the feline leukemia virus (Fe.LV — see page 111).

The cat's lymphoid tissue is responsible for the production of antibodies, which give immunity against many bacterial and viral diseases. Lymph tissue includes the tonsils and adenoids and many other lymph nodes or 'glands' that are spread right throughout the body. Their role is to filter body fluid (or 'lymph') before it is returned to the bloodstream to continue circulating. The thymus and spleen are also lymphoid tissue.

The feline leukemia virus can induce cancer in this lymphoid tissue. Because lymphoid tissue is so widespread, the sites of tumour formation, and therefore the clinical signs, are very variable. The most common organs to be affected are the intestines, thymus gland (in the neck and chest), kidneys, spleen and brain or spinal cord. Some breeds, notably the Siamese, have a much higher than average incidence of lymphosarcoma.

Treatment

Treatment is not usually recommended. This is for two reasons:

1. The tumour is usually not surgically accessible. There may be many secondary tumours, so detection and removal of all tumours may be impossible.

2. The affected cat is likely to be a source of Fe.LV infection to other cats.

THE OLD CAT

As your cat moves into old age there are many ways in which you can help to keep it healthy and comfortable. For example, there are some simple additions to its diet that will minimise the risk of deficiencies and significantly reduce stresses on vital organs such as the liver and kidney.

Ageing is a gradual process. Warning signs of organ deterioration are usually not dramatic, but rather insidious in onset. In humans it is often the heart and arteries that are the first to fail. In cats, the kidneys are their Achilles heel.

How long does a cat live?
The average lifespan of an unneutered male cat living in the wild is less than four years. A domestic cat, neutered, and living in a protected situation will usually live to twelve or fifteen years of age. Many reach eighteen or twenty. The oldest known cat was 'Puss' from Devon, England, who died the day after his thirty-sixth birthday.

Changes that occur as a cat grows old
A pessimist once described life as 'a terminal condition'. There is some truth in his view. All of the body's organs must slowly deteriorate and become less efficient. Muscles waste, the colour of the coat changes, the skin loses its elasticity and tone. It is not possible to give a precise age at which a cat is considered 'old'. Individuals vary. Some of the changes that occur in a cat's later life include the following:

  ● The senses deteriorate. Smell, taste, sight and hearing are all impaired to some degree, although it is rare for a cat to lose one of these senses entirely.

  ● The skin becomes less elastic, the coat loses its glossy sheen and the hairs tend to clump together and stick up. Because the cat is less inclined to groom, discharges may build up around the eyes, ears and anus.

238

- Muscle tone deteriorates. This includes not only the skeletal muscles of the limbs and trunk, but also the muscles within the bowel wall and others such as the bladder sphincter. The bowel may become less effective in propelling food through the digestive tract, which results in the cat becoming liable to bouts of constipation and/or diarrhoea. If the muscle tone of the bladder sphincter is reduced, the cat will start to dribble urine. If the anal sphincter is affected it may pass a lot of foul gas or occasionally inadvertently pass faeces.

- The liver and pancreas gradually deteriorate. In some old cats, one of these organs may eventually fail to produce enough digestive enzymes to digest food adequately. The cat usually continues to eat well but loses weight. The faeces of these cats are usually loose or ill formed, yellow and greasy.
- Decrease in energy levels and agility. The old cat is content to spend most of its day sleeping.
- Teeth may be lost. This is usually due to gum disease, but is also partly due to loosening of the teeth within their sockets as the jaw bones become less flexible and more chalky.
- Resistance to disease decreases. Old cats are more susceptible to diseases such as cat 'flu. When they are sick they deteriorate faster, having less strength and stamina than young cats. Healing takes longer.
- Resistance to parasites decreases. Cats that have never previously been troubled by fleas can develop heavy burdens. Similarly, internal worm parasites such as hookworm can multiply to infest in numbers that significantly affect the cat's health.
- Old cats are less adaptable to changes such as moving house, a new pet, a new baby or even just a rearrangement of the furniture. A change in diet is often no problem for a young cat, but a considerable stress for an old one.
- The old cat is likely to suffer from:
— Kidney disease.
— Mouth conditions.
— Skin tumours.
— Arthritis.
— Heart disease (rare).

LOOKING AFTER AN OLD CAT

Some routine measures that can be taken with any older cat include the following:

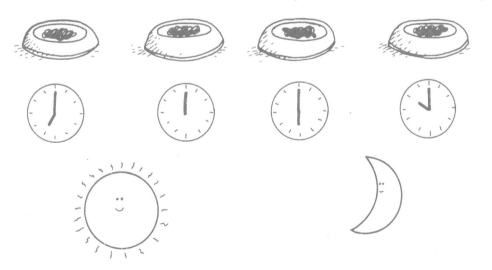

Feed an old cat a little at a time to spread the work load of the vital organs

● Feed smaller meals, more often. This gives the digestive system a better chance to digest the food effectively, and it evens out the stresses on vital organs such as the kidney and liver.

● Do not feed large amounts of rich red meats such as beef heart. White meats and fish are more easily digested, and have less toxic wastes for the kidney to excrete.

● A multi-vitamin/mineral supplement is an excellent idea. Cats make most of their own vitamins. As they get older, a supplement of vitamins significantly improves the health of many cats. Perhaps their production has fallen below optimum, or perhaps the requirements of old tissues for vitamins are higher. The levels of various minerals such as copper, zinc and iron can become depleted, so a supplement that provides both vitamins and minerals, and probably also some trace elements, is often successful in rejuvenating an old cat. It is better to use a preparation formulated specifically for cats than to use a human preparation, as feline requirements are significantly different from ours.

● Add a pinch of salt to the daily ration. This supplies sodium and also encourages drinking, which keeps the kidney flushing and also reduces the incidence of constipation. Do not add more than ⅛ teaspoon per day, and do not add any if the cat has a heart condition and your vet has advised salt restriction.

● Pamper the cat a little. Make sure the sleeping area is warm and draught-free. You might even allow the cat to sleep near a source of warmth such as a water heater or heat bank.

● Constipation is a common problem. If this is the case with your cat, read pages 184–186. Some roughage (such as bran) added to the diet can effectively prevent recurrences. Avoid excessive amounts of dry food and bones. You may occasionally have to give a laxative such as liquid paraffin.

● Groom the cat daily. Regular combing and brushing will keep your cat more comfortable by removing dead hairs that irritate the skin, or which could otherwise be ingested and lead to constipation.

● Clear away any discharges from the eyes. If necessary, clean the ears. Check the anal area for soiled or matted fur.

● Worm the old cat every six months. Your vet will supply a suitable preparation.

VETERINARY CHECK UPS

VET TREATMENT
URGENT

BOOSTER

A regular check up of an old cat can be well worthwhile. Because vets are very familiar with the problems an old cat is liable to encounter, they may be able to pick up subtle warning signs long before you do. Some of the points your vet will pay particular attention to include:
● *Teeth*
Gum disease and the formation of tartar or dental calculus is a common cause of discomfort. Early treatment can save teeth, and the cat will certainly be more comfortable without inflamed gums.
● *Vaccination*
Booster vaccinations are sensible because the old cat's immune system gradually becomes less efficient.
● *Parasites*
Internal and external parasites can build up to affect an old cat's health significantly.
● *Diet*
Your vet may discuss possible deficiencies or changes needed.
● A general check may indicate possible problems in organs such as the

240

kidney, liver and lungs. Your vet may want to run some tests to check on possible problems.

SOME SPECIFIC CONDITIONS OF OLD AGE

Kidney disease or deterioration
Warning signs could include:
- Increased thirst.
- Increased appetite (later in the course the appetite may decline or be lost).
- Bad breath.
- Weight loss.
- Deterioration of the coat — becomes lifeless and dehydrated.
- Mouth ulcers.
- Weakness, lethargy, disinclination to exercise.
- Change in character. May become more affectionate, but usually becomes moody and prefers to hide away. May even dig a hole and sit in the cold and rain.

For more details see 'Kidney and Bladder' (page 198).

Oral disease
Warning signs could include:
- Drooling saliva.
- Reluctance to eat or pain when eating. The cat may seem interested, walk up to the food bowl, but then walk away again.
- Bad breath.
- Weight loss.

To check the teeth, lift the side of your cat's lip back to expose one side of the mouth. It is not necessary to open the mouth. Look especially at the gum/tooth margin for evidence of redness, discharge, ulceration or build up of a tartar deposit.

For more details see 'Teeth and Mouth' (page 123).

Arthritis
The signs of arthritis are usually most obvious early in the morning, when the cat arises from a long rest or during damp, changeable weather.

Warning signs could include:
- Wasting of the pelvic muscles.
- Reluctance to get up from rest or to sit down again.
- Stiff, stilted gait.
- Difficulty or inability to jump up. You may, for example, note that the cat stops using a favoured chair and prefers to lie on the floor.
- Disinclination to groom, especially around the base of the tail.

For more details see 'Bones and Joints' (page 216).

Heart disease
When the heart is diseased, all the organs are affected to some extent, so the signs can be confusing. Fortunately, heart disease is not common in cats. Vets find it difficult to evaluate the cat's heart effectively because it beats rapidly and is very small.

Warning signs could include:
- Decreased exercise tolerance. Cat becomes reluctant to move about, or

moves only short distances before lying down. In some cases the cat may appear to have difficulty in getting comfortable.

- Cough — especially on awakening or starting to move around.
- Fluid retention in chest or abdomen. If the chest is affected the cat could have short, laboured breaths and perhaps a cough. If the abdomen is affected it may swell with fluid to give a pot bellied appearance.
- Palor of gums.
- Lethargy, depression, dullness.

In some cases, clots (thrombus) may form in a major blood vessel. In these cases, signs could include:

- Cold leg. No detectable pulse.
- Pain in affected leg or legs (could be both hind-limbs).
- Loss of function of affected leg(s).

For more details, see 'Heart and Lungs' (page 207).

Euthanasia (mercy killing, 'putting to sleep', 'putting down')
There may come a time when you have to consider having your old cat humanely and painlessly euthanised. This will inevitably be a difficult time for you, and a decision you will understandably be loath to make. However, for the sake of your pet you should try to be objective and to make the decision based on whether there is any joy left for your cat. Consider whether the cat is suffering unnecessarily.

Euthanasia is painless and quick. The cat will know nothing about it. Your vet will give the cat a large overdose of an anaesthetic which will put it deeply to sleep, then stop all functions permanently.

If there is no real joy left for the cat or if there is no treatment available that will give a reasonable chance of it recovering to near normal life, then you must seriously consider whether it would be kinder to put your cat down.

How to tell if your cat is dead
- Breathing stops. Look for any movement of the chest or abdomen. You could hold a mirror next to the nose. Breathing will cause fogging of the glass.
- Heart stops. Check the femoral artery, which runs inside the cat's thigh. Or feel for the heart itself. This is on the left side, just behind and above the point of the elbow.
- Eyes. Reflexes go. The cat's eyes are open after death. Gently touch the eyeball with your finger. If the cat is dead there will be no reflex blink. The eye feels soft. Compare it with the tone of your own eyeball. The pupil of a dead cat is wide open.
- *Rigor mortis:* fifteen to thirty minutes after death the cat's muscles begin to stiffen and the cat eventually becomes rigid. This rigor wears off to some degree several hours later.

Touch the cornea. After death there is no reflex blink

GLOSSARY

By Dr. N. Koch B.V.Sc

Based on:
  The A-Z of Australian Family Medicines, Rosalind Spencer, Butterworths, 1980.
  Black's *Veterinary Dictionary*, edited by Geoffrey West, 13th ed., Adam & Charles Black, London, 1979.
The Eye in Veterinary Practice, J. R. Blogg, Saunders, Philadelphia, 1980.

Purpose of this glossary:
To assist all your reading and help you understand your vet.

Abdomen: the portion of the body that lies between the chest and the pelvis
Abiotrophy: hereditary degenerative disease of late onset
Abnormality: an irregularity in any organ or system
Abortion: premature expulsion of the foetus before it is fully developed
Abrasion: removal of surface layers of skin or eyeball
Abscess: a localized collection of pus, usually enclosed in a wall of fibrous tissue
Accommodation: the adjustment of vision for seeing at different distances. Produced by change in shape of lens
Acetylsalicylic acid: asprin
Acidosis: chemical imbalance due to excess acid
Acquired immunity: immunity resulting from either vaccination or a previous attack of the disease which makes the body resistant to further infection
Action: the way in which a cat moves
Acuity: visual ability to distinguish shapes; applies to central vision
Acute disease: a disease which is rapid in onset
Adhesion: the joining of two structures by fibrous (scar) tissue
Adipose tissue: fat
Adrenal glands: two small organs found next to the kidneys; they secrete various hormones
Adrenalin: a hormone produced in the adrenal gland which has various functions including constriction of blood vessels and stimulation of the heart
Aetiology: the study of causes of a disease
Afterbirth: the matter delivered after the newborn kitten. It comprises fluids and the membranes that surrounded the kitten in the uterus.
Agenesis: absence of an organ
Agouti: the colour between the stripes on a tabby cat
Ailurophile: cat lover

Ailurophobe: cat hater

Albino: an animal lacking in the pigment melanin, so it is white

Albumin: one of the proteins found in blood

Alimentary canal: digestive system

Allele: one of two or more contrasting:
  1. genes (on the same locus in homologous chromosomes)
  2. characters transmitted by alternative genes

Allergen: a compound (usually a protein) that can cause an allergic reaction in susceptible individuals

Allergy: a specific sensitivity which results from exposure to a particular allergen

Alopecia: absence of hair from an area normally covered with hair

Alter: sometimes used in place of 'neuter' (U.S.)

Alveoli: the small air sacs within the lung

Amaurosis: blindness, especially blindness without apparent reason – from disease of the retina, optic nerve or brain

Amino acids: the building blocks which form proteins

Amylase: pancreatic enzyme which helps to digest starch

Anabolic: build up, growth, tissue building

Anaerobe: a bacteria that grows in conditions of no, or very low, oxygen

Anaemia: a deficiency of red blood cells

Anaesthetic: a compound that produces contracted insensibility or unconsciousness

Anal: referring to the anus

Analgesic: a drug which causes loss of pain without loss of consciousness

Anaphylactic: possessing anaphylaxis

Anaphylaxis: an unusual or exaggerated reaction of the animal to a substance, e.g., a severe allergic reaction to a bee sting, or an acute allergic reaction to penicillin

Androgen: male sex hormone

Aneurysm: abnormal localized widening of a blood vessel following weakening of its walls

Ankylosing spondylitis: inflammation of the joints in the backbone which leads to loss of mobility

Anoestrus: the state in the female when it is not 'in season'

Anomaly: marked deviation from the normal

Anorexia: loss of appetite

Anoxia: lack of oxygen

Antacid: substances which decrease the acidity of the stomach

Anterior: towards the head (a term used in anatomical descriptions)

Anterior chamber: the space filled with fluid (aqueous) in the front part of the eye, behind the cornea

Anthelmintic: a substance used to kill parasitic worms

Antibiotic: a substance derived from a living organism which is capable of killing or inhibiting growth of another organism, especially bacteria

Antibody: a substance found in the blood or other body fluids which has a specific restrictive or destructive action on a foreign protein, i.e., fights against infection

Anticoagulant: substances which prevent blood clotting

Antidote: a compound which neutralizes a poison

Antiemetic: substances which prevent vomiting

Antigen: a protein which enters the body from outside which leads to the formation of antibodies by the white blood cells

Antihistamine: a drug which neutralizes the effect of excess histamine

244

release which can be caused by an allergic reaction

Antipruritic: substances which prevent itching

Antipyretic: substances which lower body temperature in fever

Antiseptic: a compound which kills bacteria and/or virus, used to prevent the harmful results of infection in living tissue

Antitussive: substances which relieve coughing

Anuria: lack of urine production

Anus: the posterior opening of the digestive system

Aorta: the main artery of the body

Aplasia: lack of development of an organ

Aqueous humour, aqueous: clear, watery fluid which fills the front chamber of the eye

Arrhythmia: irregular beating of the heart

Arteriosclerosis: hardening of the arteries

Artery: a blood vessel which carries blood away from the heart. This blood is rich in oxygen

Arthritis: inflammation of a joint

Ascites: swelling of the abdomen with fluid

Ascorbic acid: vitamin C

Asphyxia: suffocation, due to lack of oxygen in the blood

Aspirin: a pain relieving, fever reducing, anti-inflammatory drug (acetylsalicilic acid)

Astigmatism: faulty vision due to lack of focus

Astringent: substances which shrink the outer layers of the skin in order to slow discharges from below the skin

Ataxia: loss of the power of movement, so a staggering step results

Atony: loss of muscle tone

Atopic dermatitis: skin inflammation due to hereditary allergy

Atopy: a form of allergy which is hereditary, e.g., asthma, eczema

Atria: the two chambers at the top of the heart. These receive blood from large veins

Atrial septal defect: defect between two of the chambers or atria of the heart

Atrophy:
1. a defect or failure of nutrition seen as a wasting away
2. decrease in size of the cell, tissue, organ or part

Atropine: potent drug used to enlarge pupil and reduce eye pain. Bottle of these eye drops can be fatal to children

Aural: relating to the ear

Auricles: another name for atria

Ausculation: a method of diagnosis by which internal organs are examined by listening to the sound they produce, usually with a stethoscope

Auto-immune disease: disease caused by the body producing antibodies against its own cells

Auto-immunity: a disease whereby the body's defence mechanisms act on normal tissues

Auto-immunization: reaction to its own tissues

Autolysis: self digestion

Autopsy: examination of the internal organs of the body after death

Autosomal: attached to an ordinary paired chromosome as distinct from a sex chromosome

Avitiaminosis: the condition caused by lack of a vitamin in the diet

Awn hairs: coarse type of secondary hair with thickened tips

Axilla: armpit

Bacteraemia: bacteria in the blood stream

Bacteria: a type of micro-organism. Some bacteria cause disease

Bacteriocidal: an agent that kills bacteria

Bacteriostatic: an agent that stops bacteria from growing without actively killing the bacteria

Back-cross: the offspring resulting from mating an animal to one of its parents

Ball & socket: a type of joint where a sphere of bone moves within a cup, e.g., hip

Barbiturates: a family of drugs which can cause sedation or anaesthesia

Basophil: type of white blood cell

Benign: mild or not serious; not malignant

Beta blockers: drugs used in various heart and circulatory disturbances

Bilateral: on both sides

Bile: a fluid formed in the liver and stored in the gall bladder which aids in digestion

Binocular vision: the ability to use the two eyes simultaneously to focus on the same object and to fuse the two images into a single image

Biopsy: the examination of a specimen from live tissue, usually with a microscope

Bladder: a sac used for storing fluids, e.g., urinary bladder

Blepharitis: inflammation of the eyelids

Blindness: lack or loss of ability to see due to disorder of the eye, the pathways from the eye to the brain or in the brain

Bloat: a distended stomach, usually in cattle or sheep

Blood group: Classification of blood according to red blood cell type

Blood poisoning: septicaemia

Blood pressure: the pressure in the arteries

Bone pinning: a method of treating fractures whereby a pointed, stainless steel pin is driven down the centre of the bone to hold the broken ends in place

Booster vaccination: injections given after the first vaccination to help increase immunity

Boracic acid: a mild antiseptic, now replaced by better drugs

Bowels: intestine

Bow-legs: the long limb bones bend outwards

Bradycardia: slow heart beat

Breech birth: a birth where the hind feet appear first (rather than the head)

Brisket (sternum): the bone in the centre of the chest joining the ribs

Broad spectrum antibiotic: an antibiotic which acts against a wide range of micro-organisms

Bronchi: the main tubes into which the windpipe divides

Bronchioles: small conducting tubes within the lung

Bronchitis: inflammation of the lining of the tubes in the lung

Bruise: an injury caused by a blow which leads to discolouration of the skin due to a localized collection of blood

Burn: an injury caused by dry heat

Bursa: a small fluid-filled cavity found where unusual pressure occurs, e.g., elbow

Bursitis: inflammation of a bursa

Buttocks: the rump or hips

Caecum: a blind ending sac found at the junction of the small and large intestine

Caesarean section: removal of unborn young from the mother by surgical incision into the uterus

Calamine: a substance used as an astringent and protective agent

Calcification: deposition of calcium salts in a tissue where it is not normally found

Calculi: stones composed of mineral salts found in various parts of the body, e.g., urinary or gall bladder

Calculus: a 'stone' formed by the crystallization of certain salts

Callus: a piece of new bone laid down around the ends of a broken bone during the first few weeks after fracture

Calorie: a unit of heat used to give an indication as to the amount of energy in a food

Canaliculus: a small tear drainage tube at the inner corner of the upper and lower eyelids leading from the tear duct opening to the tear sac

Cancer: a malignant tumour, i.e., a tumour which continues to grow and spread at a rapid rate eventually leading to death of the animal, if corrective measures are not undertaken. See also Neoplasm

Candida: a type of fungus

Canine teeth: also called eye teeth. They are the large curved teeth seen towards the front of the mouth

Canker: an old term used to describe inflammation of the external ear

Canthus: the angle at either end of the eyelid opening

Capsule:
1. a soluble case made of gelatin which contains small doses of medicine
2. a protective envelope of fibrous tissue which surrounds certain organs such as the kidney, liver or lens

Carbohydrates: a group of chemical substances including sugars and starches used as an energy source for the body

Carbolic acid: a disinfectant

Carcinoma: a malignant growth which is derived from epithelial tissue, for instance skin or lung tissue

Cardiac: referring to the heart

Cardiac arrhythmia: an irregularity in the heartbeat

Cardiac output: the volume of blood pumped through the heart per minute

Cardiography: the recording of the phases of the heartbeat

Caries: a process of decay of teeth

Carrier: an animal which has a genetic defect without showing it; or an animal which possesses disease-causing organisms without being affected

Cartilage: a hard but flexible tissue found in certain parts of the skeleton, such as nose, ear or windpipe

Caruncle: small prominence at the corner of the eye near the nose

Castration: the removal of the testicles of male animals

Cataract: clouding of the lens

Cataract, immature: a cataract where only part of the lens is involved

Cataract, mature (or ripe): a cataract in which the whole lens is involved

Cataract, senile: lens cloudy due to old age. (Note that *all* old lenses become more 'blue' with age and this is not disease)

Catarrh: inflammation of mucous membranes, especially the air passages, which leads to the secretion of mucus

Catheter: a soft, flexible tube which is passed into organs or blood vessels, e.g., into the bladder and used to remove urine when the animal is unable to urinate on its own

Caudal: towards the tail (a term used in anatomical descriptions)

Cell: the microscopic unit of which all plant and animal tissues are composed

Cellulitis: a rapidly spreading infection found just under the skin

Central nervous system (CNS): the brain and spinal cord

Cerebellar hypoplasia: underdeveloped part of the brain called the cerebellum

Cerebral: referring to that part of the brain containing its higher functions, e.g., thought

Cerebrospinal fluid: the fluid bathing the brain and spinal cord

Cervical: referring to the neck

Cervix: situated between vagina and uterus. Seals the uterus. Opens when queen is on heat and at parturition

Chemotherapy: the treatment of disease with chemical substances, especially in relation to cancer

Cherry eye: prolapsed gland of the third eyelid

Chlorhixidine: an antiseptic

Choking: obstruction of breathing

Cholecystitis: inflammation of the gall bladder

Cholesterol: a type of fat present in the blood

Chondrodysplasia: faulty cartilage and bone development

Choroid: the middle of the three coats of the eye. It possesses blood vessels which are responsible for nutrition of the retina

Chromosomes: minute bodies found within the cell nucleus which store genetic information

Chronic disease: a disease which lasts for a long time (weeks/months)

Chronic superficial keratitis (CSK): inflamed red mass on the cornea (and third eyelid may also be inflamed)

Ciliary body: a structure in the eye found between the iris and the choroid. It produces aqueous humour and contains the ciliary muscle

Cilium: eyelash

Cleft palate: a defect where the two halves of the mouth do not fuse

Clotting of blood: the process whereby the fluid portion of blood becomes jelly-like

Coagulation: another name for clotting

Cocaine: a local anaesthetic

Cochlea: the region of the ear where sounds are converted to electrical impulses

Codeine: a pain killer

Cod liver oil: an oil rich in Vitamins A and D

Coitus: sexual intercourse

Coliform enteritis: gut infection due to E. coli

Colitis: inflammation of the first part of the large intestine

Collagen: the fibrillar substance of the connective tissue

Collapsed trachea: deformed windpipe

Colobomas of the optic disc: pits in the head of the optic nerve in the eye

Colon: large intestine

Colostrum: the milk secreted by the mother, the first few days after birth. It is different to normal milk and provides the newborn with some defence against infection

Concussion: a temporary loss of consciousness due to an injury to the head

Cones: part of the layer of retina responsible for vision in bright light

Conformation: structure

Congenital: present at birth, not necessarily inherited

Congestion: excessive amount of fluid in a part of the body

Congestive heart failure: the heart is unable to maintain normal pumping of blood, resulting in fluid build-up in lungs and/or abdomen

Conjunctiva: the membrane which lines the eyelids and front of the eyeball

Conjunctivitis: inflammation of the conjunctiva

Connective tissue: the structural elements of the body
Constipation: inability to defaecate
Convulsions: powerful involuntary contractions of muscles
Cornea: transparent portion of the outer coat of the front of the eyeball forming the eye window
Corneal graft (keratoplasty): operation to restore vision by replacing a section of opaque cornea with transparent cornea
Corticosteroid: drug used to reduce inflammation; harmful side-effects exist
Cortisone: one of the corticosteroids. It is also a hormone produced naturally in the adrenal gland
Costal: referring to the ribs
Cow-hocks: hocks pointing inwards
Craniomandibular osteopathy: deformity of the jaw
Crepitus: the grating of the broken ends of bones
Cruciate ligaments: a pair of ligaments in the stifle joint which prevent the joint from over-extending
Cryptorchid: a male with one or both undescended testes
CSF: cerebro-spinal fluid
CSK: chronic superficial keratitis – inflamed red mass, e.g., on the cornea and third eyelid
Cushing's disease: condition which results from production of excess cortisol by the adrenal glands. A similar condition results from prolonged corticosteroid therapy
Cutaneous: pertaining to the skin
Cyanosis: lack of oxygen to the tissues which results in a bluish appearance of the gums and tongue
Cyst: a swelling which contains fluid other than pus, whose walls are not inflamed
Cystine: Dicysteine, an amino acid produced by the digestion or acid hydrolysis of proteins. It is sometimes found in the urine and in the kidneys in the form of minute crystals
Cystinuria: cystine crystals in urine
Cystitis: inflammation of the bladder

Dacryoadenitis: inflammation of the tear gland (tear-producing gland)
Dam: mother
Dark adaptation: ability of the eye to adjust to dim light
Day blindness: blindness during the day, due to faulty cones of the eye
Debridement: removal of damaged tissue from the surface of a wound
Defibrillator: a device which produces an electric shock used for restoring normal activity to the heart
Deformity: disfigurement
Degeneration: a deterioration. A change of a tissue from a higher to a lower or less active functional form
Degenerative pannus: an inflamed red mass, e.g., on the cornea
Dehydration: loss of water from the tissues
Demodex: a type of mite causing skin irritation
Depressed: decreased
Dermatitis: any inflammation of the skin
Dermatology: the branch of medicine concerned with disorders of the skin
Dermoid: a small tumour of skin present at birth on the eye
Dermoid cyst: cyst in the skin
Developmental abnormality: one which occurs between the time of fertilization and the adult stages of development

Dew claw: the first digit, found on the inside of the leg above the foot. It is often absent on the hind paw. It is functionless

Dextrose: a type of sugar

Diabetes insipidus: a disease due to disorder of the hypothalamus gland. The sufferer is unable to concentrate the urine and passes large volumes of very dilute urine

Diabetes mellitus: the more common form of diabetes. There is excessive glucose in the blood stream but cells are unable to utilise it, usually due to a lack of insulin

Dialysis: an artificial means of carrying out kidney function

Diamond eye: greatly oversized eyelid opening

Diaphragm: the structure which separates the chest from the abdomen

Diarrhoea: increased amounts of and very fluid faeces (stools)

Digestion: the process of breaking down food into components small enough to be absorbed through the gut wall

Digitalis: a drug used for heart stimulation

Digits: toes

Dilation: to increase the size of a structure

Di-oestrus: the last part of the oestrus cycle. During this phase much progesterone is produced, a hormone which allows the maintenance of pregnancy

Diploid: the number of chromosomes found in most cells. There is a paired set of chromosomes, one of each pair comes from the sire, the other from the dam

Dislocation: abnormal separation of two bones at a joint

Distension: increase in size, usually of a hollow organ

Distichiasis: the presence of two rows of eyelashes on the one eyelid

Diuretic: a substance which promotes the production of urine

Diverticulum: a small outpouching of a hollow organ

DNA: a substance which makes up chromosomes

Doctoring: euphemism for neutering

Docking: removal of all or part of an extremity such as the tail or an ear

Dominant inheritance: member of a gene pair which is capable of overriding the other member

Dropsy: see Oedema

Duct: an enclosed channel used for conducting fluid

Duodenum: the first part of the small intestine

Dys-: a prefix meaning painful or difficult

Dysentery: a condition of the colon where blood is passed in the faeces

Dyspepsia: disturbance to digestion

Dysphagia: difficulty in swallowing

Dysplasia: abnormal development of some part of the body

Dyspnoea: difficulty in breathing

Dystocia (or Dystokia): difficulty in giving birth

Dystrophy: inherited degeneration

Ear mange: ear irritation caused by a species of mite

Eclampsia: a disease occurring during late pregnancy or after birthing which causes muscle tremors, loss of consciousness, fits and can lead to sudden death. It is due to deficiency of calcium

Ectasia: dilation, distension

Ectropion: turning out of the eyelid

Eczema: a type of inflammatory disease of the skin which causes irritation and itching

Edema: see Oedema

Effusion: a collection of fluid in a space where it does not belong

Electro-cardiogram (ECG): a record of the different electrical phases of a heartbeat

Electro-encephalogram (EEG): recording of the electrical activity of the brain

Electrolyte: essential minerals present in body fluids

Elizabethan collar: a collar made of cardboard or plastic fitted over the head, which prevents the animal interfering with wounds, dressings, etc.

Embolism: the plugging of a small blood vessel by a piece of material from another part of the blood stream. It can lead to a heart attack if the plugging occurs in the heart, or a stroke if it occurs in the brain

Embryo: an undeveloped foetus, i.e., the future individual soon after fertilization

Emisis: vomiting

Emetic: a substance which causes vomiting

Emollient: a substance which softens and soothes the skin

Emphysema: the abnormal presence of air in some part of the body. It usually refers to abnormally large air spaces being found in the lungs

Empyema: a collection of pus and fluid within a cavity

Endocarditis: inflammation of the inner lining of the heart

Endocrine glands: glands which secrete hormones

Endothelium: the membrane lining certain vessels and cavities of the body

Endotracheal anaesthesia: the anaesthetic gas is passed down a rubber tube directly into the windpipe

Enema: introduction of fluid into the rectum usually to evacuate the bowels or loosen a constipated mass of faeces

Enteritis: inflammation of the intestines

Entire: not castrated or spayed (not neutered)

Entropion: a turning inward of the eyelid

Enucleation: removal of the eyeball

Enzymes: substances formed within living cells which speed up biochemical reactions

Eosinophil: a type of white blood cell

Eosinophilia: the presence of abnormally large numbers of eosinophils in the blood

Epi-: a prefix meaning outside of

Epidermis: outer layer of skin

Epididymis: a structure associated with the testicle in which sperms mature

Epididymitis: inflammation of the epididymis

Epidural anaesthesia: a local anaesthetic is introduced into the spinal canal

Epiglottis: a structure in the throat which prevents material from passing into the larynx

Epilation: removal of hair

Epilepsy: abnormal electrical activity within the brain which can lead to sudden fits

Epiphora: overflow of tears, a watery eye

Epiphysis: the end of a long bone

Epithelium: the layer or layers of cells of which skin and mucous membranes are composed

ERG: electroretinogram, records retinal function

Erosion: an eating or gnawing away, ulceration

Erythema: redness

Erythrocyte: a red blood cell

Euthanasia: humane killing

Everted third eyelid: turned out third eyelid
Excretion: disposal of waste materials
Expectorant: a substance used to clear phlegm
External parasites: organisms such as lice, ticks and mites which cause damage outside the body
Exudate: a fluid, usually produced by disease, which escapes from the site of production
Eye shine: reflection from the eye seen at night
Eyelashes, extra: an additional row of eyelashes

Faeces: solid excreta from the anus
Fallopian tubes: fine tubes which carry the egg from the ovary to the uterus
False pregnancy: a condition where all the signs of pregnancy are visible but the queen is not in fact pregnant
Far-sighted (hyperopia): blurred close vision
Fascia: sheets or bands of fibrous tissue which surround muscles
Febrile: raised body temperature, fever
Femur: the thigh bone
Feral: a domestic animal that has been born in the wild or reverted to it
Fever: increased body temperature (for cats, over 39°C)
Fibrin: a component of the blood which forms a meshwork which is a vital part of clot formation in the control of bleeding
Fibrosis: the formation of fibrous (scar) tissue
Fibrous tissue: one of the most abundant tissues of the body. It is composed of collagen (which when boiled gives gelatin), elastic fibres and fibroblasts surrounded by tissue fluid
Field of vision: the area which can be seen without moving the eyes
Filtration angle: See Iridocorneal angle
Fissure: a splitting or discontinuity of a surface, especially one that persists
Fistula: an abnormal passage often leading into an internal hollow organ
Fit: a seizure
Flank: the side of the body between the last rib and the hip
Flatulence: passing wind
Flehmen reaction: a characteristic facial gesture that occurs when Jacobsens organ is stimulated
Flexor: a muscle that bends or flexes a limb or part of it
Foetus: a fully developed individual within the uterus, i.e., one where all of the organs, limbs, etc., are similar in appearance to those of an adult
Follicle: a tiny sac-like structure. Also refers to the structure which houses the hair
Follicular mange: another name for demodectic mange
Fracture: a break in a bone
Fundus: the back of the eyeball, includes retina
Fungal: caused by or relating to a fungus. Synonymous with the adjective fungous
Fungicidal: an agent that kills fungi
Fungistatic: an agent that stops the growth of fungi
Fungus (pl. fungi): a primitive form of plant life

Gait: any of the co-ordinated leg actions of movement
Gall-bladder: a bag-like structure lying near the liver which stores bile
Gall-stones: hard masses formed in the gall-bladder
Gangrene: death of a part of the body accompanied by bacterial infection

Gastric: anything to do with the stomach

Gastritis: inflammation of the stomach

Gastro-enteritis: inflammation of the stomach and intestines

Gene: the unit of heredity found on a specific position on the chromosome

Genital organs: external reproductive organs

Genotype: the hereditary assortment of genes of an individual

Gestation: period of pregnancy

Gingival hyperplasia: overgrowth of the gums

Gingivitis: inflammation of the gums

Gland of the third eyelid: a gland surrounding the base of the third eyelid cartilage

Glands: groups of cells which secrete substances which act on other organs

Glaucoma: increased pressure in the eye which harms vision

Globe: eyeball

Glycosuria: the presence of glucose in the urine

Goitre: enlargement of the thyroid gland due to iodine deficiency

Gonad: the ovary or testis

Goniolens: a lens placed on the cornea for gonioscopy

Gonioscopy: examination of the angle inside of the eyeball for the disease which causes glaucoma

Granuloma: a granular tumour

Growth: any formation of abnormal or new tissue

Haematemesis: the vomiting of blood

Haematocrit value: the percentage of whole blood which is composed of red blood cells

Haematology: the study of blood and blood producing tissues

Haematoma: an area of swelling that is filled with blood

Haematuria: blood in the urine

Haemoglobin: an iron-containing molecule found in red blood cells which transports oxygen

Haemolysis: the rupture of red blood cells

Haemoptysis: coughing up blood

Haemorrhage: bleeding

Haploid: half the number of chromosomes found in ordinary cells. The sperm and ova are 'haploid'

Hare lip: a malformation in the upper lip where the two halves do not fuse

Haws: protrusion of the third eyelid

Heart block: disturbance of electrical conductivity through the heart

Heat: popular term for a queen in oestrus or in season

Heat-stroke: a condition caused by excess heat

Helminths: a class of parasitic worms

Hemeralopia: day blindness; defective vision in bright light

Hemiplegia: paralysis on one side of the body only

Hepatitis: inflammation of the liver

Hereditary: a condition passed on from generation to generation (not always evident at birth)

Heritable: a condition that can be inherited

Hernia: the pushing out through the abdominal walls or natural opening of any of the abdominal organs

Heterochromia: the eyes having a different colour

Heterozygous: each gene pair is composed of two different gene types

Hexachlorophene: a powerful antiseptic

Histamine: a substance release by damaged tissues which causes part of the inflammatory response

Histology: the study of the microscopic structure of tissues

Hock: the joint in the cat corresponding to the human ankle

Hordeolum: stye or inflammation of the sebaceous glands of the lids

Hormone: a substance produced in a particular region, which is carried by the blood and exerts its influence on another tissue away from the site of production

Horner's syndrome: damage to the sympathetic pathway which supplies sympathetic nerves to the eye. It is characterized by one sunken eye, prominent third eyelid, small pupil, drooping upper lid

Hot spot: an inflamed raw patch of skin that appears during hot weather

Humerus: the long bone found between the shoulder joint and elbow joint

Humour: any fluid of the body

Hydrocephalus: a condition where large amounts of fluid collect within the brain cavity

Hydronephrosis: blockage of the ureter leads to accumulation of urine within the kidney which causes it to expand and damages the kidney

Hygroma: a swelling occurring within a joint

Hyoid apparatus: the series of bones which support the tongue and larynx

Hyper-: a prefix meaning too much

Hyperaemia: an excess amount of blood, still contained within blood vessels, in a part of the body

Hyperglycaemia: an excess of glucose in the blood

Hyperopia (hypermetropia): far-sightedness

Hyperplasia: an increase in the size of an organ or part due to an increase in the number of cells

Hypersensitivity: allergy. The body reacts to a foreign agent more strongly than normal

Hypertension: high blood pressure

Hyperthermia: increased body temperature

Hypertrophy: an increase in size of an organ or part due to an increase in the size of its cells

Hypervitaminosis: an excess of a particular vitamin

Hyphemia: haemorrhage into the front chamber of the eye

Hypnotic: a drug which produces drowsiness

Hypo-: a prefix indicating too little

Hypocalcaemia: a deficiency of calcium in the blood

Hypoglycaemia: a deficiency of glucose in the blood

Hypomagnesaemia: a deficiency of magnesium in the blood

Hypoplasia: malformation due to insufficient development

Hypopyon: pus in the front chamber of the eye

Hypotension: low blood pressure

Hypothalamus: the part of the brain which regulates body temperature

Hypotony: a soft eye, reduced pressure in the eye

Hypoxia: decreased oxygen carriage in the blood

Hysterectomy: surgery involving removal of the uterus

Icterus: jaundice•

Ichthyosis: dry scaly skin

Idiopathic: a disease with unknown cause

Ileum: the last part of the small intestine

Ileus: distended intestine

Ilium: one of the pelvic bones

254

Immune response: the body's reaction to infection

Immunization: the production of artificial resistance to an infection

Immunosuppressant: a substance which blocks the body's defence mechanism

Impaction: a condition where two things are firmly lodged together, e.g., faeces

Impetigo: a skin disorder, characterized by blocked skin pores

Implantation: the burrowing of the fertilized egg into the wall of the uterus

Inbreeding: the mating of closely related animals

Incisors: the cutting teeth at the front of each jaw

Incompetence, cardiac: the inability of the heart valves to function properly due to disease

Incontinence: the inability to control urination or defaecation

Incubation period: the time between exposure to a disease-causing agent and the development of symptoms

Infarction: changes which occur in a tissue after its blood supply has been cut off

Infection: exposure to potentially disease-causing organisms

Infectious: a disease caused by micro-organisms which may or may not be contagious

Infertility: the inability to breed successfully

Inflammation: the series of changes which occur within a tissue after injury, providing that the injury has not caused death of the tissue. Inflammation is characterized by pain, swelling, redness, heat and loss of function

Inguinal hernia: a hernia usually made up of fat or intestines through the inguinal canal (between hind leg and the body wall)

Inguinal region: on either side of the groin

Inherited: due to genetic influences (not always evident at birth)

Injection:
    1. use of a hypodermic needle to give drugs
    2. congestion, e.g., injected blood vessel

Insulin: a hormone produced by the pancreas which causes a decrease in blood sugar levels. It is administered artificially to control diabetic mellitus

Interbreeding: the mating of animals of different varieties

Intercostal: between the ribs

Internal haemorrhage: bleeding into one of the body cavities

Internal parasites: worms

Intestine: a long hollow tube through which food passes and where most usable compounds are absorbed

Intervertebral disc: cartilage pads between the vertebrae

Intra-: a prefix meaning within

Intubation: the placement of a tube into the windpipe by way of the mouth, usually part of anaesthetic procedure

Intussusception: a form of bowel obstruction in which part of the intestine folds in on itself; a telescoping of the bowels

In vitro: outside the living body – perhaps in a test tube or laboratory

In vivo: in the living body

Iridocorneal angle: the angle between the iris and the cornea

Iris: the coloured circular membrane, the inner border of which forms the pupil behind the cornea and in front of the lens

Iris atrophy: a thin iris, loss of iris tissue

Iritis: inflammation of the iris

Irradiation: exposure to radiation, usually using X-rays

Irrigation: the washing out of wounds or body cavities with large amounts of warm water containing some antiseptic

Ischium: one of the pelvic bones

Ischemia: lack of adequate blood flow to a region or organ

-itis: suffix meaning inflammation of that particular part

Jacobsens organ: also called vomeronasal organ. A sense organ of cats, somewhere between smell and taste. Situated in the roof of the cat's mouth

Jaundice: yellow colouration of the visible mucous membranes due to liver diseases, or due to blood conditions in the newborn

Jaws: the bones which carry the teeth

Jejunum: the central region of the small intestine

Jugular veins: the large veins running on either side of the neck

Kaolin: a powder used to absorb toxins from the alimentary canal

Keratoconjunctivitis, proliferative: inflamed cornea and conjunctiva which grow in size from inflammation

Keratoconjunctivitis sicca (KCS): dry eye

Ketone bodies: abnormal intermediates in the breakdown of fatty acids, found during diabetes, starvation and other conditions

Ketosis: the presence of ketone bodies in the blood and body tissues

Knee: the lay name for the joint in the foreleg of a cat between the elbow and the paw. Correct name: carpus. Equivalent to wrist in humans

Laceration: cut

Lacrimal: relating to tears and the glands which secrete them

Lacrimal puncta: tear duct openings inside the upper and lower lids near the nose

Lacrimal sac: the dilated area at the start of the tear duct below the corner of the eye near the nose

Lacrimation: production of tears

Lactation: production of milk

Lactose: the main sugar found in milk

Lameness: abnormal movement of limbs

Laminectomy: a surgical procedure whereby the top or part of the backbone is removed to relieve pressure from the spinal cord

Lanolin: a grease used as the base for many skin preparations

Laparotomy: surgical opening of the abdomen

Larynx: the 'voice box'. It also prevents food from going down into the lungs

Lavage: washing out of the stomach or intestines

Laxative: a drug which promotes bowel evacuation

Lens: the structure in the eye which focuses light

Lens suture: a potential cleft inside the lens

Lesion: all changes to tissues produced by disease or injury; any abnormality

Leucocytes: white blood cells. These are involved in defence against invasion by micro-organisms

Leucopenia: a condition in which there are less than normal numbers of white blood cells

Leukaemia: a condition where large numbers of abnormal white cells are released into the blood stream, a malignant disease

'Lick granuloma': a condition which arises due to the excessive licking of a wound, preventing healing. Large masses of scar tissue may form

Ligaments: strong bands of tissue which bind certain bones together

Limbus: a border in the eye, the edge of the cornea

Line breeding: the mating of cats within a family to a common ancestor

Lipid: fatty material

Lipoma: a benign tumour of fat tissue

Lipoprotein: a complex molecule consisting of a lipid associated with a protein

Litter:
1. a family of kittens
2. absorbent material used for cat's toilet box or tray

Liver: a large organ lying in the abdomen whose functions are to aid in digestion of food, to break down harmful substances in the blood stream and to break down worn red blood cells

Local anaesthetic: a substance which insensitizes one portion of the body leaving the rest of the animal fully conscious

Long sighted: inability to focus on objects nearby

Lubricant: an oily substance used to reduce friction between opposing surfaces

Lumbar: the region of the back between the ribs and the pelvis

Lumen: the 'hole' in a tubular organ

Lungs: the organs involved in oxygen and carbon dioxide exchange between the body and the atmosphere

Luxation: dislocation

Lymph: the excess fluid removed from body tissues

Lymph nodes, glands: structures distributed along lymphatic vessels which filter lymph

Lymphatics: the vessels which carry lymph

Lymphocyte: a type of white blood cell involved in defending the body from infection

Lymphosarcoma: a malignant tumour of lymph tissue origin. Often associated with feline leukaemia virus infection

Mandible: the lower jaw bone

Manx: tail-less kind of cat thought to have originated in Isle of Man (U.K.)

Mask: the darker coloured areas of the face, for example in the Siamese

Mastication: chewing

Maxilla: upper jaw bone

Mediastinum: the space in the chest between the two lungs. It contains the heart, major blood vessels, trachea, oesophagus, nerves and other structures

-megaly: a suffix meaning an abnormal enlargement

Melanin: a dark pigment produced by cells called melanocytes which give rise to the colour of skin, hair, eyes, etc.

Melanoma: a tumour of melanocytes

Membrana nictitans: third eyelid

Meninges: the protective membranes that surround the brain

Meningitis: inflammation of the meninges

Meniscus: a crescent-shaped piece of cartilage found in some joints which helps form a smooth surface for free joint movement

Mesentery: the sheets of tissue which support the intestines

Metabolism: all the physical and chemical processes which occur in order to maintain the living body

Metacarpal: the bones between the wrist and the digits of the forelimb

Metaplasia: the abnormal change of one tissue type into another

Metastasis: the spread of a tumour to an area away from the original site of that tumour

Metatarsal: the bones between the hock and the digits in the hind limb

Micro: (prefix) small

Micro-organism: a lower form of life so small it can only be seen under a microscope

Microphthalmia: small eye

Micturition: the act of passing urine

Milk teeth: the temporary teeth of young animals

Minerals: chemical elements of which small amounts are present in food

Miosis: excessive contraction of the pupil

Miotic: drug which makes pupil small, used to treat glaucoma

Mitosis: the process of cell reproduction

Mitral valve defect: defect in valves in the heart called mitral valves

Moggy: a cat of mixed or unknown parentage

Moniliasis: infection with monilia, a yeast

Monorchid: a male animal which has only one descended testicle

Morphine: a painkiller

Muco-purulent: consisting of pus and mucus

Mucous membrane: the tissue lining hollow organs and also covering the inside of the mouth

Mucus: the slimy secretion produced by mucous membranes

Murmur: a heart sound caused by abnormal flow of blood through the heart

Muscular dystrophy: a disease causing muscle weakness and wasting

Mutation: a permanent change in the characteristics of an animal caused by a change to the genetic information

Mydriatic: a drug that dilates the pupil, e.g., atropine

Myelin: the insulation surrounding many nerves

Myocardial infarction: death of a portion of heart muscle, i.e., heart attack

Myocardium: heart muscle

Myopia: near-sighted, i.e., can only see clearly things which are close

Narcotics: drugs which induce a sleep-like state

Nasal solar dermatitis: skin of the nose is inflamed and made worse by the sun

Nasopharynx: the upper part of the throat which lies behind the nasal cavity

Nausea: the desire to vomit

Near-sighted: can only see things clearly which are close

Necropsy: post mortem examination

Necrosis: death of cells or tissue while it is still within the living body

Neonatal: the period just after birth

Neoplasia: the formation of new tissue, the growth of which is not co-ordinated with the rest of the tissues of the body. This term is synonymous with tumour

Neoplasm: a new abnormal growth

Nephritis: inflammation of the kidney

Nerve block: a local anaesthetic applied near a nerve to block conduction along that nerve

Nervous system: the communication system of the body

Neuritis: inflammation in a nerve

Neurone: nerve cell

Neurophil: a common white blood cell which can move into tissues and eat foreign or damaged tissue or cells

Nictitans gland: gland of the third eyelid

Nictitating membrane: the third eyelid which the animal may pull across its eye

Nocturnal: active at night
Nodule: a small, firm swelling
Nyctalopia: night blindness
Nystagmus: a condition in which the eyeballs show constant fine jerky involuntary movements

Obese: overweight
Obstetrics: the branch of medicine dealing with pregnancy, labour, delivery and care of the newborn
Obstruction: blockage
Occiput: the part of the head which meets the neck
Ocular: pertaining to the eye
Oculist: eye doctor
Oedema: the localized accumulation of fluid
Oesophagus: it is the tube which conveys food and drink down into the stomach; the gullet
Oestrogens: female sex hormones
Oestrus: season or heat
Olfactory nerve: the nerve concerned with smell
Oliguria: a decrease in the amount of urine produced
Oncology: the study of tumours
Opacity: cloudy area
Ophathalmia: severe inflammation of the whole eye
Ophthalmia neonatorum: purulent conjunctivitis in the newborn
Ophthalmic: pertaining to the eye
Ophthalmologist: eye specialist
Ophthalmology: study of the eye
Ophthalmoscopy: examination of the interior of the eye with an ophthalmoscope
Optic disc: the part of the optic nerve which can be seen in the eyeball
Optic nerve: the nerve which sends signals from the eye to the brain
Oral: pertaining to the mouth
Orbit: the bony socket which contains the eye
Orchitis: inflammation of the testicle
Organ: any discrete part of the body which has a specialized function
Organism: anything that can survive on its own
Orifice: an opening
Orthopaedics: the branch of medicine dealing with bones and joints
Ossification: formation of bone tissue. This occurs normally in bone formation but may occur abnormally in other organs
Osteitis: inflammation of bone
Osteo: pertaining to bone
Osteochondritis: inflammation of bone and cartilage
Osteogenic sarcoma: bone cancer
Osteomyelitis: inflammation of bone and its marrow
Osteoporosis: brittle bones
Otitis externa: inflammation of the part of the ear outside the eardrum
Otitis media: middle ear infection
Ovaries: the organs in the female which produce the eggs
Ovariohysterectomy: surgical removal of the uterus and ovaries. This is also called spaying
Overshot jaw: lower jaw protrudes abnormally
Ovulation: release of eggs from the ovary
Ovum: an egg

Oxytocin: a hormone causing the uterus to contract during birth. It also stimulates milk letdown

Papilloma: a wart
Paracentesis: the removal of fluid from the chest or abdomen
Paraffin, liquid: a lubricant often used to aid in defaecation
Paralysis: the loss or impairment of the function of a part
Paraplegia: paralysis of the hind limbs
Parasite: an organism living totally off another
Parasympathetic nervous system: the portion of the nervous system which controls the minute-to-minute functioning of the body
Parathyroid glands: four small glands which secrete hormones involved in bone metabolism
Parenteral: the administration of a substance by a route other than the digestive tract, e.g., injection
Paresis: slight or incomplete paralysis
Parotid gland: one of the saliva-producing glands
Paroxysm: a violent attack
Parti colour: includes bicolours, tortoiseshells and tortie and whites. Has to have a solid block of colour
Parturition: birth
Patella: kneecap
Patella luxation: slipping kneecap
Patent ductus arteriosus: a small blood vessel in the chest between pulmonary artery and aorta which should close over at birth but remains open
Pathogen: an organism capable of causing disease
Pathology: the study of disease
Pelvis: the large bony structure supporting the hind limbs
Penetrance: the frequency with which an inherited trait is shown in animals carrying the gene which causes it
Penicillin: a commonly used antibiotic
Pepsin: a stomach enzyme which breaks down proteins
Perforation: a hole punched through a tubular organ
Pericarditis: inflammation of the covering membrane of the heart
Perineum: the region between the genitalia and the anus
Peripheral: away from the centre
Peripheral nervous system: the part of the nervous system outside the brain and spinal cord
Peristalsis: the characteristic movement that takes place in muscular tubular organs. It causes the contents of the tube to be propelled in one direction
Peritoneum: the membrane lining the abdominal cavity
Peritonitis: inflammation of the peritoneum
Persistent hyperplastic primary vitreous (PHPV): tissue persists in the eyeball causing cloudy vitreous
Persistent pupillary membrane (PPM): strands which persist in the front of the eye which may cause opacity of the cornea or lens
Persistent right aortic arch: congenital defect in which the aorta in the chest is displaced forming a ring that can compress the windpipe and gullet
Pethidine: a strong pain killer
Pharmacology: the study of action of drugs
Pharynx: irregular funnel-shaped passage at the back of the mouth
Phenotype: the outward visible expression of the hereditary make-up
Phlebitis: inflammation of a vein
Photophobia: abnormal sensitivity to and discomfort from light
Photoreceptor: a nerve end organ sensitive to light – rod or cone

Piebald: white spotting. Usually black and white

Pigmentary keratitis: deposition of brown pigment into the cornea

Pinkeye: conjunctivitis

Pinking up: nipples of queen take on a rosy halo three weeks after mating. Useful in determining due date

Pinna: the major part of the external ear

Pituitary gland: a small gland found at the base of the brain which produces various hormones

Placenta: the organ which allows exchange of food, oxygen and wastes between mother and foetus

Plasma: the fluid portion of blood

Platelets: small structures found in the blood which help arrest bleeding

Pleura: the thin membrane which covers the lungs

Pleurisy: inflammation of the pleura

Pneumonia: inflammation of the lung

Pneumothorax: a collection of air in the pleural cavity. It occurs after a puncture wound to the chest

Polydipsia: excessive thirst

Polygenic: influenced by more than one gene

Polymorph: type of white blood cell

Polyuria: excessive urination

Popliteal: back of the knee

Post-: a prefix meaning after or behind

PPM: persistent pupillary membrane

Pre-: prefix meaning before

Prenatal: before birth

Prepuce: the sheath of the penis

Progesterone: the hormone involved with the maintenance of pregnancy

Prognosis: a forecast of the probable outcome of an attack of disease

Prolapse: the slipping down of an organ or structure

Proliferative keratoconjunctivitis: inflamed growths on the cornea and conjunctiva tissue

Prophylaxis: measures undertaken to prevent disease

Prosthesis: artificial replacement of a body part

Proximal: closer to a given point

Pruritis: intense and persistent itching

Puberty: maturation of sexual function

Pulmonary: pertaining to the lungs

Pulmonic stenosis: narrowing of the opening between the heart and the artery to the lungs

Pulse: the result of the heart rapidly forcing blood into the major arteries

Pupil: the round hole in the centre of the iris which corresponds to the lens aperture in the camera

Purgative: a substance which causes emptying of the gastro-intestinal tract. It may cause vomiting or have a laxative effect

Pus: a thick yellowish fluid resulting from certain types of inflammation. It contains dead and dying white blood cells plus dead and dying tissue and tissue fluid

Pyelonephritis: inflammation of the kidney and first portion of the urinary collecting system

Pyloric stenosis: narrowing of the opening between the stomach and duodenum

Pyogenic: producing pus

Pyo: (prefix) pus

Quadriplegia: paralysis to all four limbs
Queen: un-neutered female cat

Radius: the inner of the two bones of the forearm. It is the weight-bearing bone of the forearm
Rales: moist sounds heard in the chest during various diseases
Ranula: a swelling under the tongue caused by collection of large amounts of saliva
Receptor: the end of a nerve which is sensitive to a particular stimulus
Recessive: a gene which is not expressed unless both members of a pair of chromosomes carry this gene
Rectum: the last few centimetres of the digestive tract
Red eye: inflamed eye
Reduction: refers to the realignment of the ends of the broken bone
Reflux: the backflow of stomach contents into the oesophagus
Refraction:
    1. deviation in the course of rays of light passing from one transparent medium into another of different density
    2. determination of refractive errors of the eye and correction by glasses
Renal: relating to the kidney
Renal cortical hypoplasia: undeveloped part of the kidney called the cortex
Renal tubular dysfunction: faulty function of part of the kidneys called the tubules
Resection: the removal of part of an organ
Respiration: the processes associated with intake of oxygen into the blood stream and removal of carbon dioxide, i.e., breathing
Retina: the innermost coat of the back of the eye, formed of light-sensitive nerve elements
Retinal atrophy: thin retina
Retinal degeneration: a degeneration (thinning) of the retina
Retinal detachment: the separation of the retina from tissue behind it
Retinal dysplasia: abnormal development of retinal layers
Retro-: a prefix signifying behind
Rheumatism: a general term indicating pain and disability of muscles, joints, bones
Rhinitis: inflammation of the lining of the nose
Rickets: a disease of bone found in young animals due to a deficiency of calcium, phosphorus or Vitamin D
Rickettsia: a group of micro-organisms
Rigor mortis: temporary stiffening of the muscles several hours after death
Rigors: shivering fits
Ringworm: a contagious skin disease caused by a type of fungus
Rods: the part of the outer retina responsible for vision in dim light
-rrhaphy: a suffix meaning that an opening is being closed with sutures
Rupture: the bursting open of a body part

Sac: bag-like
Sacrum: the portion of the back just before the tail
Salicylic acid: an anti-bacterial and anti-fungal agent used on the skin
Saline: a salt solution used to replace body fluids
Saliva: fluid secreted in the mouth
Salmonella: a type of bacteria that can cause food poisoning
Sarcoma: a malignant tumour of tissues such as muscle, bone, cartilage
Sarcoptes: a genus of mite which causes mange in animals and man

Scapula: shoulder blade

Scar: fibrous tissue which has grown to repair injured tissue

Schirmer tear test: a method of measuring tear production

Scirrhus: the term applied to a hard growth

Sclera: the white part of the eyeball

Sclerosis: hardening

Scrotum: the pouch in which the testes are found

Seborrhoea: a condition of the skin characterized by an accumulation of dry scurf, or an excessive oily deposit on the skin

Sebum: the oil produced by skin glands

Secretion: a substance produced in a cell and then pushed out

-sectomy: a suffix meaning removal of

Sedative: a drug used to calm an animal

Self: coat of one colour. Also termed 'solid'

Semen: the fluid produced by the male which contains sperm

Semicircular canals: the portion of the ear responsible for balance

Sensitization: the process of developing immunity by giving a small amount of a substance; for example, an allergen, bacteria or virus

Sepsis: infection

Septicaemia: carriage of bacteria or toxins through the blood stream, i.e., blood poisoning

Septum: a partition

Sequelae: effects which may follow a disease or injury

Sequestrum: a splinter of bone which has broken off bone. It dies and causes the formation of pus

Serous membrane: smooth glistening membranes lining certain organs

Serum: the fluid portion of blood with clotting factors removed

Shock: the condition of collapse following such things as injury or bleeding

Short-sightedness: the inability to focus on objects close to the eye

Sicca: dry eye

Side-effects: effects of a drug other than those desired

Sinus: a narrow, hollow cavity

Sire: father

Slit lamp: provides a narrow beam of light used to aid in examination of the eye

Slough: the separation of a dead part from the healthy tissue

Smooth muscle: muscle not under voluntary control

Solar: pertaining to the sun

Solid: self colour. Coat of one colour only

Spasm: involuntary muscle contraction

Spaying: the removal of the ovaries (and usually the uterus) of the female

Sphincter: a ring of muscle surrounding the opening of an organ

Sphygmomanometer: a device which measures blood pressure

Spinal cord: the collection of nerves running within the backbone

Spleen: an organ found on the left side of the abdomen which functions partly as a blood filter

Spondylitis: inflammation of the vertebrae

Sprains: the tearing of a ligament usually caused by the wrenching of a joint

Squamous cell carcinoma: a type of skin cancer. Commonly seen on tips of ears, on nose or lips of white cats living in sunny climates

Squint:
    1. screwed up eyes – lids half closed
    2. deviated eyeball

Staphylococcus: a type of bacteria

Staring coat: a dry, non-shiny coat

Steatorrhoea: fat in the faeces

Stenosis: unnatural narrowing of a body passage or opening, usually used in connection with blood vessels

Sternum: breastbone

Steroids: drugs closely related to certain chemicals produced by the body, such as the sex hormones, or some of the hormones produced by the adrenal glands

Stomach tube: a rubber tube inserted down the oesophagus and into the stomach

Stomatitis: inflammation of the mouth

Stool: solid material passed from the anus

Strabismus: turned eyeball

Streptococcus: a type of bacteria

Streptomycin: a type of antibiotic

Stricture: narrowing of a body passage such as the bowel

Stroke: sudden rupture or occlusion of a blood vessel in the brain

Stud: an animal used for breeding

Stye: infection of the glands of the eyelid edge

Subaortic stenosis: obstruction in the heart below the aortic valve

Subluxation: (e.g., of lens or a joint) incompletely removed from its correct position

Sub clinical: disease occuring in a very mild form. Cat shows no overt signs of disease

Sulphonamides: a group of antibacterial drugs

Superinfection: an infection which occurs even though the animal is already receiving antibiotics

Suppository: a mass which contains drugs which is inserted in the rectum

Suppuration: the formation of pus

Suspension: a pharmaceutical preparation in which ingredients are dispersed as visible particles and which is consequently turbid

Sutures: stitches

Sympathetic nervous system: the part of the nervous system which prepares the body for a reaction to fright, flight or fear

Syncope: fainting

Syndrome: a group of symptoms occurring together

Synergists: drugs whose action together is more than the sum of their individual actions

Synovial membranes: the lining membrane of joints

Synovitis: inflammation of the lining of the joint

Systole: the contraction phase of a heartbeat

Tabby: striped, blotched or spotted

Tachycardia: speeding up of the heart rate

Tachypnoea: speeding up of breathing

Tapetum: a layer at the back of the eye which helps night vision

Taurine: an amino acid the cat cannot produce itself. Must be supplied in diet. Lack of taurine produces visual disturbances

Tear spill: overflow of tears down the face

Tear stain: white or lightly pigmented animals show facial staining from tear overflow

Tears: watery secretion of the tear glands

Tearing: excessive tear production

Tendon: the attachment of muscle to bone

Tenesmus: straining of the bowel in attempt to defaecate

Teratogen: an agent which can cause foetus malformation

Testes: the male gonads which produce spermatozoa and male hormones

Testosterone: male sex hormone

Tetany: localized spasmodic muscle contractions

Tetralogy of Fallot: a combination of four congenital heart defects, including a hole in the heart

Thorax: chest

Thrombocytes: platelets

Thrombocytopaemia: a deficiency of platelets in the blood stream. Leads to prolonged bleeding before clot forms

Thrombosis: the formation of a blood clot within the heart or blood vessel of a living animal

Thrombus: a blood clot within a vessel

Thymus gland: a gland found in the chest which helps in immunity

Thyroid gland: a gland found in the neck which produces certain hormones which control metabolism

Tibia: one of the bones of the hind leg. It is equivalent to the human shin bone

Tincture: a diluted alcoholic solution of certain medications

Tissue: the substance of an organ, e.g., liver, skin, bone formed by cells

-tomy: a suffix indicating an operation by cutting

Tom: un-neutered male cat

Tonometry, eye: measurement of pressure within the eye

Tonsillectomy: the removal of the tonsils

Topical: a drug applied to the outside of the body

Torsion: twisting, usually of the intestine

Toxaemia: the presence of a toxin in the bloodstream

Toxin: a bacterial poison

Toxoid: a toxin made harmless by physical or chemical means (used in the treatment of some conditions)

Trachea: air passage from the throat to the lungs

Tract: a collection of nerves having the same origin, function and termination

Traction: pull

Trauma: a disorder which is the result of direct injury

Tremors: very fine, jerky muscle contractions

Trichiasis: a condition where the eyelashes turn inwards and rub on the eyeball

Trypsin: one of the digestive enzymes

Tumour: a solid swelling resulting from abnormal growth, or a hollow swelling containing fluid

Tympanic membrane: ear drum

Tympany: the expansion of a hollow organ with gas

Ulcer: a breach in a surface which tends not to heal

Ulcer, corneal: a break in continuity of the cornea. It is often slow to heal and may suddenly deepen to cause perforation of the eye

Ulna: the longer of the two bones of the forearm

Umbilical cord: the connection between foetus and placenta

Umbilical hernia: a hernia of fat and sometimes intestines in region of the navel, where the umbilical (birth) cord exited

Umbilicus: navel

Undershot jaw: upper jaw protrudes abnormally

Uraemia: build-up of waste products in the blood due to kidney disease

Urea: the substance which mammals use to excrete nitrogen-containing wastes. The level of urea in the bloodstream is a useful measure of kidney function

Ureter: the tube from the kidney to the bladder

Urethra: tube carrying urine from the bladder to the exterior

Urinalysis: testing of the chemical and cellular elements of urine

Urination: the act of voiding urine

Urinary: pertaining to urine

Urinary calculi: concretions of mineral or 'stones' found in the urinary tract – usually the bladder – of cats

Urine: the excretion produced by the kidneys

Urolithiasis: formation of kidney or bladder stones

Urticaria: a skin rash characterized by small raised red lumps

Uterus: womb

Uvea: the bloody coat within the outer wall of the eyeball. Includes the iris

Uveitis: inflammation within the eye of the iris, ciliary body, choroid

Vagina: the muscular canal extending from the uterus to the outside of the body

Vagus nerve: an important nerve which sends branches to the heart, lungs, liver, stomach and bowels

Vascular: pertaining to blood vessels

Vasoconstrictor: a drug which decreases the diameter of blood vessels

Vasodilator: a drug which increases the diameter of blood vessels

Vasopressor: a drug which raises blood pressure

Vertebrae: the bones of the back

Vesicle: blister

Viscera: the internal organs of the body

Voluntary muscles: the muscles under conscious control

Volvulus: twisting of a loop of bowel around itself

Vomeronasal organ: Jacobsens organ (see above)

Vulva: external female genitals. Opening of urogenital tract

Wart: small, solid growth arising upon the skin or mucous membrane

Weal: raised white area of skin with a reddened edge

Weaning: the separation of young animals from the mother

Winking: quick closing and opening of the eyelids

X-rays: rays of electromagnetic energy used to display internal structures within the body

Y-Chromosome: the chromosome which causes the development of male characteristics

Zonules: the numerous fine tissue strands (ligaments) which hold the lens in place in the eye

Zoonosis: a disease of animals which may be communicated to man

INDEX